Montaigne and the Quality of Mercy

———————————

Montaigne and the Quality of Mercy

ETHICAL AND POLITICAL THEMES
IN THE *ESSAIS*

David Quint

PRINCETON UNIVERSITY PRESS
PRINCETON, NEW JERSEY

Copyright © 1998 by Princeton University Press
Published by Princeton University Press, 41 William Street,
Princeton, New Jersey 08540
In the United Kingdom: Princeton University Press, Chichester, West Sussex

All Rights Reserved

Library of Congress Cataloging-in-Publication Data

Quint, David, 1950– Montaigne and the quality of mercy :
ethical and political themes in the Essais / David Quint.
p. cm.
Includes biographical references and index.
ISBN 0-691-04836-3 (cloth : alk. paper)
1. Montaigne, Michel de, 1533–1592. Essais.
2. Montaigne, Michel de, 1533–1592—Ethics.
3. Montaigne, Michel de, 1533–1592—
Political and social views.   I. Title.
PQ1643.Q5 1998 844'.3—dc21   97-36185

This book has been composed in Galliard

Princeton University Press books are printed on acid-
free paper and meet the guidelines for permanence and
durability of the Committee on Production Guidelines
for Book Longevity of the Council on Library Resources

http://pup.princeton.edu

Printed in the United States of America

1 3 5 7 9 10 8 6 4 2

For my mother, Eleanor Dolsky Quint

CONTENTS

Preface	ix
Acknowledgments	xvii
CHAPTER ONE Clemency and Revenge: The First Essay and Its Place in Montaigne's Book	3
CHAPTER TWO Cruelty and Noblesse: "De la cruauté" and "Couardise mere de la cruauté"	42
CHAPTER THREE The Culture That Cannot Pardon: "Des cannibales" in the Larger *Essais*	75
CHAPTER FOUR An Ethics of Yielding: "De l'art de conferer" and "De la phisionomie"	102
Notes	145
Index	169

PREFACE

FROM ITS first essay, Montaigne's book places the reader in a world of violent political conflict, a scene reminiscent of the French Wars of Religion through which Montaigne lived and wrote. Two adversaries confront one another in battle. One has the upper hand and is intent on vengeance. Can they be reconciled? Watching the spectacle of warring Catholics and Huguenots, Montaigne will recall the emperor Julian: "from the cruelty of some Christians to one another, he had learned that there is no beast in the world so much to be feared by man as man himself" (671; 509).

Montaigne responds to the contemporary crisis of a civil war by propounding in the *Essais* a new ethics to counter the model of heroic virtue that prevailed in his culture and his noble class. Against the hard-liner who never yields, even in the face of death—the constant Stoic, the honor-bound aristocrat, the religious zealot—he offers a pliant goodness that is the product not of heroic effort and philosophical discipline, not even of Christian charity or meekness, but rather of ordinary fellow feeling. Where the old virtue was autarchic and self-reliant, the new moral behavior that Montaigne advocates is accommodating to other human beings. The affect it does most to inculcate is trust.

Politically conditioned, Montaigne's moral doctrine has political consequences. The focus of ethical discussion in the *Essais* is willingness or refusal to submit to the power and will of others. Montaigne argues that the choice whether to yield belongs not only to the defeated but to the conqueror, whose accommodation takes the form of showing mercy to those he might otherwise punish. And he seeks to persuade his French countrymen that they have no choice except to give way to one another. In practice, Montaigne urges all parties to swallow their pride—for pride and self-interest are what their obstinate virtue has boiled down to—and to submit to the authority of the French monarchy, the only possible guarantor of civil order.

For this reason, Montaigne's ethical reform is directed most pointedly at his own class, the rebellious French nobility whose leading role in the Wars of Religion was only a chapter in what would be a century-long struggle for independence from the crown. The moral teaching of the *Essais* is engaged in the "civilizing process," to use the term of Norbert Elias, the process of taming an early modern aristocratic culture of violence and cruelty. The relative parvenu and *robin* Montaigne adapts the pose of a traditional noble of the sword not merely out of snobbery but in order to provide a new ethical basis for the political conduct of the nobleman, a morality that teaches him the honor and nobility of yielding.

The *Essais* articulate a grammar of consent against a historical background of religious and political obstinacy. This ethical doctrine is at least as important to Montaigne's book as its explorations of skepticism and the development of the essayist's self-portrait—two projects of the *Essais* to which a good deal more critical attention has been paid. The easygoing morality of yielding that Montaigne advocates may be the ground and condition, rather than the result, of his skepticism. It may be the ground as well of his self-portrait, rhetorically designed to show that morality in action and to persuade us to follow it—whether or not the portrait corresponds to the behavior of the historical Montaigne.

It is a self-portrait of the essayist-as-everyman. "How trifling of Montaigne to have written that he preferred white wine," his contemporary Joseph Scaliger is supposed to have commented. But the very banality of Montaigne's experience is meant to reassure us of his—and our—normality. It reflects the efforts of a humanist to dissociate humanism from the competitive indvidualism that fostered it and which it fostered in turn, the more general Renaissance individualism that fascinated Jacob Burckhardt in its earlier phase in Italy. For the humanist idea that man could be the maker of himself—carried to its furthest logic in the Stoic striving for perfect self-mastery—could easily appear to sanction the aggrandizement of the individual: particularly in rivalry with and at the expense of others. The Huguenots who have propelled France into civil war must, Montaigne comments, have been motivated by "great self-love and presumption" (120; 87), but the personal religious inspiration of the Protestant is just one manifestation of an indvidualism that when it pervades an entire society will eventually turn into a Hobbesian war of every man against every man: such is, in fact, the case of the society of the Brazilian cannibals, each in jealous pursuit of individual martial honor, that Montaigne describes in his famous essay.

In the name of a shared humanity, Montaigne deflates the humanist aspirations that lead to such divisive individualism. This is the aim of the massive manifesto on skepticism that is embedded in the middle of his book, the "Apologie de Raimond Sebond." That essay's conclusion that only God, not Stoic virtue, can, through a "miraculous metamorphosis" (604; 457), raise humans above their humanity reappears in the very last pages of the larger *Essais*, where Montaigne rings sarcastic changes on the famous claim of Pico della Mirandola that human dignity consists in the individual's Protean ability "to transform himself into an angel" or a beast: if you seek to be more than human, he suggests, you are *sure* to turn into a beast (1115; 856). Yet Montaigne knows that some form of human dignity is indispensable. His morality of yielding ultimately finds a place within it for the individual's demand for respect—from others, from oneself—that lies at the basis of aristocratic honor and Stoic virtue. He argues that you can swallow your pride and have it too, provided you learn how to be a good loser.

This book can be read as an extended commentary on Montaigne's first essay. Or rather, it demonstrates how the *Essais* themselves provide such a commentary by identifying a series of subsequent essays that replay with variations the opening scenario of warring enemies. Related among themselves by theme and verbal echoes, these pertinent essays arc from the beginning to the penultimate chapter of Montaigne's book and develop a sustained moral argument. This can be traced across the pages of the *Essais*. But we can also watch the argument evolve and settle into place in the book's successive editions, the so-called A (1580), B (1588), and C (1595) texts. What emerges is a structure of coherent design inside a book noted for its heterogeneity and loose ends.

The relationship between conqueror and conquered that Montaigne describes in the first essay, "Par divers moyens on arrive a pareille fin," shows the two becoming more and more alike. They have become virtually interchangeable in a subsequent essay that itself bears a reciprocal relationship to the first, "Divers evenemens de mesme conseil" (1:24). My opening chapter explores how these two essays mirror each other in order to spell out the imperative of clemency in political relationships and in human behavior in general. It also looks at how the figure of Alexander the Great, evoked by both essays, keeps reappearing, along with the idealized figure of the Theban commander Epaminondas, in the larger framework of the *Essais* to repeat their central opposition between hard-line vengeance and lenient mercy.

Chapter Two similarly looks at two linked essays, Montaigne's explorations of cruelty in "De la cruauté" (2:11) and "Couardise mere de la cruauté" (2:27). The former essay, perhaps the central moral statement of the *Essais*, attacks the cruelty of philosophical and particularly Stoic virtue; from the perspective of the latter essay, which returns explicitly to the issue of vengeance, this discussion of cruelty can be seen to overlap with a critique of the violent culture of the French nobility, the culture of the hunt and the duel. As he enjoins his noble peers to live up to the standards of their ancestors, Montaigne seeks to inculcate what are, in fact, *new* values of mildness and civility.

What France will come to if Frenchmen, the nobility in particular, do not reform themselves is the cannibalistic society of the Brazilians discussed in "Des cannibales" (1:31). The Wars of Religion, Montaigne declares, have already seen worse atrocities than the cannibalism of the New World. But, as Chapter Three argues, the cannibals, like the ancient Romans with their gladiatorial culture discussed in "Des mauvais moyens employez a bonne fin" (2:23), demonstrate the self-destructive consequences that overtake a society of perfect martial virtue and diehard Stoic constancy when that society has no word for pardon. In a further analogy to the sectarian conflict in his France, Montaigne's cannibals, who defy their captors and are cooked and eaten, bear an unsettling resemblance to the religious martyrs of "De l'yvrongnerie" (2:2), who call upon their persecutors to roast them to a turn.

The last chapter examines Montaigne's ethic of yielding in practice, notably as embodied by the author in two essays from Book Three, where the essayist's self-portrait has taken center stage. In "De l'art de conferer" (3:8), the confrontation of adversaries has been reimagined as a peaceable conversation whose speakers are willing to yield to one another for the sake of orderly discussion itself. The essay suggests how these conversational habits may be transferred to the political situation of the subject who submits to the monarch for the sake of social order and peace. "De la phisionomie" (3:12) presents two culminating versions of the showdown that opens the *Essais*; it contrasts the refusal of Socrates to submit to his hostile Athenian judges with the course of least resistance that Montaigne himself adopted when he fell into enemy hands in two episodes during the civil wars. Montaigne's open yielding produces the reciprocal response of clemency from his captors and the essayist asserts that it is more natural and efficacious than the irony and defiance of Socrates. Yet the contrast between modern and ancient moral heroism is not one-sided and the essay ends with a partial reversal and qualification that acknowledges the value of sticking to principles, as Socrates did. Montaigne also acknowledges the limits of the ethical stance—embodying humaneness, submission, trust, but also passivity—for which he has argued through the course of the *Essais*. It is not a perfect morality, merely the best available. Its premise is a giving up of the quest for an inhuman perfection.

Studies of Montaigne have taken two general approaches to reading the *Essais*; the two are sometimes combined, and I have tried to combine them here. One, which can be called the literary approach, has analyzed the individual essay, identifying its formal and logical structures, its semantic field, and Montaigne's characteristic contradictions and qualifications of meaning. The second approach, more closely allied to the history of ideas and philosophy, collects related passages throughout the *Essais* in order to discuss thematic continuities and the book's overall meaning. Taken separately, each method has limitations. The literary method that confines itself to one essay at a time can detach the essay from the context of the book as a whole and from any larger critical picture of it. A tendency of this approach has been to focus less on the thematic content of the essay than on second-order subjects, appropriate enough for analysis in their own right, such as the problem of judgment or the status of the narrative "I." In the deconstructionist criticism of the last two decades close reading has become identified with the demonstration of the single essay's incoherence or excess of meaning—rather than of paradox or multiple points of view—in a way that effectively rules out larger patterns of coherence among essays, apart from a blanket skepticism or the problem of writing itself. As for the broader philosophical method, it commonly depends on passages removed from contexts that can greatly complicate their meaning in the single essays from which they are drawn. Moreover, such criticism cannot convey the extent to which Montaigne's use of the essay form—his style and a way of writing that leads his reader through ironic reversals of logic and perspective—itself contributes to the experience of meaning in the *Essais*. The latter, philosophical method has been nonetheless predominant in the strongest recent studies of Montaigne, those of Gérald Nakam, Judith Shklar, and Jean Starobinski.

Nakam is the reader of Montaigne with whom I find I most frequently agree: she similarly notes his emphasis on the building of human trust. I share above all her premise that the *Essais* need to be read as a response to the horror of the French civil wars. They may be the first sustained meditation on the implications of a permanent schism in Western Christianity, and I would suggest that the insistently secular terms of Montaigne's argument claim a new role for an ethical humanism when accord on Christian principles no longer seems possible. I have tried to place Montaigne's ideas and terms in their historical surroundings, and I have particularly emphasized their relationship to the noble culture which he both shared in and criticized. While Montaigne may state that all topics are equally good grist for his mill (302; 219), my reading presupposes that what he chooses to discuss can be as important as how he writes about it. For all of its willed diversity, his book can be read as a book, and its individual essays, which Montaigne called chapters, should be related to a continuing argument.

My aim as a literary critic is, nevertheless, to derive this argument from the *Essais* through readings that seek to do justice to their verbal art and formal complexity. I analyze single essays on their own terms, to show how Montaigne's moral doctrine emerges from their play of logic and metaphor, allusion and anecdote. I have paid special attention to how Montaigne uses his sources—including instances where, allowing himself a kind of interpretative license, he embellishes or even makes those sources up. I take into account, too, Montaigne's additions and rewriting through the three strata of the text. Furthermore, I suggest that Montaigne links essays to one another by means that are as much literary as thematic: the repetition of similar scenes, the reappearance of the same protagonists, the echoing of specific terms and motifs. Each of my chapters juxtaposes two essays, read singly and read together, and I show how all the essays I treat suggest a single focus of thought that is implicit elsewhere in the *Essais*. This demonstration of textual unity rests on the conclusion that, as Pierre Villey argued long ago, Montaigne got over his skeptical phase. He had something positive to say and something urgent.

What of the moral and political doctrine itself? Montaigne is his own best critic when he opposes himself to Socrates, the greatest classical figure of dissent within the state and the quester after justice. For the morality that Montaigne advocates appears already to depend on the political consensus that it seeks to build and put into place. In his time the main obstacle to this consensus was religious conviction. Montaigne may try to persuade us that such stubborn conviction quickly reduces to mere self-interest and perverse malignity, but for many of his contemporaries, the salvation of one's soul outweighed the essayist's concern for social peace. When Montaigne's position is translated out of its historical context, it can look, as Max Horkheimer noted, like the political morality of the privileged that urges acquiescence in the status quo. Furthermore, while it is salutary for Montaigne to remind us how easily our sense of justice and honor can be confused with revenge and cruelty, we may still not be reconciled to watching others commit cruelty and escape reckoning. They will get away with murder.

Montaigne grounds his morality ontologically by asserting that it is part of a common human nature, and culturally by arguing that it is the index of a genuine nobility: all men naturally share humane impulses, but the nobleman has the largest share. The argument about nobility is clearly strategic, aimed at the reform of aristocratic behavior. We may suspect that the same is true of Montaigne's claims about a human nature that underlies the variety of custom that he elsewhere acknowledges and documents. His famous assertion in "Du repentir" (3:2) that every man bears the entire form of the human condition can cut two ways. It warrants the exemplarity of Montaigne's own compassion for and trust in others and suggests to his readers that they can summon up these same qualities in their own nature. But it may also suggest that the cruelty he deplores is equally natural to human beings and that a "common" human nature is, in fact, an ambiguous base on which to construct an ethics. The essay on the Brazilian cannibals looms for this reason all the larger in the *Essais*, at least in my account of them, for the culture of ruthless competition and pitiless valor—what makes the cannibals noble savages—offers a disturbingly antithetical view of a human behavior close to nature.

Yet we want to believe that people are good at heart; perhaps we must believe it. Some such impulse drives the very wish to respond to Montaigne's appeal to our best instincts. There is something perennially cheering and hopeful in his faith in humanity, which is as close, I think, as he may come to a profession of religious faith. Montaigne, the real-life negotiator between Catholic and Protestant forces, asserts that it takes more, not less, courage to yield, to seek compromise and dialogue with one's adversary rather than dominate or be dominated. The desire for conquest that the *Essais* show to be identical with a desire for self-destruction in the stoical martyr, the tyrant, the man of honor is, in fact, Montaigne claims, the product of a pathological fear of mortality. Even more, it is a fear of living itself. At a moment when renewed ethnic and religious conflicts threaten relations of human society that we, like Montaigne, wish to think of as ordinary and normal—in Bosnia, in Rwanda, but I am thinking of hardening race relations and identity politics closer to home as well—Montaigne's message seems no less urgent for us than for his sixteenth-century readers. Live and let live may be as good a start as we shall ever find in thinking about morality.

ACKNOWLEDGMENTS

THIS BOOK was largely shaped in the classroom. At Princeton University I had the good fortune to learn from four exceptional Montaignistes: John Archer, Timothy Hampton, Eric MacPhail, and David Posner. Robert Hollander shared with me his deep knowledge of, and his enthusiasm for, the *Essais* in the undergraduate course in which we taught together. I subsequently presented an early and very rough version of the book's ideas to a seminar at the Folger Shakespeare Library. I am grateful to the seminar participants, especially Marianne Meijer, Ellen Ginsberg, Philip Berk, and Nicole Minnick, for suggestions that enabled me to see my thesis and for objections that prodded me to clarify it.

The writing of the book was made possible by two paid leaves from Yale University. I am particularly thankful to the generosity, social and intellectual, of my Pisan friends, Lina Bolzoni, Sergio Zatti, and Gian Biagio Conte, and of Paola Colaiacomo in Rome: I lifted more than one sentence into this book from my conversations with them. I want to acknowledge the hospitality of the American Academy in Rome and of its director, Caroline Bruzelius.

Many friends and colleagues have generously read and commented on the manuscript. My special gratitude goes to Timothy Hampton for his encouragement of this project from its beginning; he and Edwin Duval provided expert readings and suggestions, and pointed me through the critical literature on Montaigne. Anthony Grafton gave me the benefit of his learning and intelligence and tried to keep me from oversimplification of historical issues. Ronald Levao, Victoria Kahn, Lawrence Manley, Michael Murrin, Constance Jordan, and Marianne Meijer improved my thinking and writing with their careful comments. David Bromwich did yeoman's work: he gave my prose and ideas a final going-over and helped me through the process of writing the Introduction. To all of these friends my debts are much more than intellectual. I have benefitted likewise from the advice of the Press readers, Robert Cottrell and Sabine MacCormack, and I am thankful to Robert Brown for his careful work on a manuscript with numerous inconsistencies. For comments on an earlier version of the chapter on "Des cannibales," I am indebted to François Rigolot, Stephen Greenblatt, Claude Rawson, John Christian Laursen, David Armitage, and Marshall Brown.

The earlier version of Chapter 3 was published as a "A Reconsideration of Montaigne's *Des cannibales*" in *Modern Language Quarterly* 51 (1990): 459–89. It was also published, with the same title, in *America in European Consciousness 1493–1750*, ed. Karen Ordahl Kupperman (Chapel Hill: University of North Carolina Press, 1995), pp. 166–191.

Montaigne and the Quality of Mercy

Chapter One

CLEMENCY AND REVENGE: THE FIRST ESSAY AND ITS PLACE IN MONTAIGNE'S BOOK

THE *ESSAIS* BEGIN with a fearful showdown. Put yourself, Montaigne asks his reader in the opening essay, in the position of the defeated, face to face with your enemy, who "has vengeance in hand." By which tactic can you soften the heart of your foe and save your life: by humble submission that seeks to stir pity and commiseration, or by a brave defiance and constancy that will impress your foe with your valor?

Which, indeed, of these "entirely contrary means," those of the essay's title, "Par divers moyens on arrive a pareille fin" ("By Diverse Means We Arrive at the Same End")? The answer changes subtly through the progressive revisions of the essay from the so-called A text of the 1580 first edition to the later B and C texts of 1588 and 1595. These changes are both shifts of emphasis and a rethinking: they suggest both an evolution and a filling out of Montaigne's reflections upon moral and political issues that, through links between this first essay and subsequent ones, will become one of the central strands of his book. We shall watch this initial showdown between victor and vanquished reappear through the pages of the *Essais* with changing protagonists: Stoics, cannibals, gladiators, martyrs, Socrates before his judges, and finally Montaigne himself. How these encounters will end—with life or death, with clemency or revenge?—is the repeated question of Montaigne's book.

This first chapter looks in detail at "Par divers moyens" and at a later essay in Book One that symmetrically responds to it, "Divers evenemens de mesme conseil" (1:24). The focus of the first essay on the question of how you may *obtain* clemency from your foe—by submission or valorous defiance—shifts in the second to whether or not you, in turn, should *grant* clemency to a dangerous enemy. Montaigne cites, only to attack, the Stoic doctrine that condemns the fellow-feeling of pity and detaches it from virtue, and, in doing so, he links the Stoic drive for ethical self-sufficiency with the code of personal honor of the sixteenth century warrior-noble: both are inhuman, neither is apt to be merciful. Nonetheless, Montaigne acknowledges and seeks to preserve the self-respect that is the desired goal of this Stoic/aristocratic ethos even as he advances the paradox in "Divers evenemens" that you will most fully respect yourself when you freely submit to and acknowledge the power of others. The reciprocal arguments of the two essays allow Montaigne in "Divers evenemens" to overturn the terms of "Par divers moyens" and to argue that clemency requires more courage than revenge, since the enemy you leave alive may continue to be a threat to you, that submission is more valorous than defiant valor itself, since it means disarming yourself and trusting in your foes. We shall see that this difficult ethical and political balance—yielding with honor—is one that Montaigne repeatedly prescribes through the course of the *Essais*: a prescription to cure his France of the malady of civil war. A coda to the chapter shows how the inexplicably vengeful Alexander who appears at the end of "Par divers moyens" is subsequently contrasted in the *Essais* with the idealized figure of another ancient hero: the Theban captain Epaminondas, who perfectly balanced valor and clemency in himself and in his actions. The reappearances of Alexander and Epaminondas at the beginnings and endings of the books of the *Essais* constitute a framing device, intended or not, that writes large the central ethical issue of mercy raised by Montaigne's text.

1:1, The A-Text Version

La plus commune façon d'amollir les coeurs de ceux qu'on a offensez, lors qu'ayant la vengeance en main, il nous tiennent à leur mercy, c'est de les esmouvoir par submission à commiseration et à pitié. Toutesfois la braverie, et la constance, moyens tous contraires, ont quelquefois servi à ce mesme effect.[1] (7)

The commonest way of softening the hearts of those we have offended, when, vengeance in hand, they hold us at their mercy, is by submission and pity. However, bravery and steadfastness—entirely contrary means—have sometimes served to produced the same effect. (3)

In these opening sentences of the *Essais*, Montaigne acknowledges that submission is the most common ("commune") recourse of the vanquished; nonetheless bravery and constancy have *sometimes* worked to obtain the same clemency, and in the first 1580 version of "Par divers moyens" he appears to be fascinated by this latter stance of unbending resolve.[2] Montaigne cites three historical examples of courage and fighting spirit changing the anger of the conqueror into mercy: Edward, prince of Wales, who only stopped the butchery of the unresisting people, women, and children of Limoges at the sight of three French noblemen continuing the fight; Scanderbeg, the Albanian prince, who pardoned his soldier when the latter, after vain supplication, resolved to fight for his life; the Emperor Conrad, who abated his wrath when the women of Bavaria carried their husbands and their duke on their shoulders and brought them out of their besieged city under safe-conduct. The 1580 essay next pauses to comment on these cases.

Or ces exemples me semblent plus à propos, d'autant qu'on voit ces ames assaillies et essayées par ces deux moyens, en soustenir l'un sans s'esbranler, et courber sous l'autre. Il se peut dire, que de rompre son coeur à la commiseration, c'est l'efect de la facilité, débonnaireté, et mollesse, d'où il advient que les natures plus foibles, commes celles des femmes, des enfans, et du vulgaire y sont plus subjettes; mais ayant eu à desdaing les larmes et les prières, de se rendre à la seule reverence de la saincte image de la vertu, que c'est l'effect d'une ame forte et imployable, ayant en affection et en honneur une vigueur masle, et obstinée. (8)

Now these examples seem to me more to the point, inasmuch as we see these souls, assailed and tested by these two means, hold up unshaken against one and bow beneath the other. It may be said that to subdue your heart to commiseration is the act of easygoing indulgence and softness, which is why the weaker natures, such as those of women, children, and the common herd are the most subject to it; but that, having disdained tears and prayers, to surrender simply to reverence for the sacred image of valor is the act of a strong and inflexible soul which holds in affection and honor a masculine and obstinate vigor. (4)

As opposed to a weak-hearted commiseration that is an identification with the weakness and misfortune of the defeated, the admiration for your foe's courage is virtually an act of aesthetic appreciation: for the "sacred image of valor" abstracted from the individual foeman. The victor does not appear to take the continuing resistance of his enemy personally, and this allows for a disinterested veneration of bravery itself. Yet another kind of identification seems to occur as well. It takes one to know one, Montaigne suggests: only the noble male rather than a commoner or a woman, would be able to appreciate a behavior that is also characterized as noble and male—the resistance of those three "gentils-hommes François" that stopped the prince of Wales. If the most common way of obtaining pardon is to submit and to seek to arouse pity and commiseration—if it is the means, that is, of commoners—it is precisely commoners who will be most likely to be susceptible to such appeals for pity. And therefore the nobleman will, perhaps *must*, try other means, those of constancy and courage. For Montaigne will observe in a subsequent essay, "Que le goust des biens et des maux depend en bonne partie de l'opinion que nous en avons" (1:14), it is precisely by this kind of martial valor that the aristocracy defines itself as a class. If the occasions to demonstrate physical courage did not exist, he asks,

> qui auroit mis en credit parmy nous la vertu, la vaillance, la force, la magnanimité et la resolution? Où jouëroyent elles leur rolle, s'il n'y a plus de douleur à deffier: "*avida est periculi virtus.*" S'il ne faut coucher sur la dure, soustenir

armé de toutes pieces la chaleur du midy, se paistre d'un cheval et d'un asne, se voir detailler en pieces, et arracher une balle d'entre les os, se souffrir recoudre, cauterizer et sonder, par où s'acquerra l'advantage que nous voulons avoir sur le vulgaire? (56–57)

who would have brought into credit among us virtue, valor, strength, magnanimity, and resolution? Where would these play their part, if there were no more pain to defy? *Courage is greedy of dangers* [Seneca]. If we need not sleep on hard ground, sustain fully armed the heat of noon, feed on a horse or an ass, watch ourselves being sliced to pieces and a bullet torn out from between our bones, let ourselves be sewn up again, cauterized, and probed, how shall we acquire the advantage that we wish to have over the common herd? (38)

The nobleman's claim to moral superiority, and to a privileged place in the social hierarchy, depends upon his valor as a soldier, his willingness to pledge his body for his honor. Or, put another way, his pursuit of martial virtue reaffirms an identity that aspires to greatness above others. Montaigne's tone in this passage makes it hard to decide just what he thinks of the trade-off of the aristocrat's body for his social position, just as the ambiguity of the phrase, "nous voulons avoir," may question whether he is really entitled to that position; but one should note for further consideration that Montaigne includes himself in this "we."[3]

This class and gender distinction is nonetheless already and immediately put in question by the other two cited cases in "Par divers moyens": Scanderbeg's soldier, presumably from the rank and file, and the Bavarian women are able, when the situation demands it, to put on a "masculine and obstinate vigor." There is also a problem in the very terminology that links women and commoners with weak softness ("mollesse"), males and aristocrats with inflexible ("imployable"), obstinate strength. For, these latter noble souls, if they are unshaken by supplication, may nonetheless bow and bend ("courber") before the sight of valor. In the next sentence, furthermore, Montaigne concedes that less aristocratic souls—"ames moins genereuses"—can also be impressed by shows of valor and defiance, and he cites, as a fourth historical example, the people of Thebes who put their noble generals on trial: after just barely pardoning their general Pelopidas, who had himself bowed ("plioit") beneath their accusations and resorted to supplication, they refrained even from judging Epaminondas, who braved them with reproaches and arrogance. Here, too, plebeians are capable of acting like their aristocratic betters.

This refusal of individuals to live up to tight and fast social roles appears to lead to the most famous sentence of the essay:

Certes c'est un subject merveilleusement vain, divers et ondoyant, que l'homme. Il est malaisé d'y fonder jugement constant et uniforme. (9)

Truly man is a marvelously vain, diverse, and undulating object. It is hard to found any constant and uniform judgment upon him. (5)

But the cause of this celebrated skepticism as it unfolds in the A-text essay's final paragraph is, in fact, much more dark and pessimistic. Montaigne adds two further historical examples. Because of his admiration for the valor of the Mamertine Zeno, who offered himself for punishment in place of his fellow citizens, Pompey spared their city and thus conformed to the cases of clemency so far recorded in the essay. But, the essayist notes, on another analogous occasion, when a Perusine citizen, who had once hosted the conquering general Sulla, demonstrated a similar valor, he obtained no mercy, either for himself or for the other citizens of the city: "ny pour soy ny pour les autres." And here the first version of the essay abruptly ended, with a contrary example of clemency denied, of bravery failing to soften the heart of an implacable enemy.

The skeptical turn at the end of the essay, and the understated horror of the fate of the Perusines, lumped together for slaughter into the chillingly impersonal "les autres," already suggests what, in the subsequent B and C exfoliations of the essay, will be one of its twin themes: the difficulty of finding counsel for present experience in the historical example, itself. That it is Montaigne's present which is at stake is to be inferred from these last two stories drawn from the Roman civil wars, wars that throughout the *Essais* are paralleled with the French Wars of Religion through which the essayist lived: the parallel was, in fact, a commonplace repeatedly invoked by Montaigne's contemporaries.[4] In a later essay of 1588, where Montaigne brings up the Roman wars in the context of a discussion of the contemporary French conflict, he similarly contrasts the chivalry and moderation of Pompey to the murderous behavior of Sulla (3.10; 1014; 775–76). But if the evocation of the two Roman generals here seems to suggest the present-day relevance of the whole sequence of historical examples of the essay, these final anecdotes nonetheless question what lessons can be learned from history, a history that according to a prevailing Renaissance humanism of Montaigne's time was supposed to teach one the rules of life—*Historia magistra vitae*. In two parallel historical situations, similar behavior—the demonstration of valor—produced directly contrary results, neatly reversing the proposal of the essay's title. The moral seems to be that no two situations are exactly parallel—neither the two Roman cases nor, more importantly, the Roman past and the French present—and therefore history can provide no constant and uniform maxims about the proper course of human action. History is an inadequate teacher of life's lessons, Montaigne suggests: it is no help to you when your life is on the line.[5]

The counterexample of Sulla, moreover, unsettles the wishful thinking in which the first version of the essay has theretofore indulged: the idea that one can obtain clemency without suing for it, that it is possible to survive without yielding to the victor and relinquishing a pose of defiant autonomy. Such integrity of the self is identified with the masculine, aristocratic valor that turns the defeated but undaunted warrior into the mirror of his princely conqueror and that wins the latter's reverence and mercy. This noble selfhood defines itself by self-assertion and aggression, and by indifference, bordering on disdain, toward any other human being: it can take or leave the pardon it receives (and receives pardon for just this attitude.) The constancy ("constance") that is said to win pardon in the second sentence of the essay already links such autonomy to the language and doctrine of Roman Stoicism—Seneca devoted a whole treatise, *De Constantia*, to the virtue of remaining the same and refusing to yield to outside pressure. The link, as we shall see, is made explicit by Montaigne's first addition to the essay in the B text of 1588, and the connection between Stoic philosophy and the codes of martial honor espoused by the sixteenth-century aristocracy is a recurring feature of the *Essais*. It is tempting to read Montaigne's apparent fascination with this model of selfhood in the original version of his opening essay—particularly with the gratifying fantasy that such reckless and independent behavior can sometimes succeed in the social world with impunity—as part of what Pierre Villey, in his classic study of the evolution of Montaigne's thought, detected as an early flirtation with Stoicism, later replaced by skeptical and then "Epicurean" phases. The final turn of the A-text essay, the story of Sulla that dispels this fantasy, would show Montaigne's skepticism already bearing down upon the Stoic currents of his thinking.[6]

Indeed, it can be argued that Montaigne's examination of Stoic precepts in the *Essais* was never free from criticism, skeptical and otherwise, for all of his own professed reverence for the "sacred image of valor."[7] The essay, we have seen, questions the assumptions that this valor is exclusively aristocratic and male. Moreover, the example of the Theban populace, who pardon *both* the general who supplicates them and the general who haughtily faces them down, suggests that it is better to fall into the hands of the common people than of princes. Or, to put this another way, the same great-souled, aristocratic valor that in defeat disdains commiseration from others, may be unlikely, in the person of the victor, to extend commiseration to others in turn, "having disdained" their "tears and prayers": the essay has shown *no* examples of noble rulers forgoing vengeance for the sake of pity.

1:1 Revisited, the B and C Additions

The issue of pitiless valor becomes central in the 1588 and 1595 additions to the essay. Here the focus lies as much upon the attitudes of those with the power to grant or withhold pardon as upon the actions and perspective of the defeated whose lives are at stake.[8] In the first of the B-text interpolations, Montaigne confesses his own probable behavior in such a situation: it is now the first and I would suggest, from an ethical standpoint, the single most important contribution to the self-portrait that will be a major project of his book.

> L'un et l'autre de ces deux moyens m'emporteroit aysement. Car j'ay une merveilleuse lascheté vers la misericorde et la mansuetude. Tant y a qu'à mon advis, je serois pour me rendre plus naturellement à la compassion, qu'à l'estimation: si est la pitié passion vitieuse aux Stoïques: ils veulent qu'on secoure les affligez, mais non pas qu'on flechisse et compatisse avec eux. (8)

> Either of these two ways would easily win me, for I am wonderfully lax in the direction of mercy and gentleness. As a matter of fact, I believe that I should be likely to surrender more naturally to compassion than to esteem. Yet to the Stoics pity is a vicious passion; they want us to succor the afflicted, but not to bend and sympathize with them. (4)

Were *he* in the position of power as victor, Montaigne asserts, he would let off his foe, whether the latter begged for his life or remained defiant. He links himself here not with the soldier-aristocrat—as he does in "Que le goust des biens"—but with the weak common people and women whom he will describe in the directly ensuing A-text passage that we have already seen, with the Theban people who forgave both Pelopidas and Epaminondas—and he may go the latter one better in weak-heartedness, for he is more naturally moved by the sight that arouses pity rather than admiration. Montaigne confesses that his compassion *is* a weakness, a "lascheté" that is linked semantically to the other terms of the essay suggesting laxness or bending from an inflexible hardness. At least it is so in the eyes of Stoic philosophy, and he here explicitly contrasts his own disposition with the unbending virtue—"non pas qu'on *fléchisse*"—preached by Stoicism.

It becomes possible to hear in the "mollesse," the softness that Montaigne attributes to commoners, women, children, and now, by extension, to himself, the technical force of *mollitia*, the Stoic Seneca's favorite term of reproach that is often translated as "effeminacy." Montaigne declares himself to be a softie. He is so by nature, and as the *Essais* go on to vindicate nature over the teachings of philosophy, it is especially this softness, this willingness to yield that they substitute for what designates itself as a more masculine, more tough-minded virtue. Already in this opening essay, Montaigne calls the very terms of virtue and vice into question. Carrying the force of its Latin etymology, "virtus," "vertu" is conceived throughout the essay in terms of force and power, and must be translated as martial valor. But is it a properly ethical virtue?[9]

What now, from 1588 onward, becomes the first appeal to classical authority in Montaigne's book is a passage from near the end of Seneca's unfinished *De Clementia*. This is a key text of ancient philosophy to which we will see Montaigne repeatedly return. Its evocation here at the opening of the first book of the *Essais* now balances the A-text beginning of the first essay of the second book, where Montaigne cites Seneca's story from the same treatise (2:1.2–3) about Nero, who, when signing the death warrant of two criminals, complained, "Would to God I had never learned how to write!" (2:1, 332; 239)—this, comments Montaigne, even though Nero was "the true image of cruelty"—"cette vraie image de la cruauté." Seneca, in fact, dedicated and directed the *De Clementia* to Nero. In it, he tries to find a philosophical basis for mercy, especially for the absolute ruler who has vengeance entirely in his hand and can do as he pleases with his power. The all-powerful emperor becomes in this manner a figure for the ideal Stoic who has complete control over himself and can be totally indifferent to the outside world.[10] Seneca's larger argument is that the victor only magnifies—and also demonstrates to the world—this power over himself and others by sparing the vanquished. He both flatters and tries to educate Nero by telling him that

> a prince's fortune is too exalted for him to feel the need of compensation, and his power is too evident to lead him to seek a reputation for power by injury to another ... for that man has lost his life who owes it to another, and whosoever, having been cast down from high estate at his enemy's feet, has awaited the verdict of another upon his life and throne, lives on to the glory of his preserver, and by being saved confers more upon the other's name than if he had been removed from the eyes of men. For he is a lasting spectacle of another's prowess ... the praise of him who was content to take from a conquered king nothing but his glory will rise in increasing greatness. This is to triumph even over his own victory, and to attest that he found among the vanquished nothing that was worthy of the victor.[11] (*De Clem.* 1.21.1–3)

Mercy aggrandizes the merciful as it reduces its recipient to total insignificance, even to a kind of death-in-life. Or, rather, the vanquished has become a living trophy testifying to the greatness of the conqueror who has spared him.

Now it is important to note that this is an argument that Montaigne takes seriously. In "De la diversion," the fourth essay of the third book added to the *Essais* in 1588, he suggests that when he lately counseled a young prince, presumably Henri of Navarre—as Seneca had counseled Nero—he used similar reasoning to dissuade him from the course of vengeance.

> C'est une douce passion que la vengeance, de grande impression et naturelle: je le voy bien, encore que je n'en aye aucune experience. Pour en distraire

dernierement un jeune prince, je ne luy allois pas disant qu'il falloit prester la jouë à celuy qui vous avoit frappé l'autre, pour le devoir de charité; ny ne luy allois representer les tragiques evenemens que la poësie attribue à cette passion. Je la laissay là et m'amusay à luy faire gouster la beauté d'une image contraire: l'honneur, la faveur, la bien-veillance qu'il acquerroit par clemence et bonté: je le destournay à l'ambition. Voylà comment on en faict. (835)

Vengeance is a sweet passion, whose impact is great and natural: I see this well enough, though I have no experience of it in myself. Recently, in order to lead a young prince away from it, I did not tell him that we must turn our cheek to the man who has just struck the other one, for charity's sake, nor did I represent to him the tragic results that poetry attributes to this passion. I let the passion alone and applied myself to making him relish the beauty of a contrary picture, the honor, favor, and good will he would acquire by clemency and kindness. I diverted him to ambition. That is how it is done. (634)

It's as simple as that, Montaigne declares with some satisfaction, as he dismisses the efficacy of preaching Christian humility and rather resorts to Seneca's ploy of promising the merciful ruler an enhanced reputation. At the same time, Montaigne treats the philosophical argument of the *De Clementia* that he is recalling here precisely as a ploy, a saving diversion of the kind described by his essay's title. The persuasive power of the "image" that he paints for the young prince—like the "sacred image of valor" of the first essay—is as much aesthetic as it is philosophical, and it is presented as a pleasant alternative to the fictions of tragic poetry, perhaps too heavy reading for the princely student. This more enjoyable and flattering image, an image of flattery itself—the honors and adulation that will be heaped on the merciful ruler—deters the prince from revenge; the essayist is content to make use of whatever will do the trick. We may come to feel that the *Essais* will similarly use any kind of argument available to persuade the reader to the course of clemency.[12]

Where Montaigne, to return to "Par divers moyens," marks his distance from the *De Clementia* is at the moment where Seneca translates the gratuitous, unconstrained nature of imperial mercy into a general Stoic principle that distinguishes such mercy, indifferent to the sufferings of others, from a vicious pity that identifies and even partakes in that suffering.

> good men will all display mercy and gentleness, but pity [misericordiam] they will avoid; for it is the failing of a weak nature [vitium pusilli animi] that succumbs to the sight of others' ills. And so it is most often seen in the poorest types of persons; there are old women and wretched females who are moved by the tears of the worst criminals. (*De Clem.* 2.5.1)

Montaigne's B-text addition that directly invokes this Senecan passage also lets us see that the same passage already lay behind the class and gender distinctions drawn in the essay's first version: the lower classes and women are subject to pity, the aristocracy, an aristocracy of Stoic sages and supermen, show leniency but do not let their serenity of mind be disturbed.[13] Seneca goes on to say that he is aware that such doctrine has been criticized because "it does not permit a wise man to be pitiful, does not permit him to pardon" (2.5.2). When Montaigne ironically confesses his own effeminate "weakness" vis-à-vis such Stoic virtue, he renews the force of this criticism, and the rest of his additions to the first essay examine its implications.

The weak point of Seneca's argument is easy enough to spot. If the holder of power, whether the all-powerful emperor or the Stoic all-powerful over himself, is indifferent to the world outside him, he will be indifferent, too, to whether the world speaks well or ill of his choice of clemency or vengeance. And the fact that the emperor in question was the cruel Nero, who eventually ordered his philosopher-counselor Seneca to commit suicide in A.D. 65, casts considerable historical irony upon the latter's treatise on mercy. Moreover, the satisfaction of granting mercy to your enemy, a satisfaction that is supposed to derive from rendering the enemy into your dependent and a virtual non-entity, will be diminished if he refuses to acknowledge himself as such: the defiant opposition of the other—the other's insistence that he is still very much there as other—challenges the very autonomy of the self to which the victor-as-Stoic-sage is supposed to aspire. It is this scenario that Montaigne now explores in the new historical examples he adds to the B and C versions of his first essay. They show the princely conqueror unmoved by the valor shown by those at his mercy. Or rather he is moved to further revenge.

In the 1595 C-text, Montaigne includes toward the middle of the essay the story of the tyrant Dionysius of Syracuse who, having conquered the city of Rhegium, wanted to make a "tragic example of vengeance" of the city's obstinate captain and defender, Phyto.

> Il luy dict premierement comment, le jour avant, il avoit faict noyer son fils et tous ceux de sa parenté. A quoi Phyton respondit seulement, qu'ils en estoient d'un jour plus heureux que luy. Apres il le fit despouiller et saisir à des bourreaux et le trainer par la ville en le foitant tres ignominieusement et cruellement, et en outre le chargeant de felonnes paroles et contumelieuses. Mais il eut le courage tousjours constant, sans se perdre; et d'un visage ferme, alloit au contraire ramentevant à haute voix l'honorable et glorieuse cause de sa mort, pour n'avoir voulu rendre son païs entre les mains d'un tyran; le menaçant d'une prochaine punition des dieux. Dionysius, lisant dans les yeux de la commune de son armée qu'au lieu de s'animer des bravades de cet ennemy vaincu, au mespris de leur chef et de son triomphe, elle alloit s'amollissant par l'estonnement d'une si rare vertu, et marchandoit de se mutiner, estant à mesme d'arracher Phyton d'entre les mains de ses sergens, feit cesser ce martyre, et à cachettes l'envoya noyer en la mer. (9)

First he told him how the day before he had his son and all his relatives drowned. To which Phyto replied only that they were happier than he by one day. After that he had him stripped and seized by executioners, who dragged him through the town, whipping him very ignominiously and cruelly and, in addition, heaping on him slanderous and insulting words. But Phyto kept his courage steadfast, not letting himself go, and with a firm countenance persisted in recalling loudly the honorable and glorious cause of his death—that he had refused to surrender his country into the hands of a tyrant—and in threatening that tyrant with prompt punishment by the gods. Instead of growing angry at this defiance of a conquered enemy, the rank and file of Dionysius's army showed in their countenances that, disregarding their leader and his triumph, they were softened by astonishment at such rare valor; so that, seeing them on the point of mutiny and about to snatch Phyto from the hands of his sergeants, Dionysius had his martyrdom stopped and secretly sent him to be drowned in the sea. (4)

Phyto's response to Dionysius, proclaiming his indifference both to the death of his family and to his own impending demise, his constant courage and firm countenance: these all reek of Stoicism and Stoic constancy. He closely resembles the philosopher Stilbo, one of the heroes of Seneca's *De Constantia* (5.6–7), whose exemplary story Montaigne cites in "De la solitude" (1:39), perhaps the most Stoic in flavor of all the *Essais*. After the fall of his city, Megara, and the loss of his wife, children, property, Stilbo is confonted by the victorious Demetrius Poliorcetes who

le voyant en une si grande ruine de sa patrie le visage non effrayé, luy demanda s'il n'avoit pas eu du dommage. Il respondit que non, et qu'il n'y avoit, Dieu mercy, rien perdu de sien. (240)

seeing him unperturbed in expression amid the great ruin of his country, asked him if he had not suffered loss. No, he replied, thanks to God he had lost nothing of his own. (177)

That is, he had lost none of his personal virtue. So, Seneca writes in *De Constantia*, "he wrested the victory from the conqueror, and bore witness that, though his city had been captured, he himself was not only unconquered but unharmed." (5.7) And Seneca introduces the anecdote by describing the nature of virtue itself: "Virtue is free, inviolable, unmoved, unshaken, so steeled against the blows of chance that she cannot be bent, much less broken. Facing the instruments of torture she holds her gaze unflinching, her countenance changes not at all." (5.4–5) The imperturbable Stoic cannot be defeated.

The display of this virtue by Phyto does nearly wrest victory—"au mespris . . . de son triomphe"—from Dionysius; his troops, the "commune," are astonished by the valor of their defeated enemy, and are even on the point of saving him. But in a reversal of the essay's terms, it is now the commoners who are impressed by the spectacle of constancy, while the ruler Dionysius remains intent on his revenge and seems to want to break the spirit of his captive; failing that, he has Phyto killed. Like the people of Thebes who pardoned Epaminondas, and like Montaigne himself, the Syracusan rank and file show that they can be softened ("alloit s'amollissant") to clemency by the courage of their foe: such commoners are inclined to pity in any case by the weakness of their nature. The strongman Dionysius, however, fails to hold in reverence the image of a similar strength. For, Montaigne suggests, the unflinching, unbending Stoic virtue of Phyto may very well mirror the political power of his conqueror—the analogy that Seneca develops in the *De Clementia*—but this analogy is not necessarily reversible: Dionysius is no Stoic. His power to do as he wills does not imply the capacity to control his will and to relent. Rather the confrontation of Phyto and Dionysius becomes a contest of two wills, one Stoic, one tyrannical.

The disturbing similarity between these two wills is explored at greater length in the final section of the essay that Montaigne acknowledges runs "directly counter to my first examples" and that is devoted to the figure of Alexander the Great, "the most valorous ['hardi'] of men and the most gracious to the defeated." In an earlier A-text passage in "Que philosopher c'est apprendre à mourir" (1:20) Alexander is called the greatest man that was simply a man—"le plus grand homme, simplement homme" (85; 58)—of history. Alexander's presence at the end of the essay balances the description of Edward, prince of Wales, the protagonist of its first historical anecdote, "whose traits and fortune have in them many notable elements of greatness" (p. 3)—"duquel les conditions et la fortune ont beaucoup de notables parties de grandeur" (p. 7). The essay has thus by its ending, and through Montaigne's process of revision, turned not least of all into an investigation of the behavior of greatness: "They that have power to hurt and will do none," in Shakespeare's memorable verse from the *Sonnets*. In his final two anecdotes concerning the usually gracious Alexander, Montaigne suggests, to the contrary, not only to Shakespeare but also to the argument of the *De Clementia*, that the more power you have, the more hurt you are likely to do.

After taking the city of Gaza with great difficulty, Alexander addresses the enemy commander Betis, who was still fighting on indomitably and alone, surrounded by the victorious Macedonian troops.

> Tu ne mourras pas comme tu as voulu, Betis; fais estat qu'il te faut souffrir toutes les sortes de tourmens qui se pourront inventer contre un captif. L'autre, d'une mine non seulement asseurée mais rogue et altiere, se tint sans mot dire à ces menaces. Lors Alexandre, voyant son fier et obstiné silence: A-il flechi un genouil? lui est-il eschappé quelque voix suppliante? Vrayment je

vainqueray ta taciturnité; et si je n'en puis arracher parole, j'en arracheray au moins du gemissement. Et tournant sa cholere en rage, commanda qu'on luy perçast les talons, et le fit ainsi trainer tout vif, deschirer et desmembrer au cul d'une charrette. Seroit-ce que la hardiesse luy fut si commune que, pour ne l'admirer point, il la respectast moins? (9–10)

"You shall not die as you wanted, Betis; prepare yourself to suffer every kind of torment that can be invented against a captive." The other, with a look not only confident but insolent and haughty, stood without saying a word to these threats. Then Alexander, seeing his proud and obstinate silence: "Has he bent a knee? Has any suppliant cry escaped him? I'll conquer your muteness yet; and if I cannot wring a word from it, at least I'll wring a groan." And turning his anger into rage, he ordered Betis' heels be pierced through and had him thus dragged alive, torn and dismembered, behind a cart.

Could it be that hardihood was so common to Alexander that, not marveling at it, he respected it the less? (5)

Where Phyto had loudly voiced his defiance of Dionysius, Betis defies his conqueror with a silence that Alexander finds intolerable. He demands a sign, bodily or verbal, of the other's submission: and the kneeling ("flechi") and pleading ("une voix suppliante") he looks for pick up the semantics of bending that the essay has opposed to the rigid virtue of the man of valor. It is not the image of such valor, but rather the spectacle of its breakdown that Alexander wants to watch by subjecting Betis to torture: what finally becomes a literal breaking apart and dismemberment of his body. And here, as well, the cruelty practiced upon the captive has a kind of aesthetic logic since, in the account of this episode given by the historian Quintus Curtius (*History of Alexander* 4.6.29), Alexander imitates Achilles' treatment of Hector's body in the *Iliad*—though Hector was already dead, as Montaigne reminds us by the insistent qualification, "tout vif," applied to the unfortunate Betis.

The 1588 B-text version of the essay ended with an ironic rhetorical question that sought to explain Alexander's behavior in just such aesthetic terms: was valor so common to Alexander that he did not admire it?—and "admirer" bears both the sense of wonder and veneration. In the story of Phyto that is, we recall, a still later C-text addition, the troops of Dionysius are struck by the "rare vertu" of the captive. Here Montaigne speculates that valor is a kind of second nature to Alexander, so much so that he could not reverence it as a virtue, much less recognize it as extraordinary when possessed by another person. Once again, the terms of the essay have been turned on their head, as the adjective "commune" suggests. It turns out to be the common people, not the prince, who can best appreciate a princely virtue—precisely because they normally fall short of it themselves. And by now the suspicion that the A-text version of the essay already implicitly voiced has been confirmed: it is better to be at the mercy of commoners, susceptible both to pity and to admiration for brave resistance, than to seek forbearance from princes who are unpredictable and capable of inexplicable cruelty. It cannot be excluded that Montaigne plays upon the etymological origins of the term "hardiesse" (cf. the German "hart" and the English "hard") which he has substituted here for "vertu," continuing the essay's contrast between the firm, unbending virtue of the prince and aristocrat and the commoners' lax and flaccid weakness—with all of the sexual implications of these metaphors.[14] Montaigne may himself be a softie, but Alexander, in a similar modern parlance, was a real prick.

A lack of satisfaction with this effort to explain Alexander's cruelty seems to motivate the C-text addition that now brings the essay, in its final form, to its thunderous, horrifying end. Montaigne asks two more questions of Alexander, as if unsatisfied with the query/explanation that had ended the essay's B-text version.

> Ou, qu'il l'estimast si proprement sienne qu'en cette hauteur il ne peust souffrir de la veoir en un autre sans le despit d'une passion envieuse, ou que l'impetuosité naturelle de sa cholere fust incapable d'opposition? De vrai, si elle eust receu la bride, il est à croire qu'en la prinse et desolation de la ville de Thebes elle l'eust receue, à veoir cruellement mettre au fil de l'espée tant de vaillans hommes perdus et n'ayans plus moyen de desfense publique. Car il en fut tué bien six mille, desquels nul ne fut veu ny fuiant ny demandant merci, au rebours cerchans, qui çà, qui là, par les rues, à affronter les ennemis victorieux, les provoquant à les faire mourir d'une mort honorable. Nul ne fut veu si abatu de blessures qui n'essaiast en son dernier soupir de se venger encores, et à tout les armes du desespoir consoler sa mort en la mort de quelque ennemi. Si ne trouva l'affliction de leur vertu aucune pitié, et ne suffit la longueur d'un jour à assouvir sa vengeance. Dura ce carnage jusques à la derniere goute de sang qui se trouva espandable, et ne s'arresta que aux personnnes desarmées, vieillards, femmes et enfans, pour en tirer trente mille esclaves. (10)

> Or did he consider it so peculiarly his own that he could not bear to see it at this height in another without passionately envious spite? Or was the natural impetuosity of his anger incapable of brooking opposition? In truth, if it could have been bridled, it is probable that it would have been in the capture and desolation of the city of Thebes, at the sight of so many valiant men, lost and without any further means of common defense, cruelly put to the sword. For fully six thousand of them were killed, of whom not one was seen fleeing or asking for mercy, but who were on the contrary seeking, some here, some there, through the streets, to confront the victorious enemy and to provoke an honorable death at his hands. Not one was seen so beaten down with wounds as not to try even in his last gasp to avenge himself, and with the

weapons of despair to assuage his death in the death of some enemy. Yet the distress of their valor found no pity, and the length of a day was not enough to satiate Alexander's revenge. This slaughter went on to the last drop of blood that could be shed, and stopped only at the unarmed people, old men, women, and children, so that thirty thousand of them might be taken as slaves. (5)

In this final tableau of Thebes, still another city at the mercy of its conqueror, Montaigne has managed to find the historical example that completely reverses his preceding ones, particularly the story of the prince of Wales and Limoges that opens the essay. Where Edward did not spare the women and children and only abated his vengeance toward the city at the sight of three lone gentlemen fighting on against his entire army, Alexander shows no mercy to the six thousand Thebans fiercely resisting him and only spares the women and children—though he spares them only to enslave them, desolating Thebes and completing his revenge. In this case, valor really has become "common," since it is displayed by the entire adult male population of the doomed city. These are, ironically, the same Thebans who, in the A-text version of the essay, had shown themselves capable of reverencing—and sparing—their valorous fellow citizen Epaminondas. Their own valor induces no such mercy in their conqueror.

The first of Montaigne's new questions/explanations about Alexander's behavior now suggests that Alexander was able enough to see and recognize the extraordinary valor of Betis, but could not bear what he saw. For Alexander may have considered valor to be his own exclusive property that set him above other men. Seneca had argued that the almighty emperor-Stoic measures his autonomy from those to whom he grants mercy, abasing them to near nonbeing. But Betis, the other ("un autre") who obstinately refuses to capitulate or go away, challenges this imperious selfhood that would acknowledge only its own will and consciousness. Alexander finds in Betis a double or mirror image that enrages him precisely because it would deny his own uniqueness and omnipotence: what he envies in Betis is finally *anything*—valor, selfhood, will—that Betis might claim as his own, independent and beyond the control of his conqueror. And so Alexander reduces Betis to literal nonbeing.[15]

Alexander's behavior may be glossed by the brief fifteenth essay of the first book, "On est puny pour s'opiniastrer à une place sans raison" ("One is punished for defending a place obstinately without reason"). Dated by Villey to an earlier phase of the composition of the *Essais*, it can be read as a streamlined, brutally simplified first draft of "Par divers moyens." The essay describes the custom of war that punishes—and punishes by death— those who stubbornly defend a place which cannot be held by the rules of war.[16] In three anecdotes drawn from the French wars in Italy earlier in

Montaigne's century, angry commanders order the massacre of those enemies, captains as well as rank and file, who they feel have held out unreasonably against them and their superior forces, against the fortune of war. This military realism makes us look at the valor of the defeated in "Par divers moyens" in a somewhat different light: was it, according to codified norms of war, merely a mad obstinacy? Did Phyto, Betis, and the Thebans—the victims of their conquerors' wrath in the anecdotes that Montaigne would add into the later B-text version of that essay—receive the treatment they had every reason to expect? Should they not have submitted, the most common way of softening the hearts of the victors, once the odds of war were clear? But now Montaigne returns to the problem of making a calculus of those odds, of distinguishing reasonable defense from desperate obstinacy.

> Mais, d'autant que le jugement de la valeur et foiblesse du lieu se prend par l'estimation et contrepois des forces qui l'assaillent, car tel s'opiniatreroit justement contre deux couleuvrines, qui feroit l'enragé d'attendre trente cannons; où se met encore en conte la grandeur du prince conquerant, sa reputation, le respect qu'on luy doit, il y a danger qu'on presse un peu la balance de ce costé la. Et en advient par ces mesmes termes, que tels ont si grande opinion d'eux et de leurs moiens, que, ne leur semblant point raisonnables qu'il y ait rien digne de leur faire teste, passent le cousteau par tout, où ils trouvent resistance, autant que fortune leur dure; (68)

> But the judgment of the strength or weakness of a place is formed by estimating the comparative strength of the forces attacking it; a man might properly hold out against two culverins who would be crazy to resist thirty cannon. Moreover, there comes into account also the greatness of the conquering prince, his reputation, the respect that is owed to him, whence there is a danger that the balance will be weighed too heavily on the side of the attackers. And it happens because of these same conditions that some have so great an opinion of themselves and their power that, since it seems unreasonable to them that there should be anything worthy to stand up against them, they put everyone to the sword wherever they find resistance, as long as their fortune lasts; (48)

So how do you know when to put up a fight? If anything you will probably incline not to stubborn and insensate resistance, but rather to the other extreme of giving up your position too easily and too soon, impressed as you will be by the greatness of your enemy. But it still may not be soon enough to suit the victor: and here, as in "Par divers moyens," the focus shifts from the beleaguered defender to the conqueror, and, as it does so, becomes more pessimistic. The "grande opinion" that the great have of themselves causes them to regard all opposition to their power as culpable stubbornness. This exaggerated "opinion" of the aggressor is, in fact, the counterpart or mirror of the "opiniastrer" of the obstinate defender: the more the former (unreasonably) thinks of himself the more unreasonable he will view the latter's resistance. Was it the very "greatness" of Alexander the Great that made him brook no opposition: would he have massacred the defeated Thebans whether they submitted to him or continued to fight?

Or, Montaigne asks in his third rhetorical question, was this simply the case of an uncontrollable anger, "incapable d'opposition": whether, as the ambiguous syntax quibbles, the opposition of Betis, who stands in the way of Alexander's power, or the opposition of virtue that Alexander might impose upon his impetuous nature? If Alexander could not control himself—as Stoicism preaches—how could he be expected to be merciful to others? And if the "virtue" of Alexander—his valor and "hardiesse"—can fail to produce clemency, better the compassionate pity of Montaigne and other "weaker natures."

But perhaps Betis does ask for it by his stubborn silence, as Phyto undeniably does with his loud imprecations against Dionysius. If the nature of the victorious rulers has darkly changed in the historical anecdotes added to the B and C versions of the essay, so has that of their valorous victims. Their defiance has acquired a new level of aggression that is generalized in the desperate prowess of the Thebans who sought "to provoke an honorable death" at the hands of their enemy—and to bring down as many of the enemy with them as they can. There can be, the essay acknowledges, something provocative in this valor that rouses feelings other than reverence in its beholder. If you ask for no quarter, no quarter is what you may get.

Once again, then, the essay has made the defiant foe into the mirror image of the victorious conqueror, both equally implacable. The actions of both, moreover, offer distorted reflections of a virtue that is "Stoic": the conqueror who does not stoop to pity (nor, for that matter, rise to disdainful clemency), the vanquished who refuses to acknowledge defeat. Perhaps, Montaigne suggests, their confrontation is what behavior based on Stoic teachings might quickly degenerate into, when the wish to attain power over the self becomes confused with a general will to power. The warfare in which the essay is set is almost a metaphor: it seems to be the inevitable result as much as the condition of a collision of two would-be autonomous selves, neither of whom is willing to acknowledge, much less yield to, the claims of the other upon itself, both of whom express this supposed indifference to the outside world in terms of aggression.[17] Where the two are unevenly matched in power, the conqueror is apt to turn into a cruel tyrant (and the essay suggests that there is not much to choose from between Dionysius and Alexander), the vanquished just as apt to invite, and become complicit in, his own destruction. If the victor refuses pity—and pardon as well—the defeated may prove just as pitiless toward himself.

It may be time to step back from this first of the *Essais*, whose extraordinary verbal artistry and complexity crowded into the space of three pages compares with the greatest of prose poems. The careful elaboration of the essay through its three versions has produced two separate, if, I shall argue, connected arguments. One of these arguments, we have seen, is skeptical, and it is reinforced in the later B and C texts by the new historical anecdotes that, joined to the story of Sulla and his former Perusine host in the essay's first version, all counter the essay's opening examples by showing the valor and defiance of the defeated failing to gain mercy from their victors. The essay thus mounts an attack on prudential wisdom: the idea that one can use historical analogy to determine the proper course of present behavior. As Victoria Kahn has shown, Montaigne exploits the humanist practice of arguing and mustering examples on both sides of a question—*in utramque partem*—to demonstrate how this debating process can lead not to consensus but to a suspension of judgment.[18] In the perfectly symmetrical antithesis between the opening story of the siege of Limoges and the last account of the destruction of Thebes, the essay formally spells out the contradictory quality of historical examples, and reaffirms its earlier view of the diverse, undulating, and unpredictable nature of human behavior.

The second argument, the one that I have spent more time unfolding and examining, concerns Montaigne's shifting attitude toward a model of heroic selfhood, a model that combines and demonstrates an analogy between aristocratic concepts of martial honor and Stoic philosophical doctrines of personal autonomy. The essayist is initially attracted to this rugged individualism when it is displayed in the valor of the defeated, unconcerned for their own lives, subsequently repelled when the same individualism in the person of the conqueror (and perhaps of the vanquished, too) puts the lives of others in disregard. Central to Montaigne's revision of the essay is his evocation and critique of the Stoic's avoidance of pity, an identification with other persons and their weaknesses that would require a bending or relaxation from that commitment to virtue which is supposed to make the self its own godlike master. Montaigne intuits that this self-sufficiency is self-aggrandizing: it separates the Stoic as well as the valorous aristocrat "from the common herd": the commoners and women—and Montaigne himself—among whom the "vicious passion" of pity summons up feelings of common humanity. In the case of Alexander, who would make valor exclusively his own, it separates the pitiless tyrant from *all* other human beings. The essayist notes in the "Apologie de Raimond Sebond" (2:12) that the "vice" of compassion can be a spur to clemency—[A] "La compassion sert d'aiguillon à la [B] clemence" (567; 427). The later additions to "Par divers moyens" suggest that without pity no mercy may be forthcoming at all. The terrible scenes of cruelty and human devastation that conclude the essay suggest the ethical and political drawbacks of a self obstinately intent on "virtue" to the point of inflexibility.

The two arguments of the essay are interrelated. For in the skeptical reversals of its examples Montaigne provides a portrait of the flexibility of mind, the capacity to see more than one side of an issue, that is part and parcel of the "softness" he attributes to himself and that he opposes to the rigid commitment to one position characterizing the attitudes of the noble protagonists in the various showdowns that those examples recount. A voice of skeptical moderation, the essayist's own voice, has a say in what is otherwise a drama of unyielding wills, and it may offer a way out of the impasse that those contending wills create. To use Villey's terms, we can watch a Skeptical phase of Montaigne's thought succeeding a Stoical one, but we need to see how this skepticism helps to constitute a particular personal style or way of being in the world that the essayist will depict as his own and that he will hold up as a pointed alternative to—or, better, revision and recuperation of—the aristocratic-Stoic model of selfhood that the first essay of his collection has examined and found wanting. The self-portrait has decidedly moral and political purposes, as we shall eventually see in the autobiographical anecdote that Montaigne inserted into the essay that directly responds to 1:1, "Divers evenemens de mesme conseil."

Clemency in "Divers evenemens de mesme conseil" (1:24)

Essay 1:24 answers "Par divers moyens," and not only in its title—"Various outcomes of the same plan"—which reverses the title of the opening essay.[19] This essay, which is also concerned with the problem of pardon and directly cites a central, perhaps *the* central passage of Seneca's *De Clementia*, also reverses the perspective of the showdown of adversaries in "Par divers moyens." We are asked to identify with the prince who must decide whether or not to pardon, rather than with those at his mercy. But in this case, the principal life that is at stake is that of the prince himself, who is menaced by plots to assassinate him. How should you act when, for all of your power, you are constantly at risk? The essay notes that for the most part, history shows princes heading off conspiracies with "vengeance and executions"—"par vengeance et par supplices" (128; 94). But Montaigne chooses instead to present instances of clemency. Here, too, we can trace the development of Montaigne's thought on mercy versus revenge by reading first the original A-text version of the essay, and then by examining the additions and revisions of the B text of 1588. It is in the latter that Montaigne turns to the authority of his personal experience and recounts his own showdown with potential foes.

"Divers evenemens" opens with an anecdote that is set in the time of "nos premiers troubles" (124), that is, at the beginning of the French Wars of Religion. For the first time, but not the last, we shall see Montaigne's meditations on the showdown of obstinate opponents, on vengeance and mercy, placed explicitly in the particular contemporary context to which, I argue, they are all, however indirectly, addressed. He is always talking about, though he may be talking around, the civil strife between Catholics and Protestants in his own France. Montaigne tells of how Jacques Amyot had once recounted to him a "story to the honor" of François, the duke of Guise. During the Catholic siege of a Huguenot-held Rouen in 1562, this prince had been informed by Catherine de' Medici of a conspiracy against his life and the identity of his would-be assassin, a gentleman in his camp. When the duke confronted this gentleman with the proofs of his betrayal, the latter, his spirit entirely broken, begged for mercy and would have thrown himself in supplication at the duke's feet.

> mais il l'en garda, suyvant ainsi son propos: Venez ça; vous ay-je autre-fois fait desplaisir? ay-je offensé quelqu'un des vostres par haine particuliere? Il n'y a pas trois semaines que je vous congnois, quelle raison vous a peu mouvoir à entreprendre ma mort? Le gentil'homme respondit à cela d'une voix tremblante, que ce n'estoit aucune occasion particuliere qu'il en eust, mais l'interest de la cause generale de son party; et qu'aucuns luy avoyent persuadé que ce seroit une execution pleine de pieté, d'extirper, en quelque maniere que ce fut, un si puissant ennemy de leur religion. Or, suyvit ce Prince, je vous veux montrer combien la religion que je tiens est plus douce que celle dequoy vous faictes profession. La vostre vous a conseillé de me tuer sans m'ouïr, n'ayant receu de moy aucune offence; et la mienne me commande que je vous pardonne, tout convaincu que vous estes de m'avoir voulu homicider sans raison. Allez vous en, retirez vous, que je ne vous voye plus icy; et, si vous estes sage, prenez doresnavant en voz entreprinses des conseillers plus gens de bien que ceux là. (125)

But the prince kept him from doing so, and continued his talk thus: "Come here. Have I ever done anything against you? Have I harmed one of your family through private hatred? I haven't known you three weeks; what reason can have moved you to undertake my death?" To that the gentleman replied in a trembling voice that it was no personal cause that he had for it, but the interest of the general cause of his party; and that some persons had persuaded him that it would be an act of piety to extirpate by any means whatever so powerful an enemy of their religion. "Now," went on this prince, "I want to show you how much gentler is the religion I hold than the one that you profess. Yours has advised you to kill me without a hearing, having received no harm from me; and mine commands me to pardon you, convicted though you are of having wanted to murder me without reason. Go away, get out, don't let me see you here again; and if you are wise, henceforth take more decent counselors for your enterprises." (90–91)

The Catholic teaches the Protestant a lesson in Christian forgiveness. His clemency seems, however, as much an act of *noblesse oblige* as of charity. Although the treacherous gentleman confesses that there was nothing personal in his assassination plot—war is war—the duke has insisted upon a private relationship between two individuals: "What did I ever do to you to deserve this?" He implies that there would indeed have been some justification for vendetta if he, the duke, had done some injury to the gentleman or to the gentleman's clan. The claims of personal honor seem to counterbalance an imperative to forgive the trespasses of others. The duke's beau geste that brings him "honor" similarly takes on the guise of aristocratic magnanimity and condescension: it asserts as much the prince's superiority of rank as an equality of the two men in Christian brotherhood. The overlap of the two ethical codes may be felt in the duke's admonition to the gentleman to associate henceforth with "gens de bien," which primarily connotes the nobility and those who live up to noble standards of behavior. The duke suggests that the gentleman has been led astray by Huguenots who are not gentlemen: assassination—except, perhaps, in affairs of family honor—is something just not done. He teaches him a lesson in nobility.

The honorable nature of the duke's action links his story to the anecdote that immediately follows, one that Montaigne translates almost verbatim from the *De Clementia* (1.9). It is the story of Augustus and Cinna, later to be the subject of Corneille's famous play. The Roman emperor has discovered a plot against his life led by Cinna, and had asked himself when the cycle of vengeance and cruelty that had founded his reign would come to an end. At this point his wife Livia advised him to try the expedient of mercy.

> Et les conseils des femmes y seront-ils receuz, lui fit elle? Fais ce que font les medecins, quand les receptes accoustumées ne peuvent servir: ils en essayent de contraires. Par severité tu n'as jusques à cette heure rien profité: Lepidus a suivy Salvidienus; Murena, Lepidus; Caepio, Murena; Egnatius, Caepio. Commence à experimenter comment te succederont la douceur et la clemence. Cinna est convaincu: pardonne luy; de te nuire desormais il ne pourra, et profitera à ta gloire. (125–26)

> Are women's counsels to be admitted? Do what the doctors do when the accustomed prescriptions will not serve: they try the opposite. By severity up to now you have not gained a thing: Lepidus has followed Salvidienus, Murena Lepidus, Caepio Murena, Egnatius Caepio. Now try how gentleness and clemency will succeed. Cinna is convicted; pardon him; harm you henceforth he cannot, and it will profit your glory. (91)

This woman's counsel confirms the course to which Augustus had already been inclined. Livia appeals to Augustus, as Seneca does to Nero in the larger *De Clementia*, to consider the glory that he will accrue by showing clemency, and, in addition, she suggests that a course of mercy may be politically more opportune than severity. Sure enough, after a lengthy colloquy with Cinna similar to the one between the duke of Guise and the Huguenot gentleman, Augustus wins not only the eternal friendship of Cinna but also security for his reign, for from that time onward there were no more conspiracies against him, and he "received a just reward for this clemency of his" (126; 92). The essay thus juxtaposes a modern instance of forgiveness during the Wars of Religion with Seneca's archetypal story of imperial clemency, and appears to assure us that mercy is the best policy.

But the next sentence effects a brilliant and unexpected reversal: the mildness of the duke of Guise did not prevent him from soon being assassinated in another, similar act of treason.[20] Montaigne spells out the grim moral.

> Tant c'est chose vaine et frivole que l'humaine prudence; et au travers de tous nos projects, de nos conseils et precautions, la fortune maintient tousjours la possession des evenemens.
>
> Nous appellons les medecins heureux, quand ils arrivent à quelque bonne fin; comme s'il n'y avoit que leur art, qui ne se peut maintenir d'elle mesme, et qui eust les fondemens trop frailes pour s'appuyer de sa propre force; et comme s'il n'y avoit qu'elle, qui aye besoin que la fortune preste la main à ses operations. Je croy d'elle tout le pis ou le mieux qu'on voudra. Car nous n'avons, Dieu mercy, nul commerce ensemble: (127)

> So vain and frivolous a thing is human prudence; and athwart all our plans, counsels, and precautions, Fortune still maintains her grasp on the results.
>
> We call doctors fortunate when they attain some good end, as if their art alone could not stand on its own feet and had too weak a foundation to support itself by its own strength; and as if no other needed a helping hand from Fortune. Of medicine I believe all the bad or good you like, for we have, thank God, no dealings whatever. (92)

We are back on the skeptical ground of "Par divers moyens," and the link between the two essays is fairly clear. That first essay also ended up describing how the same behavior, the stubborn resistance of the defeated, could obtain different results, their pardon or their deaths, in different situations. Here, the roles are switched but the alternative results are the same: the pardoning ruler wins security by his mercy—or his death. If in the earlier essay man was vain and undulating, here his prudence is equally vain and frivolous. The ensuing discussion of doctors picks up the medical metaphor in the speech of Seneca's Livia, who remembers that physicians often try out contrary remedies. It announces an attack on medicine that becomes a favorite theme of the *Essais*.[21] Life and death are once again at stake, but Montaigne remains skeptical about the help afforded by the doctors' art: he does not call on them. The failure of medicine, in turn, becomes a figure for the inefficacy and capriciousness of all prudential arts, none of them immune from Fortune.

But this skeptical moment yields in turn to ethical reflection.

> Voylà pourquoy, en cette incertitude et perplexité que nous aporte l'impuissance de voir et choisir ce qui est le plus commode, pour les difficultez que les divers accidens et circonstances de chaque chose tirent, le plus seur, quand autre consideration ne nous y convieroit, est, à mon advis, de se rejetter au parti où il y a plus d'honnesteté et de justice; et puis qu'on est en doute du plus court chemin, tenir tousjours le droit: comme en ces deux exemples que je vien de proposer, il n'y a point de doubte, qu'il ne fut plus beau et plus genereux à celuy qui avoit receu l'offence, de la pardonner, que s'il eust fait autrement. S'il en est mes-advenu au premier, il ne s'en faut pas prendre à ce sien bon dessein; et ne sçait on, quand il eust pris le party contraire, s'il eust eschapé la fin à laquelle son destin l'appeloit; et si eust perdu la gloire d'une si notable bonté. (128)

> That is why, when the various details and circumstances of a matter have so perplexed us that we are powerless to see and choose what is most advantageous, I find the surest thing to do, even if no other consideration invited us to it, is this: to cast ourselves into the course in which there is the most decency and justice, and since we are in doubt about the shortest path, to hold always to the straight path. Thus, in the two examples I have just advanced, it was clearly fairer and nobler in the man who had received the offense to pardon it than to do otherwise. If the first one came to grief, this good plan of his must not be blamed for it; and no one knows whether, if he had taken the opposite course, he would have escaped the end to which his destiny called him; and thus he would have lost the glory of such exceptional kindness. (93–94)

Montaigne appeals to standards of "honnesteté," a term, like "gens de bien," that was undergoing a semantic shift in the sixteenth and seventeenth centuries, gradually losing its meaning of "honor" and coming to describe a more general and mediocre ethical virtue that Frame has in both cases translated as "decency." But it is again the earlier class-determined connotation that we still hear in this passage, as we should also understand the primary meaning of "genereux" as "noble."[22] In other words, the morality that Montaigne is urging here is couched in the same terms of aristocratic honor and magnanimity that informed the behavior of the duke of Guise in the essay's opening anecdote. These are terms, we have seen, easily assimilated with Seneca's Stoic doctrine that the dispenser of mercy aggrandizes himself. The duke attains here the same "gloire" that Livia promised Augustus in the *De Clementia*.

Montaigne offers the reader his own version of the argument for mercy of the *De Clementia*, one that is both skeptically inflected and tricked out in the vestments of aristocratic honor. The unpredictability of a world of human affairs governed by Fortune becomes the ground for an ethical behavior that is pointedly not utilitarian: the policy of forgiveness does not guarantee political success. (Though neither does the more usual, contrary policy of vengeance, Montaigne goes on to note in the following sentence: one only has to look at the fates of the Roman emperors who succeeded Augustus.) Just as in the argument he will later profess in "De la diversion" to have used to convince the young prince to clemency, Montaigne evokes an aesthetics of virtue: the duke of Guise did the beautiful ("beau"), as well as the noble thing. When the A-text version of the essay picks up again, he writes that Julius Caesar, by his policy of clemency, had taken the fairest path possible toward the danger of conspiracies—"La voye qu'y tint Julius Caesar, je trouve que c'est la plus belle qu'on puisse prendre" (131; 96)— although Caesar, too, would fall victim to assassination. The duke is indeed rewarded by becoming a part of literature, the hero of a story to his own honor that Montaigne retells, just as Seneca told the story of Augustus and Cinna to Nero, both exemplary tales of pardoning meant to move others to emulate them.

This emulation is competitive, a kind of beauty contest to determine who is the fairest of them all. If clemency does not guarantee you political efficacy against conspirators, it nonetheless channels your will to power. You show yourself more noble ("genereux") not only than those whom your clemency has spared, but over other pretenders to nobility and glory. Thus mercy, like military valor in "Par divers moyens," becomes a mark of true nobility, especially since in the cases described in the essay, it expresses a similar lack of fear of death. The princes pardon even though they live in constant danger of plots against them. It is the mark of cowardice, rather than of courage, to avenge yourself on your foes by killing them, Montaigne will assert in a key passage in "Couardise mere de la cruauté" (2:27): it shows that you fear that they will come after you again—"nous craignons, s'il demeure en vie, qu'il nous recharge d'une pareille" (695; 525).

By making clemency a form, indeed the supreme expression, of true valor, Montaigne here reveals the logic behind an argument that the *Essais* make elsewhere to *substitute* clemency *for* valor as the distinguishing sign of aristocratic identity. He complains in "Des récompenses d'honneur" (2:7) that philosophical virtue has become confused with martial valor, a valor that has easily become "vulgaire" in France's civil wars, where all classes have proved valiant, not only the nobility, whose identifying and exclusive form, he comments, is nonetheless the profession of arms.[23] In a C-text addition to "De la praesumption" (2:17), Montaigne argues that true nobility must find some other way of manifesting itself above the herd.

> [C] Les marchans, les juges de villages, les artisans, nous les voyons aller à pair de vaillance et science militaire aveq la noblesse; ils rendent des combats honorables, et publiques et privez; ils battent, il defendent villes en nos guerres. Un prince estouffe sa recommendation emmy cette presse. Qu'il reluise d'humanité, de verité, de loyauté, de temperance et sur tout de justice: marques rares, inconnues et exilées . . .
>
> [A] Par cette proportion, je me fusse trouvé [C] grand et rare, comme je me trouve pygmée et populaire à la proportion d'aucuns siecles passez, ausquels il estoit vulgaire, si d'autres plus fortes qualitez n'y concurroient, de voir un homme [A] moderé en ses vengeances, mol au ressentiment des offences, religieux en l'observance de sa parolle . . . (647)
>
> [C] We see merchants, village justices, and artisans keeping up with the nobility in valor and military knowledge. They do honorably in both private and public combats; they fight, they defend cities in our wars. A prince's distinction is smothered amid this crowd. Let him shine with humanity, with truthfulness, loyalty, moderation, and especially justice, marks that are rare, unknown, and banished . . .
>
> [A] By such a comparison I would have thought myself [C] great and rare, just as I think myself dwarfish and ordinary in comparison with certain past ages, in which it was a commonplace, if other, stronger qualities did not concur, to see a man [A] moderate in his revenge, slow to resent offenses, religious in keeping his word . . . (490–91)

We can watch how Montaigne revised his essay so that the final C version ascribes to the ideal prince those qualities that he had first depicted in himself in the A text: the essay originally presented a self-portrait "moderé en *mes* vengeances, mol au ressentiment des offences, religieux en l'observance de *ma* parolle." We will see Montaigne generally use his own example to describe a new kind of noble identity. Here he sets forth the standards of nobility that, in place of martial valor, would distinguish the prince and those who emulate him from the lower classes; if he lists justice as the most important of these attributes, it is "humanité" that he names first, the quality of mercy and sympathy that, as he subsequently describes it, moderates vengeance and softens resentment. The softness that Montaigne's first essay suggested was a vicious property that he shared with commoners and women now becomes the badge of true virtue, the clemency that marks out the aristocrat. The gentleman is known by his gentleness, by the "facilité" and "debonnaireté" that the same passage of "Par divers moyens" lists and makes interchangeable with "mollesse" and that carry invariably positive connotations in the *Essais*. It is by the exhibition of clemency that a prince or nobleman can "shine;" the beauty of the act produces the honor to which the aristocrat aspires and which sets him apart in a class by himself.

"Divers evenemens" ends with an A-text passage that suddenly puts us on the other side of the story, in the vantage point of the prince's enemy. Montaigne tells the story of an unnamed Roman nobleman, who had fled from the tyranny of the Triumvirate. After a thousand escapes, he became weary of his life of constant fear, and turned himself in to the cruelty of the executioners pursuing him. Montaigne comments:

> D'appeller les mains ennemies, c'est un conseil un peu gaillard; si croy-je encore vaudroit-il mieux le prendre que de demeurer en la fievre continuelle d'un accident qui n'a point de remede. Mais, puisque les provisions qu'on y peut aporter sont pleines d'inquietude et d'incertitude, il vaut mieux d'une belle asseurance se preparer à tout ce qui en pourra advenir, et tirer quelque consolation de ce qu'on n'est pas asseuré qu'il advienne. (132)

> To call out for the hand of the enemy is a rather extreme measure, yet a better one, I think than to remain in a continual fever over an accident that has no remedy. But since all the precautions that a man can take are full of uneasiness and uncertainty, it is better to prepare with fine assurance for the worst that can happen, and derive some consolation from the fact that we are not sure that it will happen. (97)

The earlier medical metaphor reappears here, only to suggest that there is no remedy for death, the ultimate accident of fortune. The story is supposed to suggest the mirroring reciprocity between the hunted foe of the prince and the situation of the prince himself, always a target for assassins. The clement prince has placed himself in the hands of his enemies, though he does not go so far as to summon them to kill him. In a world of uncertainty the best one can do is assume a "belle asseurance": one can act nobly and beautifully and hope for the best.

But this ending, which brings us back to the horror of the opening essay, also shows what the withholding of clemency looks like: it is not beautiful at all. The story, adapted from Appian's *Civil Wars* (4.28), recounts an incident during the proscriptions of Augustus and Antony, though Montaigne's perhaps deliberately vague "tyrannie du Triumvirat" could refer to Julius Caesar as well as to Augustus: to both Caesars who are praised for their clemency in the essay. The term is further loaded with contemporary resonance and looks back to the essay's beginning, for it evokes the so-called modern "triumvirat," formed both against the Huguenots and the French crown, in which François, the duke of Guise, joined in 1561 with Anne de Montmorency and Jacques d'Albon,

Maréchal de Saint-André: the same duke of Guise who is paired with Augustus in the first two anecdotes of "Divers evenemens."[24] Appian's anecdote gives us the spectacle of the earlier career of Augustus, himself a protagonist of civil wars like the Wars of Religion in France, a career full of "vengeances" and "cruautez," that the emperor hoped to end by taking the advice of Livia. The switch in perspective here from the prince to his victim reminds us how much depends on the clement disposition of the great, how asymmetrical are the relations in question. Whatever personal risks the clement ruler may run, his life is only one compared to the many others whom the contrary policy of revenge condemns to death.

The B-text and C-text additions to the essay emphasize the lack of fear that the prince or governor should display toward his subjects, whatever his real distrust of them. These additions both reinforce the symmetry between "Divers evenemens" and "Par divers moyens," and reexamine still further the concerns of the opening essay. Montaigne introduces two anecdotes about Dionysius of Syracuse and Alexander the Great, protagonists—also in B and C additions—of the opening essay. Both show these rulers confronting possible plots against them by peaceful rather than punitive tactics. Last seen ordering the defiant Phyto secretly drowned in "Par divers moyens," Dionysius here pays a large sum of money to a stranger who publicly declares that he has a surefire means to reveal the identities of all conspirators against the tyrant's regime: there is no such means, however, except the payment itself, which convinces the citizens of Syracuse that Dionysius must have learned a political art of great worth, a secret weapon that he now holds over his enemies to keep them in fear. And, Montaigne praises other princes who make public their knowledge of plots directed at their lives, thus intimidating plotters and suggesting by inference that they, in their royal omniscience, have nothing to fear.

The gallant fearlessness of Alexander when informed of a conspiracy against him is more striking, especially after the cruelty that he displayed at the end of "Par divers moyens." Warned in a letter from his general Parmenion that Philippus, his physician, was seeking to poison him, he showed the letter to Philippus at the same time that he swallowed the drink Philippus had prepared for him.

> Fut ce pas exprimer cette resolution, que, si ses amys le vouloient tuer, il consentoit qu'ils le peussent faire? Ce prince est le souverain patron des actes hazardeux; mais je ne sçay s'il y a traict en sa vie, qui ayt plus de fermeté que cestuy-cy, ny une beauté illustre par tant de visages. (129)

> Wasn't that expressing this resolve, that if his friends wanted to kill him, he was willing to let them? This prince is the supreme model of hazardous acts; but I do not know if there is an episode in his life that shows more courage than this one, or a beauty shining in so many aspects. (94)

This shining act—the buried metaphor is of a gem with many facets—is the most beautiful in Alexander's life, one that showed more courage than all of his battlefield exploits: clemency has, in effect, replaced martial valor as the distinctive virtue of the prince. The beauty of Alexander's deed is of the same kind as that achieved by the duke of Guise and Julius Caesar. The ruler's willingness to expose his life to peril, to pursue a policy of outward trust rather than one of suspicion and reprisal, is celebrated as the utmost display of a virtue that becomes the object of aesthetic appreciation for later ages. The two inserted anecdotes about Dionysius and Alexander counterbalance the negative portraits of the two rulers in "Par divers moyens," and once again suggest the unpredictable and diverse nature of human behavior—the ever present skeptical argument of the *Essais* —at the same time that they find in clemency a corrective to the unyielding revenge and brutality of the opening essay.

Between the anecdotes of Alexander and Dionysius lies the second principal B-text addition, which draws Montaigne's own personal experience into the argument of "Divers evenemens." It anticipates—and already links this essay to—the anecdotes concerning Montaigne at the end of "De la physionomie," the penultimate essay of Book Three, that, I will argue, crown the various versions of the showdown of hostile opponents that run through the *Essais*. Eventually these stories in which the essayist himself is the hero become the "patron" or model for ethical and political behavior. Here in "Divers evenemens" he contrasts his own action while mayor of Bordeaux with that of an earlier mayor, killed when he went out to meet a riotous city mob. The latter mayor made two mistakes. First he tried a course of submission and softness—"de soubsmission et de mollesse" (130; 94)—rather than assume a more honorable stance of confidence, befitting his rank. For one cannot, Montaigne remarks, expect humanity from mobs, though they may be quieted by reverence and fear. His second mistake was to lose his nerve,

> et d'alterer encore despuis cette contenance desmise et flatteuse qu'il avoit entreprise, en une contenance effraiée: chargeant sa voix et ses yeux d'estonnement et de penitence. (130–31)

> and change once again that deflated and fawning countenance that he had assumed into a frightened one, filling his voice and his eyes with astonishment and penitence. (96)

At that moment, the mob fell upon him. By contrast, when, in 1585 during the Wars of Religion, Montaigne found himself about to attend a general review of troops at which, he had been warned, an attempt might be made on his life by disaffected adherents to the intransigent Catholic League, he chose a course of exposure and a fixed countenance that gave nothing away.

CLEMENCY AND REVENGE 31

> Le mien [conseil] fut, qu'on evitast sur tout de donner aucun tesmoignage de ce doubte et qu'on s'y trouvast et melast parmy les files, la teste droicte et le visage ouvert, et qu'au lieu d'en retrancher aucune chose (à quoy les autres opinions visoyent le plus) qu'au contraire on sollicitast les capitaines d'advertir les soldats de faire leurs salves belles et gaillardes en l'honneur des assistans, et n'espargner leur poudre. Cela servit de gratification envers ces troupes suspectes, et engendra dés lors en avant une mutuelle et utile confience. (131)

> [My plan] was that they should above all avoid giving any sign of this fear, and should show up and mingle in the ranks, head high and countenance open, and that instead of cutting out anything (as the other opinions mostly aimed to do), they should on the contrary urge the captains to instruct their soldiers to make their volleys fine and lusty in honor of the spectators, and not spare their powder. This served to gratify the suspected troops, and engendered from then on a useful mutual confidence. (96)

The exemplary stories in this B-text insertion are particularly remarkable for the way in which they repropose the scenarios of "Par divers moyens," if only to switch around the first essay's terms. Here, rather than the ruler-aristocrat, it is the common rank and file, especially once they have been incited ("agité"), who will relent through "reverence" rather than at the sight of submission; in fact, the mob, unlike the commoners to whom the opening essay ascribed a kind of natural compassion, is without a forgiving "humanité." (130; 96) Montaigne himself produced reverence by adapting an unchanging countenance that seems to echo the stoical "visage ferme" of Phyto in "Par divers moyens"—and here the essay also clearly looks forward to "De la physionomie," where Montaigne's ability to keep a straight face will save his life—and by a display of aristocratic hauteur.[25] Unlike the unfortunate earlier mayor, whose currying of the people's favor was wanting in "honneur" and "bien-seance," Montaigne gives the orders to shoot off beautiful and gallant volleys in honor of the spectators, that is, in honor of Montaigne himself, before whom they have been mustered in review. This is another beautiful act, now performed by the essayist himself: a display of self-aggrandizing honor and nobility. And, as in the initial stories of "Par divers moyens" to which we seem to have returned, this act gratifies and removes the hostility of a potential enemy.

At this point the reader may want to throw up his hands in frustration. Montaigne seems capable of contradicting not only his former propositions but of contradicting those contradictions. The stance of bravery and constancy in the face of a vindictive foe that Montaigne first celebrates and then critically questions in the opening essay reappears here, a stance taken up by Montaigne himself. But Montaigne finally is not the Pyrrhonist he describes in the "Apologie de Raimond Sebond," a proto-deconstructionist content to lead his reader into skeptical dead ends. The paradoxes of the *Essais* teach us not only that we need to see problems from many different angles; that very flexibility of thought allows us to change our way of seeing and evaluating the world itself. We need to see that a kind of dialectical argument has emerged from Montaigne's skeptical method. In these anecdotes, the positions of ruler and those at his mercy have been confused to the point where it is not clear who has power over whom: the two mayors are the ones who seem in immediate physical danger. Nonetheless it is necessary to link Montaigne's behavior to the rest of "Divers evenemens" in order to recognize that it is simultaneously an act of clemency as well as a noble gesture of constancy: for the alternative to reconciling himself with the soldiers suspected of mutiny and murderous intentions would have been to seek them out and execute them. Moreover, in the passage that prefaces these anecdotes, Montaigne suggests that his action was as much an act of submission to the soldiers—who could have killed him and his associates as they mingled with the ranks—as it was a standing up to their menace.

> C'est un excellent moyen de gaigner le coeur et volonté d'autruy, de s'y aller soubsmettre et fier, pourveu que ce soit librement et sans contrainte d'aucune necessité, et que ce soit en condition qu'on y porte une fiance pure et nette, le front au moins deschargé de tout scrupule. (130)

> To submit and entrust oneself to others is an excellent way to win their heart and will, provided it be done freely and without the constraint of any necessity, and that the situation be such that we bring to it a pure and clean trust, and at least a countenance free of any misgiving. (95)

This sentence rewrites the opening of "Par divers moyens" that opposes the two means of softening hearts, submission versus bravery. Here the two means have been dialectically combined. It is possible for you to submit with honor and to hold your head up high: in fact, if this submission is to have the desired effect of winning the other's heart, you *must* act with noble—i.e., fearless—composure. The fault of the earlier mayor lay in his submitting with a submissive demeanor—and even that he could not keep. By the same token, clemency, as Montaigne has now redefined it from the Stoic model of Seneca, also represents a similar combination of the two means. A princely or aristocratic "humanité" contains within it an act of noble courage: of "vaillance." The courage lies in your acknowledgment of your own vulnerability at the hands of the others whom you spare and in your *free* submission to this condition. In *both* cases, whether you are the clement ruler or the yielding subject—and by now they cannot be told apart—a Stoic or aristocratic sense of personal independence and self-respect is preserved even as you yield and trust in others, provided you yield freely. The crucial phrase, "librement et sans contrainte d'aucune necessité," defines the condition that Montaigne will elsewhere call "franchise," an honest dealing with the world that is based on freedom, the freedom in part of a particular noble caste, but more generally, as these essays demonstrate, freedom from the fear of death.[26]

Montaigne thus manages to salvage the liberty and integrity of the Stoic selfhood that he initially admired in "Par divers moyens" even as he imagines that selfhood in a situation that directly counters the scenes of implacable revenge and equally implacable defiance that bring that first essay to a close. Here both sides "submit" to the other, a mutual yielding that defuses potential violence. He has, that is, tried to separate the ethical search for power and control over oneself from a political will to dominate others: the confusion of the two, he had implied in "Par divers moyens," is a recipe for tyranny. The separation is not complete, as I have sugggested above. The will to power is displaced in the self-aggrandizing gesture of clemency whose beauty causes others to acknowledge the nobility and greatness of its bestower: this is Seneca's argument in the *De Clementia*. Moreover, as the example of Augustus and Cinna attests, clemency can be an instrument of political rule. Nonetheless, in contrast to the further argument that Seneca makes to Nero in his treatise, Montaigne's clement ruler does *not* show leniency as an expression of his political omnipotence, a power so great—or that wants to be so great—that it renders the other insignificant. Rather the granter of mercy recognizes the vulnerability that he shares with others, an acknowledgment both of the limits of his power and of his common mortality—and here Montaigne's medical metaphors acquire a special force. Paradoxically, you can most fully demonstrate the freedom of your own will when you acknowledge and yield to the will of others, when you entrust your physical safety to the power of someone else.

The anecdote from the period of Montaigne's mayoralty returns "Divers evenemens" to the French Wars of Religion, and it is easy enough to see how the concepts of an honorable submission and of mutual trust offer a moderate solution to the hard-line divisions that had developed between Catholics and Huguenots; in effect, Montaigne is outlining an ethics for a *politique* settlement. But the entire essay has, in fact, treated cases of internal strife—the Roman civil wars, the possibility of treachery in the camp of Alexander and Dionysus' Syracuse, the riot in Bordeaux—in contrast to the situation of foreign war that characterized most of the anecdotes of "Par divers moyens." Beyond its relevance to Montaigne's contemporary context, the scenario of civil war fits the revision that "Divers evenemens" enacts upon the opening essay of his book. For, as is suggested in both essays by the mirroring of victor and of vanquished, of pardoner and of those spared, all human conflicts are ultimately civil wars: internecine conflicts that, "Divers evenemens" implies, can only be peacefully resolved when they are recognized for what they are. The clemency the essay preaches at once allows you to exert your power over others and puts you in their power; it not only makes you act humanely toward potential foes, but also, in your shared weakness, causes you to know your common likeness and "humanité."

A Frame for the *Essais*?

The acknowledgment of a common humanity and of common human limits is the final moral wisdom taught in "De l'experience" (3:13) at the conclusion of the three-book version of the *Essais*, and their ending looks back toward their beginning. It is in the B text of 1588 that Montaigne introduces the figure of Alexander the Great at the end of "Par divers moyens" and then concludes his opening essay with a question seeking to understand the Macedonian conqueror's cruel treatment of the vanquished Betis—to which he adds two more questions in the final C-text version of the essay. In the same B text, Montaigne may offer an answer to the initial question posed by the *Essais*, an answer that comes, however, only at the very end of the collection. On the last page of "De l'experience" (3:13), Alexander reappears.

> Et je ne trouve rien si humble et si mortel en la vie d'Alexandre que ses fantasies autour de son immortalisation. Philotas le mordit plaisamment par sa responce; il s'estoit conjouy avec luy par lettre de l'oracle de Jupiter Hammon qui l'avoit logé entre les Dieux: Pour ta consideration j'en suis bien aise, mais il y a de quoy plaindre les hommes qui auront à vivre avec un homme et luy obeyr, lequel outrepasse [C] et ne se contente de [B] la mesure d'un homme. [C] *"Diis te minorem quod geris, imperas."*
> [B] La gentille inscription de quoy les Atheniens honorerent la venue de Pompeius en leur ville, se conforme à mon sens:
> > *D'autant es tu Dieu comme*
> > *Tu te recognois homme.* (1115)

And I find nothing so humble and so mortal in the life of Alexander as his fancies about his immortalization. Philotas stung him wittily by his answer. He congratulated him by letter on the oracle of Jupiter Ammon which had lodged him among the gods: "As far as you are concerned, I am very glad of it; but there is reason to pity the men who will have to live with and obey a man who exceeds [C] and is not content with [B] a man's proportions." [C] *Since you obey the gods you rule the world.* (Horace)

The nice inscription with which the Athenians honored the entry of Pompey into their city is in accord with my meaning.
> *You are as much a god as you will own*
> *That you are nothing but a man alone.*
> > (Amyot's Plutarch) (856–57)

Here, at the end of the *Essais*, Alexander's behavior finds an explanation: he thought that he was a god.[27] Woe to those men compelled to live under his rule, including Philotas himself, whose letter was all too prophetic: Alexander took the letter's comments, however witty, as a sign of disloyalty when he accused Philotas of plotting against him. He extracted a confession of guilt from Philotas in a scene of torture, described in Quintus Curtius' *History of Alexander* (6.9f.), that is as horrifying as the same historian's account of the death of Betis (4.6). Montaigne remembers the story of Philotas, who he presumes was innocent, in his argument against judiciary torture in "De la conscience" (2:5; 369; 266). The episode is also probably recalled in a B-text addition about Alexander that Montaigne added to "De l'inconstance de nos actions" ("Of the inconsistency of our actions"), the opening essay of the second book and thus one that occupies another strategic position in the *Essais*.

> [B] Il n'est point de vaillance plus extreme en son espece que celle d'Alexandre; mais elle n'est qu'en espece, ny assez pleine par tout, et universelle. [C] Toute incomparable qu'elle est, si a elle encores ses taches: [B] qui faict que nous le voyons se troubler si esperduement aux plus legieres soubçons qu'il prent des machinations des siens contre sa vie, et se porter en cette recherche d'une si vehemente et indiscrete injustice et d'une crainte qui subvertit sa raison naturelle. (336)

> [B] There is no more extreme valor of its kind than Alexander's; but it is only of one kind, and not complete and universal enough. [C] Incomparable though it is, it still has its blemishes; [B] which is why we see him worry so frantically when he conceives the slightest suspicion that his men are plotting against his life, and why he behaves in such matters with such violent and indiscriminate injustice and with a fear that subverts his natural reason. (243)

Thus the event that Montaigne holds up in "Divers evenemens" as the most beautiful of Alexander's life—Alexander's bravely drinking down the beverage that his doctor Philippus had prepared after having been informed of the latter's treachery—was also exceptional. Unlike the fearless clemency with which the various rulers celebrated in "Divers evenemens" met conspiracies against them, Alexander's normal course in similar situations was to turn into a paranoid tyrant.

Alexander's lack of clemency, both to defeated enemies and to those of his own camp he suspects of plotting against his life, is linked at the end of "De l'experience" to his fantasies of immortalization. Paradoxically, the great man's belief or desire to believe in his divinity makes him fear for his own life. Or rather his fear of death inspires his pretensions to be a god, pretensions that are supported by his political conquests, by his life-and-death power over others. Alexander's refusal to accept his mortal limitations spurs his unending aggression—and makes him so cruel. For, as Philotas had suggested and then personally experienced, the king's denial of his own humanity makes him treat those he rules with inhumanity. The pairing of Alexander with Pompey, reminded by the Athenians that the most godlike of human actions is to acknowledge oneself a mere man, may also signal a return to "Par divers moyens," which originally ended with the contrast between the clement Pompey and the vengeful Sulla. Both endings of the first essay of Montaigne's book seem to be invoked by the ending of the last.

In the context of the ending of "De l'experience," Alexander's fantasies of divinity are coupled with a more general tendency to ignore the claims of the body—the obvious reminder of human mortality. At one level, Montaigne condemns, if obliquely, an excessive religious preoccupation with otherworldly goals: and he has in mind the zealotry of Huguenots and Catholics that have torn his France apart. After allowing Christian meditation its due place for a privileged few (presumably monastics who do not act upon the world), he adds an aside to the reader in the C text: "Entre nous, ce sont choses que j'ay tousjours veuës de singulier accord: les opinions supercelestes et les meurs sousterraines" (1115)—"Between us, these are two things that I have always observed to be in singular accord: supercelestial thoughts and subterranean conduct" (856). Such attempts to escape from one's humanity, Montaigne continues, transform one not into an angel, but into a beast.

This attack on religious fanaticism is contained, however, in a larger philosophical polemic against any privilege accorded to the reasoning soul over natural bodily impulses. The most notorious, though by no means exclusive, target here is once again Stoicism. In a C-text addition, Montaigne cites, to indicate his dissent from, Seneca's Epistle 92 (4–7), where the Roman moralist is in a particularly harsh mood and preaches against the marriage of "le raisonnable avec le desraisonnable, le severe à l'indulgent, l'honneste au des-honneste, que volupté est qualité brutale, indigne que le sage la gouste" (1113)—"the reasonable with the unreasonable, the severe with the indulgent, the honorable with the dishonorable; that sensual pleasure is a brutish thing unworthy of being enjoyed by the wise man" (855). In the same letter, Seneca writes:

> Reason, however, is a common attribute of gods and men; in the gods it is already perfected, in us it is capable of being perfected.[28] (27)

Through the inflexible rule of reason, the Stoic sage can become like a god, a god unto himself. Montaigne had already attacked this Stoic presumption at the very end of the "Apologie de Raimond Sebond"; by the C text of 1595, he would label as absurd Seneca's dictum that man must be miserable unless he raise himself above his humanity.

When Alexander, with his own delusions of divinity, is placed in this context, he becomes once again a kind of mirror figure for the Stoic. The philosopher's rigorous, unpitying control over his own human frailty possesses, as Montaigne now explicitly spells out, an ethical and political analogue in the tyrant's cruel and pitiless dealings with subjects above whom he has set himself as a god. Clemency toward others begins with forgiveness toward oneself: in particular with a reconciliation with the fact of one's mortality.

If the negative figure of Alexander at the beginning and ending of the *Essais* is a product of the B text and represents a change of attitude on Montaigne's part between 1580 and 1588, the A text of 1580 had already demoted Alexander to second place among the great men of history in its penultimate essay, "Des plus excellens hommes" (2:36)—"Of the most outstanding men." The essay represents Montaigne's own version of Plutarch's parallel *Lives*. In his "Defence de Seneque et de Plutarque" (2:32), the essayist counters the charge made by Jean Bodin in his *Methodus* that Plutarch had shown favoritism to his fellow Greeks by comparing them with Romans who were not their equals (726). In "Des plus excellens hommes" Montaigne not only presents three famous Greeks (Homer, Alexander, Epaminondas); in each case he compares them favorably with Roman rivals (Virgil, Julius Caesar, Scipio Aemilianus). In the case of Epaminondas and Scipio, as a C-text addition to the essay makes clear, he has sought himself to fill in a gap created by the loss of Plutarch's own parallel biographies of the two men.

The choice of Epaminondas, the great Theban general, as the most outstanding of men, superior even to Alexander, comes as a surprise. Why Epaminondas? Perhaps because, as Timothy Hampton has suggested, the Boeotian Epaminondas may, through a play of words, recall Montaigne's lost friend, the paragon of men who was Etienne de La Boétie?[29] Or perhaps Montaigne uses Epaminondas to answer Bodin: the Greeks called Epaminondas first among themselves, and the first man of Greece is easily the first in the world, Montaigne asserts (756; 573), implying that so much did Greek virtue outshine Roman virtue that there was really no comparison, no real parallel for Plutarch to make. But Montaigne's admiration went deeper, and the reasons are suggested by the two "opinions" of Epaminondas that he cites as examples illustrating the Theban's "excessive bonté" and which formed the ending of the A-text version of the essay.

> Il ne pensoit pas qu'il fut loisible, pour recouvrer mesmes la liberté de son pays, de tuer un homme sans connoissance de cause: voylà pourquoy il fut si froid à l'entreprise de Pelopidas, son compaignon, pour la delivrance de

> Thebes. Il tenoit aussi qu'en une bataille il falloit fuyr le rencontre d'un amy qui fut au party contraire, et l'espargner. (757)

> He did not think it was permissible, even to recover the freedom of his country, to kill a man without full knowledge of the case. That is why he was so cool to the enterprise of his companion Pelopidas for the deliverance of Thebes. He also held that in battle a man should avoid encountering a friend who was on the opposite side, and spare him. (574)

The last word of the original essay tells all: Epaminondas spared friends even when they were no longer friends, but fought against him. Nor would he kill for political expedience. It is the scrupulous clemency of Epaminondas that earns him the nod over Alexander who, in the A-text version of the essay is himself described in entirely positive terms as an exemplar of virtue and military fortune.

The contrast between the two men becomes marked in the B-text additions to the essay. Parallel to his other B-text additions that demonstrate his changing his mind about Alexander, the result, Villey suggests, of his attentive reading of Quintus Curtius's *History*, Montaigne inserts a list of those actions of Alexander that are "rather hard to excuse"—"peu mal excusables"—including his massacres of the Thebans, of Persian prisoners of war, of Indian troops to whom he had given a promise of safety (754; 571).[30] Epaminondas was made of different stuff.

> [B] En cettuy-cy l'innocence est une qualité propre, maistresse, constante, uniforme, incorruptible. Au parangon de laquelle elle paroist en Alexandre subalterne, incertaine, bigarrée, molle et fortuite. (756)

> [B] In this man innocence is a key quality, sovereign, constant, uniform, incorruptible. In comparison, it appears in Alexander as subordinate, uncertain, streaky, soft, and accidental.

In this carefully constructed opposition, where the virtue of Epaminondas *is* while that of Alexander merely *seems*, the virtue in question, "innocence" should be understood here with all of its etymological force: "in-nocens." Epaminondas did not do injury to others, and this lends his actions the constancy that Alexander lacked: so Montaigne holds up Alexander's cruelties and paranoia as examples of human inconsistency in "De l'inconstance de nos actions." The essayist characteristically takes up the Stoic good of constancy, contrasted with effeminate softness ("molle") of behavior, in order to give these terms a new ethical twist. He paradoxically celebrates Epaminondas as the man of war who wouldn't harm a soul, who, as we shall shortly see, achieves constancy precisely *through* "mollesse": the quality, as Montaigne first declared in "Par divers moyens," that lends itself to pity and clemency.

This is the portrait of Epaminondas that reappears two essays later in the three-book version of the *Essais* of 1588, in the first essay of Book Three, "De l'utile et de l'honneste" ("Of the useful and the honorable"). The essay both acknowledges and resists a Machiavellian realpolitik according to which reason of state may override morality and private conscience. At its end, Montaigne evokes the figure of Epaminondas as the great teacher ("precepteur") who demonstrates that there are limits to what is lawful for the sake of king and country (802; 609). He explicitly returns to his judgment in "Des plus excellens hommes."

> J'ay autrefois logé Epaminondas au premier rang des hommes excellens, et ne m'en desdy pas. Jusques où montoit il la consideration de son particulier devoir; qui ne tua jamais homme qu'il eust vaincu; qui, pour ce bien inestimable de rendre la liberté à son pays, faisoit conscience de tuer un Tyran [C] ou ses complices [B] sans les formes de la Justice; . . . Voylà une ame de riche composition. Il marioit aux plus rudes et violentes actions humaines la bonté et l'humanité, voire la plus delicate qui se treuve en l'escole de la Philosophie. Ce courage si gros, enflé et obstiné contre la douleur, la mort, la pauvreté, estoit ce nature ou art qui l'eust attendry jusques au poinct d'une si extreme douceur et debonnaireté de complexion? Horrible de fer et de sang, il va fracassant et rompant une nation invincible contre tout autre que contre luy seul, et gauchit, au milieu d'une telle meslée, au rencontre de son hoste et de son amy. Vrayement celuy là proprement commandoit bien à la guerre, qui luy faisoit souffrir le mors de la benignité sur le poinct de sa plus forte chaleur, ainsin enflammée qu'elle estoit et escumeuse de fureur et de meurtre. C'est miracle de pouvoir mesler à telles actions quelque image de justice; mais il n'appartient qu'à la roideur d'Epaminondas d'y pouvoir mesler la douceur et la facilité des meurs les plus molles [C] et la pure innocence. (801-2)

> I once placed Epaminondas in the first rank of outstanding men, and I do not take this back. To what a height did he raise consideration for his private duty, he who never killed a man he had vanquished, who even for the inestimable good of restoring liberty to his country scrupled to kill a tyrant [C] or his accomplices [B] without due form of justice . . . There is a soul of rich composition. To the roughest and most violent of human actions he wedded goodness and humanity, indeed the most delicate that can be found in the school of philosophy. That heart, so great, full, and obstinate against pain, death, and poverty—was it nature or art that made it tender to the point of such an extreme gentleness and goodness in disposition? Terrible with blood and sword, he goes breaking and shattering a nation invincible against anyone but himself, and turns aside in the middle of such a melee on meeting his host and his friend. Truly that man was in command of war itself, who made it endure the curb of benignity at the point of its greatest heat, all inflamed as it was and foaming with frenzy and slaughter. It is a miracle to be able to mingle some

semblance of justice with such actions; but it belongs only to the strength of Epaminondas to be able to mingle with them the sweetness and ease of the gentlest ways, [C] and pure innocence. (609)

The iconic moment in which Epaminondas turns away from his Spartan friend in the heat of battle demonstrates how he manages to balance the demands of a violent political world with the ethical obligations of the private man. It is also a moment that is almost purely Montaigne's own invention. In Amyot's translation of Plutarch's *De l'esprit familier de Socrate*, it is not Epaminondas but his interlocutor Theanor who argues that "in battles one should turn away before an enemy from whom one has received a favor" ("es batailles il se faut bien destourner de devant celuy des ennemis dont on a receu quelque plaisir") as he tries to persuade Epaminondas that one should not, to the contrary, refuse gifts offered by a friend.[31] This passage, taken out of context and misattributed to the Theban hero, is the apparent source both for the "opinion" of Epaminondas cited at the end of "Des plus excellens hommes" and for this dramatic portrait of Epaminondas, clement even in the midst of raging arms, that Montaigne now imagines: no such anecdote is reported by ancient writers. The portrait suggests an ideal mixture and reconciliation of the two human natures that Montaigne sets in opposition in his opening essay. In fact, the terms of "Par divers moyens" return here: "la facilité, debonnaireté, et mollesse" that the first essay attributes to weak, effeminate natures belong as well to Epaminondas, but so, too, does a male obstinacy of courage. Yet, by now, it is the former—"la bonté et l'humanité" of Epaminondas—rather than the latter, that seems to be indispensable to virtuous behavior: and we have seen how Montaigne argues that leniency toward one's enemy is the sign of true bravery and valor.

The fact that Montaigne is largely making up this Epaminondas whom he upholds as the most excellent of men should only cause us to take this figure more seriously as the expression of the essayist's deepest preoccupations. And in this light the most telling piece of evidence proving the excellence of Epaminondas may be the one Montaigne lists first: Epaminondas spared the lives of all those whom he vanquished. For whereas Montaigne's ancient sources praise the mildness of Epaminondas and narrate incidents that attest to it, they offer, so far as I can tell, *no* direct textual basis for this blanket assertion.[32] It is rather the highest attribute that Montaigne can ascribe to a man of virtue, particularly to a public statesman, and it places the idealized Epaminondas into the series of showdowns between victors and defeated foes at their mercy that run through the *Essais* from their opening essay, his consistent clemency opposed to Alexander's outbreaks of tyrannical revenge.

Epaminondas and Alexander: weighed against each other in "Des plus excellens hommes," they appear at the end of the first and the last essay of Montaigne's third book; while the figure of Alexander, himself, seems to link the endings of the first and last essays of the larger collection. In a work so deliberately variegated, so full of loose ends as the *Essais*, it appears impossible to detect any unifying formal structure. Nonetheless, by the time of their B-text version, Montaigne's excellent and not-so excellent ancient heros seem to construct a kind of verbal frame to his book, linking first and last essays—and the pattern is more striking, if one includes the penultimate essay of Book Two:

1:1 [B] Alexander's vindictiveness, Betis; [A]Pompey's clemency
2:1 [B] Alexander's fear of conspiracies (Philotas)
2:36 [A, B] Epaminondas vs. Alexander
3:1 [B] Epaminondas's clemency
3:13 [B] Alexander thinks he is a god, Philotas; Pompey reminded he is man

It is of course possible that the pattern created by these passages is fortuitous.[33] But their symmetry and their simultaneous appearance in the B text suggest Montaigne's intentional choice and conscious artistry. The effect of such a frame is to indicate the continuing interest and development through the *Essais* of the issues placed at their forefront by "Par divers moyens" and reexamined, in a more clear-cut case of symmetry, in "Divers evenemens." The reappearance of the self-deifying Alexander at the end of the book suggests that one of its unifying aims is precisely to understand— and so to learn how to avoid—his inhuman vindictiveness, which seems so inexplicable at its beginning. The choice of pardon over revenge is the moral and political touchstone of the *Essais*, to which other issues—the nature of nobility and valor, the will of the self to power and autonomy and its relationship to others, the quest for Stoic philosophical mastery versus the acceptance and embrace of human limitations and weaknesses— become ancillary, judged according to how they will or will not result in a practice of clemency. As for the paragon Epaminondas, we shall see that his clement traits—*douceur, debonnaireté, facilité, mollesse, bonté, humanité*, and, above all, *innocence*—turn out to be identical to those of Montaigne himself, as they emerge from the self-portrait of his book.

Chapter Two

CRUELTY AND NOBLESSE: "DE LA CRUAUTÉ" AND "COUARDISE MERE DE LA CRUAUTÉ"

> L'horreur de la cruauté me rejecte plus avant en la clemence qu'aucun patron de clemence ne me sçauroit attirer. (922)

> The horror I feel for cruelty throws me back more deeply into clemency than any model of clemency could attract me to it. (703)

THIS PASSAGE from near the beginning of "De l'art de conferer" (3:8) interprets the scenes of horror that run through the *Essais* and that often, as we have seen, bring an individual essay to a gory and emphatic conclusion. The rhetorical force of such scenes of inhuman cruelty aims to persuade Montaigne's reader, as it does the essayist himself, to the course of clemency. The passage at the same time indicates how, in several central essays of his book, Montaigne will rewrite its opening opposition between clemency and revenge as a struggle between clemency and *cruelty*. The initial distinction that Montaigne makes in "De la cruauté" (2:11) between a passive, mild disposition and an active exercise of virtue depends, significantly enough, on different attitudes towards *vengeance*.

> Celuy qui, d'une douceur et facilité naturelle, mespriseroit les offences receues, feroit chose tres-belle et digne de louange; mais celuy qui, picqué et outré jusques au vif d'une offence, s'armeroit des armes de la raison contre ce furieux appetit de vengeance, et apres un grand conflict s'en rendroit en fin maistre, seroit sans doubte beaucoup plus. Celuy-là feroit bien, et cettuy-ci vertueusement: l'une action se pourroit dire bonté; l'autre vertu: car il semble que le nom de la vertu presuppose de la difficulté et du contraste, et qu'elle ne peut s'exercer sans partie. (422)

> He who, through a natural mildness and easygoingness should despise injuries received should do a very fine and praiseworthy thing; but he who, outraged and stung to the quick by an injury, should arm himself with the arms of reason against this furious appetite for vengeance, and after a great conflict should finally master it, would without doubt do much more. The former would do well, and the other virtuously; one action might be called goodness,

the other virtue. For it seems that the name of virtue presupposes difficulty and contrast, and that it cannot be exercised without opposition. (307)

Virtuous action is defined at the outset, in an essay devoted to the subject of cruelty, as the forbearance from revenge. In his second essay on cruelty, "Couardise mere de la cruauté" (2:27), Montaigne redefines revenge, itself: its true aim, he says, is to defeat and humiliate one's enemy—"le faire bouquer" (694; 524)—not cruelly to kill or torture him. Cruelty is not only the opposite of clemency; it is also contrary to a genuine vengeance. By the same terms, what we normally call vengeance is nothing but cruelty.[1]

The respective arguments of the two essays on cruelty correspond, in fact, to the two rather different positions with which we have already seen Montaigne alternately identify himself in "Par divers moyens" and "Divers evenemens." In his first essay, Montaigne confesses to a natural weakness, a compassionate disposition that associates him with women and commoners rather than with aristocratic valor and Stoic doctrine. He returns to this idea in "De la cruauté," which will characteristically go on to question its opening distinction—which I have just cited—between a true, embattled virtue and the merely natural goodness that the essayist himself claims to share: by the end of the essay we may conclude that this goodness is, in fact, preferable to philosophical virtue. In "Divers evenemens," we have watched Montaigne redefine the nature of noble valor, which manifests itself above all in the act of clemency: it takes real bravery to leave your defeated enemy alive and to live with the possibility that he may try to harm you again. As its title suggests, "Couardise mere de la cruauté" develops this argument; ascribing cruelty to the lower classes and to tyrants, it also implicitly criticizes the behavior of Montaigne's aristocratic contemporaries as not being noble enough. This issue of nobility further relates the two essays on cruelty, for the natural goodness that Montaigne claims in "De la cruauté" as a virtual birthright is itself a token of nobility. Both essays will turn out to be concerned with the nature of nobility and noble behavior.[2]

The focus on nobility, both here and elsewhere in the *Essais*, bears directly upon the political crisis of Montaigne's France, as well as upon the essayist's own class allegiances and pretensions. For the nobility were the leading protagonists of the civil wars. The Huguenots sought out protectors in high-ranking nobles who, through their networks of clients, gave their religious movement the shape of an armed political faction. The ultra-Catholic alliance that formed around the Guise family and that would later become the League was similarly held together by aristocratic patronage. Ensuing conflicts pitted not only adherents of competing faiths but also great families that were traditional rivals in the kingdom and jealous of one another's power. The wars became three-sided affairs as both Catholic and Protestant magnates opposed the weak central authority of the French monarchy. What could thus be presented as a vindication of feudal independence or of aristocratic government, i.e., where the nobility, through local *parlements* and the estates general, would dictate terms to the crown, led increasingly toward the disintegration of political authority and toward anarchy. At the local level, petty warlords rose up and carried out acts of brigandage, like the one Montaigne recounts in "De la phisionomie" in which he was himself captured and robbed. The wars likewise afforded opportunities for neighboring nobles, great and petty, to continue old vendettas and blood feuds: the other story that Montaigne tells of himself in the same essay involves the quarrel of two gentlemen of his vicinity.[3]

Montaigne's criticism of a culture of revenge and cruelty is thus specially pointed toward his noble contemporaries who had reduced France to a condition of near lawlessness. The *politique* Montaigne saw a strong royal authority as the only curb against this aristocratic violence, and in "De l'utile et de l'honneste" (3:1) he derides the presumption of a nobility that fought against its king. In the same passage he claims, as some modern scholars have done, that these nobles were less motivated by religious zeal than by private interest.[4]

> Je tiens que c'est aux Roys proprement de s'animer contre les Roys, et me moque de ces esprits qui de gayeté de coeur se presentent à querelles si disproportionnées: car on ne prend pas querelle particuliere avec un prince pour marcher contre luy ouvertement et courageusement pour son honneur et selon son devoir. . . . Mais il ne faut pas appeler devoir (comme nous faisons tous les jours) une aigreur et aspreté intestine qui naist de l'interest et passion privée; ny courage, une conduite traistresse et malitieuse. Ils nomment zele leur propension vers la malignité et violence: ce n'est pas la cause qui les eschauffe, c'est leur interest; ils attisent la guerre non par ce qu'elle est juste, mais par ce que c'est guerre. (793)

> I hold that it properly belongs to kings to quarrel with kings, and I laugh at these souls who wantonly expose themselves to such disproportionate conflicts. For a man is not picking a private quarrel with a prince in marching against him openly and courageously for the sake of his honor and according to his duty. . . . But we must not call "duty," as we do every day, an inner bitterness and asperity that is born of private interest and passion; nor "courage" a treacherous and malicious conduct. Their propensity to malignity and violence they call zeal. It is not the cause that inflames them, it is their self-interest. They kindle war not because it is just, but because it is war. (602)

As Kristen B. Neuschel has observed in a study of the fractious sixteenth-century French nobility, it was a sense of "honor," shared by minor as well as great nobles, that "legitimated the right to private violence."[5] Montaigne argues that such self-authenticating aristocratic honor has no role to play when it comes to rebellion against a king who stands above his nobility. We may recall the words of François, Duke of Guise, who in "Divers evenemens de mesme conseil" asked his would-be Protestant assassin whether a private hatred existed between their families: what might give an otherwise vile public act the excuse of honor. But in this remarkable passage Montaigne also discounts the language of feudal duty and martial honor by reducing them to self-interest and, with even greater condemnation, to violent passion and malign cruelty. At bottom, the noble combatants of the civil wars are fighting simply for the sake of fighting.

The martial ethos that gives the traditional French *noblesse d'épée* its propensity to violence is an underlying concern and object of criticism in Montaigne's two essays on cruelty (as it is also, we shall see in Chapter Three, in his famous essay on the cannibals of Brazil). As they respectively focus on his aristocratic culture's defining pursuits of the hunt and the duel, each of them a form of killing that mimics and substitutes for warfare, "De la cruauté" and "Cruauté mere de la courdise" expose and reject the brutality of this noble ethos. The later sections of this chapter will show how Montaigne's moral arguments are specifically directed at the nobility. He seeks to persuade a war-loving aristocracy to change their ways: an ethical reform of his class that is at the heart of the political project of the *Essais*. To be truly noble, Montaigne will suggest, is to forswear cruelty: and this version of *noblesse oblige* amounts to a redefinition of noble identity itself.

Cato and Socrates

"De la cruauté" contains two distinct, but peculiarly linked, propositions. Montaigne contrasts the death scenes of Cato of Utica, who after having failed to kill himself with a thrust of his sword, completed his suicide by tearing out his entrails, and of Socrates, calmly talking with his friends as he took his hemlock. The essayist claims that Socrates' death is "more beautiful" than that of Cato: this marks a turning away from a model of rigid Stoic virtue celebrated in several other essays that dwell upon Cato's suicide as that virtue's supreme embodiment. The second, larger and framing argument of the essay distinguishes *both* Cato and Socrates, who turned their habit of virtuous behavior into a second nature or "complexion" that excluded even the occasion of vice, from those practitioners of virtue who successfully struggle against vicious inclinations—and then it contrasts both of these kinds of virtue to the mere goodness of those who possess a "nature facile et debonnaire." Montaigne claims to belong to this last category: his good, innocent nature is witnessed by his hatred of cruelty. How do these two arguments of the essay fit together?[6]

Cato's suicide was beautiful. The virtuous act, we have seen, seems inseparably linked to aesthetic appreciation in Montaigne's thought, and the death of Cato elicited a particularly discriminating connoisseurship. He devotes one early essay, "Du jeune Caton" (1:37), to it and to the verse tributes paid to Cato by five Roman poets; by the 1595 edition the real subject is no longer Cato but a contest among the five poets themselves.[7] At the end of "De juger de la mort d'autruy" (2:13), Montaigne moves to another art form to consider the finer points of Cato's beautiful death scene.

> Mais, afin que le seul Caton peut fournir à tout exemple de vertu, il semble que son bon destin luy fit avoir mal en la main dequoy il se donna le coup, pour qu'il eust loisir d'affronter la mort et de la coleter, renforceant le courage au dangier, au lieu de l'amollir. Et si ç'eust à moy à le representer en sa plus superbe assiete, c'eust esté deschirant tout ensanglanté ses entrailles, plustost que l'espée au poing, comme firent les statueres de son temps. Car ce second meurtre fut bien plus furieux que le premier. (610)

> But in order that Cato alone might suffice for every example of virtue, it seems as if his good destiny gave him pain in the hand with which he gave himself the blow, that he might have leisure to confront death and collar it, strengthening his courage in the danger instead of softening it. And if it had been up to me to portray him in his proudest posture, this would have been all bloody, tearing out his own bowels, rather than sword in hand, as did the statuaries of his time. For this second murder was much more savage than the first. (462)

Montaigne does represent Cato in words, in a kind of *paragone* of writing with sculpture, to indicate the iconic moment that best captures the Roman's courage. It was when Cato, having botched his first attempt, had to resort to his bare hands that he demonstrated the strength of his Stoic will, a will that was hardened rather than mortified at the prospect of his death and the ripping apart of his body. Surpassing the sculptures that commemorated it but could not rise to its inspired fury, Cato's death was a work of art.

In "De la cruauté," Montaigne transfers this aestheticizing consideration of Cato's suicide to Cato himself. The leisure that Cato had to confront death also allowed him to appreciate his own action.

> Tesmoing le jeune Caton. Quand je le voy mourir et se deschirer les entrailles, je ne me puis contenter de croire simplement qu'il eust lors son ame exempte totalement de trouble et d'effroy, je ne puis croire qu'il se maintint seulement en cette démarche que les regles de la secte Stoique luy ordonnoient, rassise, sans émotion et impassible; il y avoit, ce me semble, en la vertu de cet homme trop de gaillardise et de verdeur pour s'en arrester là. Je croy sans doubte, qu'il sentit du plaisir et de la volupté en une si noble action, et qu'il s'y agrea plus qu'en autre de celles de sa vie: . . . Il me semble lire en cette action je ne sçay quelle esjouissance de son ame, et une émotion de plaisir extraordinaire et d'une volupté virile, lors qu'elle consideroit la noblesse et hauteur de son

entreprinse . . . pour la beauté de la chose mesme en soy: laquelle il voyoit bien plus à clair en sa perfection, lui qui manioit les ressorts, que nous ne pouvons faire. (424–25)

Witness the younger Cato. When I see him dying and tearing out his entrails, I cannot be content to believe simply that he then had his soul totally free from disturbance and fright; I cannot believe that he merely maintained himself in the attitude that the rules of the Stoic sect ordained for him, sedate, without emotion, and impassible; there was, it seems to me, in that man's virtue too much lustiness and verdancy to stop there. I believe without any doubt that he felt pleasure and bliss in so noble an action, and that he enjoyed himself more in it than in any other action of his life . . . I seem to read in that action I know what rejoicing of his soul, and an emotion of extraordinary pleasure and manly exultation, when it considered the nobility and sublimity of its enterprise: . . . for the beauty of the very thing in itself, which he, who handled the springs of it, saw much more clearly in its perfection than we can see it. (308–9)

The best judge of the beauty of Cato's suicide was Cato himself. Cato's distanced contemplation ("consideroit"; "voyoit") of his lofty deed parallels the essayist's own act of discerning spectatorship ("je le voy"; "il me semble lire") as he reads different accounts of it, enhanced by poetry and art. The pleasure that Cato takes in his own feat of virtue is the sign that this virtue surpasses a mere Stoic struggle for self-control, that Cato, having perfected his habit of virtue, has passed over to a free Epicurean embrace of pain and death. But this pleasure is also scopophilic, inseparable from the spectacle that Cato's disembowelment offers to himself as well as to Montaigne and finally to us, Montaigne's readers.

Why, then, does Cato lose the beauty contest with Socrates? The preference that the essayist voices for Socrates, in the passage that immediately followed in the A text, comes both as a surprise and as a rhetorical anticlimax.

L'aisance donc de cette mort, et cette facilité qu'il avoit acquise par la force de son ame, dirons nous qu'elle doive rabattre quelque chose du lustre de sa vertu? Et qui, de ceux qui ont la cervelle tant soit peu teinte de la vraye philosophie, peut se contenter d'imaginer Socrates seulement franc de crainte et de passion en l'accident de sa prison, de ses fers et de sa condemnation? Et qui ne reconnoit en luy non seulement de la fermeté et de la constance (c'esoit son assiette ordinaire que celle-là), mais encore je ne sçay quel contentement nouveau et une allegresse enjoüée en ses propos et façons dernieres? . . . Caton me pardonnera, s'il luy plaist; sa mort est plus tragique et plus tendue, mais cette-cy est encore, je ne sçay comment, plus belle. (425)

So the ease of this death [of Cato] and the facility that he had acquired through the strenth of his soul, shall we say that it should cut down something of the lustre of his virtue? And who that has a mind however little tinctured with true philosphy can be satisfied with imagining Socrates as merely free from fear and passion in the incident of his imprisonment, his fetters, and his condemnation? And who does not recognize in him not only firmness and constancy (that was his ordinary attitude), but also I know not what new contentment, and a blithe cheerfulness in his last words and actions? . . . Cato will pardon me, if he please; his death is more tragic and tense, but this one is still, I know not how, more beautiful. (309–10)

The rhetorical letdown registered in the essay itself from the nobility and lofty "hauteur" of Cato's gory suicide to the cheerful last moments of Socrates is deliberate and reinforces the essay's point. The pleasure that Cato feels as he contemplates his suicide exemplifies a virtue that has become identified with ease ("aisance"; "facilité"): a habit so ingrained that one acts virtuously without effort. But Cato's death nonetheless *looks* strained ("tendue") and full of exertion next to that of Socrates because it retains at least the outward *form* of the aristocratic, Stoic philosophy whose rules and ethos Cato has actually gone beyond. Cato's suicide was "tragic" in the sense that it belongs, as Aristotle's *Poetics* (Chapter 13) would have it, to a noble or princely personage: his soldierly death at swordpoint both asserts a class identity as well as a Stoic contempt for bodily pain. It was also tragic because it was stagy, providing a show for Cato himself to contemplate with pleasure.[8] Now that very theatricality yields precedence in beauty to Socrates, who similarly takes pleasure in his death scene but whose purer, even more effortless virtue expresses itself in a humbler literary genre without drama, even—as the essayist's own repeated recourse to the "je ne sçay" formula suggests—by not expressing itself at all.

Thus the iconic moment of Cato's suicide—his ripping apart of his body—turns out *not* to suffice for every example of virtue. When Montaigne asks pardon of Cato, he indicates a revision of his earlier thought, a revision that continued in two other essays—like "De la cruauté" of a date of composition subsequent to "Du jeune Caton" and "De juger de la mort d'autruy"—where Cato's death reappears at the essay's end as a climactic anecdote: much as it does in those two early essays. The emphasis, however, has changed.

> [C] L'extreme degré de traicter courageusement la mort, et le plus naturel, c'est la voir non seulement sans estonnement, mais sans soin, continuant libre le train de la vie jusques dans elle. Comme Caton qui s'amusoit à dormir et à estudier, en ayant une, violente et sanglante, presente en sa teste et en son coeur, et la tenant en sa main. (679)
> "Contre la faineantise" (2:21)
>
> [C] The extreme degree in treating death courageously, and the most natural, is to see it not only without being stunned, but without concern, continuing

the course of life freely right into death. Like Cato, who spent his time sleeping and studying, while having present in his head and heart a violent and blody death, and holding it in his hand. (515)
"Against do-nothingness"

[A] Tel estude fut celuy du jeune Caton sentant sa fin prochaine, qui se recontra au discours de Platon, de l'eternité de l'ame.... Il print cette occupation, non pour le service de sa mort, mais comme celuy qui n'interrompit pas seulement son sommeil en l'importance d'une telle deliberation, il continua aussi, sans chois et sans changement, ses estudes avec les autres actions accoustumées de sa vie.
C] La nuict qu'il vint d'estre refusé de la Preture, il la passa à jouer; celle en laquelle il devoit mourir, il la passa à lire: la perte ou de la vie ou de l'office tout luy fut un. (703-4)
"Toutes choses ont leur saison" (2:28)

[A] Such a study was that of the younger Cato when, feeling his end approaching, he came upon Plato's discussion of the eternity of the soul.... It was not to ease his death that he took up this occupation; but like a man who would not even interrupt his sleep out of concern over such a resolve, he also continued, without choice and without change, his studies together with the other customary actions of his life.
C] The night when he had just been rejected for the praetorship, he spent in play; the one in which he was to die, he spent reading. Loss of life and loss of office were equally indifferent to him. (532)
"All things have their season"

The 1595 C-text addition to "Contre la faineantise" repeats the idea already present in the 1580 A-text version of "Toutes choses ont leur saison," to which Montaigne also added a C-text coda. He returned obsessively to the story of Cato's suicide, but did so in order to transfer its focal point from the spectacular scene of death to the nocturnal vigil that preceded it. What now impresses the essayist is the lack of fuss, the sheer indifference, with which Cato approached his own demise. As Cato follows his normal daily routine of life, there is no hint, no representation at all of the violent death to follow—a death that also becomes one more indifferent act, absorbed into that routine. In its very lack of drama, Cato's death has become like the death of Socrates.

A Man of Easy Virtue

"De la cruauté" begins by contrasting two kinds of virtuous behavior: an active striving to subdue vicious inclinations that is properly termed virtue and its double or false twin, a passive goodness of nature that offers few occasions to vice.

> Il me semble que la vertu est chose autre et plus noble que les inclinations à la bonté qui naissent en nous. Les ames reglées et bien nées, elle suyvent mesme train, et representent en leurs actions mesme visage que les vertueuses. Mais la vertu sonne je ne sçay quoy de plus grand et plus actif que de se laisser, par une heureuse complexion, doucement et paisiblement conduire à la suite de la raison. (422)

> It seems to me that virtue is something other and nobler than the inclinations toward goodness that are born in us. Souls naturally regulated and wellborn follow the same path, and show the same countenance in their actions, as virtuous ones. But virtue means something greater and more active than letting oneself, by a happy disposition, be led gently and peacefully in the footsteps of reason. (306)

The paradoxical movement of the essay no sooner distinguishes active virtue from passive goodness than it upholds—in the death scene of Socrates—a perfected virtue that is as passive and uneventful as possible. We are led to question what is mirroring what: whether goodness has the same countenance as virtue, or whether virtue finds as the final goal of its striving the replication of a goodness that may be available all along in human nature.

After Montaigne has examined the virtue of Cato and Socrates, exemplified in their deaths—and it can be argued that virtue in the *Essais* always boils down to overcoming the fear of death—he concludes that there are, in fact, *three* categories of virtue and seeming virtue. For it was possible for those two men and for others to practice virtue to such an extent that it became a second nature and stamped out altogether whatever vicious disposition they might have been born with: this re-creation of one's own natural complexion was the height of virtue, on a scale where virtue is once more judged in terms of its *beauty*.

> Or qu'il ne soit plus beau, par une haute et divine resolution, d'empescher la naissance des tentations, et de s'estre formé à la vertu de maniere que les semences mesmes des vices en soyent desracinées, que d'empescher à vive force leur progrez, et, s'estant laissé surprendre aux émotions premieres des passions, s'armer et se bander pour arrester leur course et les vaincre; et que ce second effect ne soit encore plus beau que d'estre simplement garny d'une nature facile et debonnaire, et dégousteée par soy mesme de la débauche et du vice, je ne pense point qu'il y ait doubte. Car cette tierce et derniere façon, il semble bien qu'elle rende un homme innocent, mais non pas vertueux; exempt de mal faire, mais non assez apte à bien faire. Joint que cette condition est si voisine à l'imperfection et à la foiblesse que je ne sçay pas bien comment en démeler le confins et les distinguer. Les noms mesmes de bonté et d'innocence sont à cette cause aucunement noms de mespris. (426)

Now I do not think that there is any doubt that it is finer [more beautiful] to prevent the birth of temptations by a lofty and divine resolution, and to have so formed oneself to virtue that the very seeds of the vices are rooted out, than to prevent their progress by main force, and, having let oneself be surprised by the first commotions of the passions, to arm and tense oneself to stop their course and conquer them; and that this second action still is finer [more beautiful] than to be simply provided with a nature easy and affable and having an inborn distaste for debauchery and vice. For it certainly seems that this third and last type makes a man innocent, but not virtuous; exempt from doing ill, but not apt enough to do good. Besides this condition is so close to imperfection and weakness that I do not very well know how to separate their confines and distinguish them. The very names of goodness and innocence are for this reason to some extent terms of contempt. (310)

In this second schema or hierarchy of types of virtue, it is the first category, the fully achieved virtue of Cato and Socrates, that finds a mirror image in the third, the easygoing affability—"nature facile et debonnaire"—which Montaigne asserts here is not true virtue. For both of these modes of practicing goodness are effortless, the first by second nature, the last by nature itself, and they both contrast with the difficult overcoming by reason of bodily appetites and unruly affects that is the Stoic/Epicurean model of virtue and that is typically characterized in terms of military combat: the "grand conflict" described at the opening of the essay. But as Montaigne goes on to describe his own affable good nature for the remainder of the essay, we are left to wonder whether this disposition of character—virtuous or not—is not an acceptable, perhaps more than acceptable moral substitute for such a strenuous and combative virtue, whether it is not, in fact, preferable even to the facile virtue of Cato and Socrates.

To say a word about himself, Montaigne continues—and the word takes up more than half of the essay—he for his part makes almost no effort to bridle his impulses. But his good fortune, rather than his reason, has caused him to be largely free of vicious appetites.

> Ma vertu, c'est une vertu, ou innocence, pour mieux dire, accidentale et fortuite. Si je fusse nay d'une complexion plus déreglée, je crains qu'il fut allé piteusement de mon faict. Car je n'ay essayé guiere de fermeté en mon ame pour soustenir des passions, si elles eussent esté tant soit peu vehementes. Je ne sçay point nourrir des querelles et du debat chez moy. (427)

> My virtue is a virtue, or I should say an innocence, that is accidental and fortuitous. If I had been born with a more unruly disposition, I fear it would have gone pitifully with me. For I have not experienced much firmness in my soul to withstand passions, if they are even the least bit vehement. I do not know how to foster quarrels and conflicts within me. (311)

The essayist cannot quite give up on the idea that his passive innocence is a kind of virtue, even if it lacks any kind of firmness—even if, as he noted above, innocence can itself be a term of contempt. Nor can he help implying that the Stoic model of virtue that he fails to live up to necessarily does violence to one's nature by setting the self at odds with itself—however salutary such self-control may be. The etymological force of "in-nocence," which Montaigne himself glosses as the inability to do harm—"exempt de mal faire"—may apply to his relationship as much to himself as to others.[9]

It is nevertheless the effects on others of this innocence that Montaigne will underscore when he singles out his hatred of cruelty—and thus finally comes to the titular subject of the essay—as an example of the simple goodness of his nature.

> Ce que j'ay de bien, je l'ay au rebours par la sort de ma naissance. Je ne le tiens ny de loy, ny de precepte, ou autre aprentissage. B] L'innocence qui est en moy, est une innocence niaise: peu de vigueur, et point d'art. A] Je hay, entre autres vices, cruellement la cruauté, et par nature et par jugement, comme l'extreme de tous les vices. Mais c'est jusques à telle mollesse que je ne voy pas égorger un poulet sans desplaisir, et ois impatiemment gemir un lievre sous les dens de mes chiens, quoy que ce soit un plaisir violent que la chasse. (429)

> What good I have in me I have, on the contrary, by the chance of my birth. I have gotten it neither from law, nor from precept, nor from any other apprenticeship. B] The innocence that is in me is a childish innocence: little vigor and no art. A] Among other vices, I cruelly hate cruelty, both by nature and by judgment, as the extreme of all vices. But this is to such a point of softness that I do not see a chicken's neck wrung without distress, and I cannot bear to hear the scream of a hare in the teeth of my dogs, although the chase is a violent pleasure. (313)

The self-deprecatory B-text addition about Montaigne's childish, unstudied innocence nonetheless links this innocence both to the accident of his birth and to his disposition against physical cruelty: he cannot stand, he says, to behold the sufferings of animals, much less of other human beings, and he goes on memorably to condemn the use of torture in the execution of criminals. "Je me compassionne fort tendrement des afflictions d'autruy" (430), he acknowledges shortly after, and the confession here of his "mollesse" recalls "Par divers moyens," where commiseration for the sufferings of others ("les affligez") was the effect of "facilité, débonnaireté, et mollesse." Like the clemency advocated in the first essay of his book, Montaigne's hatred of cruelty is the token of a pointedly unstoic weakness—Seneca's disparaged "mollitia"—that is morally recuperated and valorized as part of the essayist's easygoing, native goodness. If this goodness or innocence is the inferior twin of philosophical virtue, it is nonetheless *practical*: it produces an aversion to cruelty that is a cornerstone of ethical behavior in general and that has, moreover, a particular moral urgency for Montaigne's contemporaries.

For such goodness—and Montaigne's own example—stand out in a France that the Wars of Religion have turned into a theater of cruelty.

> Je vy en une saison en laquelle nous foisonnons en exemples incroyables de ce vice, par la license de nos guerres civiles; et ne voit on rien aux histoires anciennes de plus extreme que ce que nous en essayons tous les jours. Mais cela ne m'y a nullement aprivoisé. A peine me pouvoy-je persuader, avant que je l'eusse veu, qu'il se fut trouvé des ames si monstrueuses, qui, pour le seul plaisir du meurtre, le voulussent commettre: hacher et détrencher les membres d'autruy; esguiser leur esprit à inventer des tourmens inusitez et des morts nouvelles, sans inimitié, sans profit, et pour cette seule fin de jouïr du plaisant spectacle des gestes et mouvemens pitoyables, des gemissemens et voix lamentables d'un homme mourant en angoisse. Car voylà l'extreme point où la cruauté puisse atteindre. C] "*Ut homo hominem, non iratus, non timens, tantum spectaturus, occidat.*" (432)

> I live in in a time when we abound in incredible examples of this vice, through the licence of our civil wars; and we see in the ancient histories nothing more extreme than what we experience of this every day. But that has not reconciled me to it at all. I could hardly be convinced, until I saw it, that there were souls so monstrous that they would commit murder for the mere pleasure of it: hack and cut off other men's limbs; sharpen their wits to invent unaccustomed torments and new forms of death, without enmity, without profit, and for the sole purpose of enjoying the pleasing spectacle of the pitiful gestures and movements, the lamentable groans and cries, of a man dying in anguish. For that is the uttermost point that cruelty can attain. C] *That man should kill man not in anger, not in fear, but only to watch the sight* [Seneca]. (315–16)

The incredulousness with which Montaigne discovers sadism does indeed attest to the innocence of his nature. Inserted in the C text, the final tag from Seneca's Epistle 90 insists on the visual pleasure of cruelty, the enjoyment of the spectacle of the sufferings of the tortured, who are turned into so many performers: Seneca has in mind the Roman gladiators who, Montaigne had already noted in a B-text addition to "De la cruauté," succeeded animals as victims in the arena (433; 316). There he further comments that the pleasure that we take in watching animals tear each other apart attests to some natural instinct of inhumanity—"quelque instinct a l'inhumanité" (433; 316.) So, at the opening of the later, 1588 B text essay, "De l'utile et de l'honneste" (3:1), he would acknowledge that this pleasure, this *schadenfreude*, is an inescapable part of the human condition.

> car, au milieu de la compassion, nous sentons au dedans je ne sçay quelle aigre douce poincte de volupté maligne à voir souffrir autruy; . . . (791)

> For in the midst of compassion we feel within us I know not what bittersweet pricking of malicious pleasure in seeing others suffer; . . . (599)

Even the compassion that puts an end to cruelty contains an element of the scopophilic pleasure that defines the vice itself. But Montaigne, who cannot bear to hear the groaning ("gemir") of a hare, and who has always found the sight of a stag at bay a very *unpleasant* spectacle, cannot reconcile himself to a practice of cruelty that has become an everyday vice in his strife-ridden France. Relative to the philosopher's studied self-control, the essayist's "innocence" may not technically be termed virtue, but relative to the debased moral standards of his own times, it nonetheless stands out. As he wryly remarks in a closely related passage in "De la praesumption," you can cheaply enough be considered virtuous—"vous estes estimé vertueux à bon marché" (646;490)—if you are born in a depraved age.

The tag at the end of Montaigne's condemnation of contemporary cruelty also tips off the reader to the imprint of Seneca on "De la cruauté." The passage appears to echo and be inspired by the Roman moralist's characterization of cruelty in the *De Clementia*.

> Cruelty is an evil thing befitting least of all a man, and is unworthy of his spirit that is so kindly; for one to take delight [*gaudere*] in blood and wounds and, throwing off the man, to change into a creature of the woods, is the madness of a wild beast. For what difference does it make, I beg of you, Alexander, whether you throw Lysimachus to a lion, or yourself tear him to pieces with your teeth? . . . The reason why brutality is most of all abhorred is this: because it transgresses first of all ordinary, and then all human, bounds, searches out new kinds of torture, calls ingenuity into play to invent devices [*nova supplicia conquirit, ingenium advocat ut instrumenta excogitet*] by which suffering may be varied and prolonged, and takes delight [*delectatur*] in the afflictions of mankind; then indeed has the dread disease of that man's mind reached the farthest limit of insanity [*ad insaniam pervenit ultimam*], when cruelty has changed into pleasure and to kill a human being now becomes a joy [*crudelitas versa est in voluptatem et iam occidere hominem iuvat*]. [*De Clem.* 1.25.1–2]

Seneca tries to persuade Nero to clemency by arguing that its alternative is cruelty, the taking of pleasure in the sufferings of another. Such cruelty is bestial, and makes tyrants like Alexander act like savage animals toward their fellow men. The converse is to treat even animals with humanity, and Montaigne will close his essay by condemning the hunt and by arguing that there is a "general duty of humanity"—"un general devoir d'humanité" (435;318)—owed to beasts and other living things. This humaneness, the capacity for mercy and kindness—"grace et benignité" (435;318)—distinguishes men from beasts of prey, and gives a particular moral charge to Montaigne's assertion that he does not take much store in the "cousinage" (434; 317) that is said to exist between humans and the animals. The essayist will advocate kindness toward animals less because of sentimental notions of creaturely kinship, than because "humanity" separates us from the cruelty of an animal world of predators and victims—which the hunt too closely resembles. Our capacity for humanity counters our bestial instinct to inhumanity.[10]

The height of cruelty ("extreme point"; "insaniam . . . ultimam") for both Seneca and Montaigne lies, however, in the perversion of human reason and intellect to further the infliction of pain. Montaigne echoes Seneca in his description of how modern practitioners of cruelty sharpen their wits ("esguiser leur esprit"; "ingenium advocat") to produce new forms of torture ("inventer des tourmens inusitez et des morts nouvelles"; "nova supplicia conquirit") in order to take pleasure in the drawn-out deaths and groans of their victims. Both Seneca's evocation of Alexander's tyranny and the description of contemporary cruelty in "De la cruauté" appear to lie behind the passage that Montaigne would add to the end of the B-text version of "Par divers moyens on arrive a pareille fin" and its portrait of an Alexander who threatens the vanquished Betis with "every kind of torment that can be invented" ("toutes les sortes de tourmens qui se pourront inventer") and demands to hear a groan ("gemissement") from his captive. Alexander's action can now be seen virtually to define cruelty. Montaigne, we recall, added a direct reference to the *De Clementia* toward the beginning of the B-text of "Par divers moyens," and then took up the story of Augustus and Cinna from Seneca's treatise on mercy in "Divers evenemens de mesme conseil." The presence of the *De Clementia* here in "De la cruauté" is another link between Montaigne's essays on cruelty and his essays on clemency and revenge.

The direct citation from Epistle 90 of the *Epistulae morales ad Lucilium* evokes a second text of Seneca with which the whole essay of "De la cruauté" is in dialogue. In his philosophical letter, Seneca attempts to demystify the myth of the Golden Age. The people of that age of innocence may have been free of many modern vices, he argues, but they were not virtuous, for virtue is an acquired habit of the philosopher's study and willpower. The passage Montaigne cites comes from the conclusion of the letter, and deserves to be quoted in its fuller context.

> For nature does not bestow virtue; it is an art to become good [*Non enim dat natura virtutem; ars est bonum fieri*]. They [the people of the Golden Age], at least, searched not in the lowest dregs of the earth for gold, nor yet for silver or transparent stones; and they were still merciful even to the dumb animals—so far removed was that epoch from the custom *that man should kill man not in anger, not in fear, but only to watch the sight!* They had yet no embroidered garments nor did they weave cloth of gold; gold was not yet even mined.
>
> What, then, is the conclusion of this matter? It was by reason of their igno-

rance of things that the men of those days were innocent [*Ignorantia rerum innocentes erant*]; and it makes a great deal of difference whether one wills not to sin or has not the knowledge to sin. Justice was unknown to them, unknown prudence, unknown also self-control and bravery; but their rude life possessed certain qualities akin to all these virtues. Virtue is not vouchsafed to a soul unless that soul has been trained and taught, and by unremitting practice brought to perfection. For the attainment of this boon, but not in the possession of it, are we born [*ad hoc quidem, sed sine hoc nascimur*]; and even in the best men, before you refine them by instruction, there is but the stuff of virtue, not virtue itself. Farewell. (*Ep.* 90.45–46) (my emphasis)

Throughout his essay Montaigne has seemed to adhere to this Stoic position and distinguished true virtue, the product of philosophy, from the natural innocence with which he claims that he himself was born. Montaigne stays very close indeed to Seneca's terms. In the passage immediately preceding the tag cited in "De la cruauté," Seneca sees such primitive innocence exemplified in a lack of cruelty to animals, in the clemency shown to dumb beasts, not yet slaughtered for public amusement in the amphitheaters—"parcebantque adhuc etiam mutis animalibus"—what Montaigne himself takes to be the test case of his own hatred of cruelty. And the essayist claims that whatever good is in him derives from his birth: in pointed contrast to Socrates who admitted that he had a natural propensity to vice that he had corrected through philosophical discipline (429; 313).

But Montaigne restates Seneca's opposition of philosophical virtue to native goodness only to question the philosopher's natural assumption that the first is superior to the second. For the same Senecan tag that links the essayist's own aversion to the spectacle of cruelty with the easy, unphilosophical innocence of the Golden Age also suggests, in the larger context of the essay, the potential cruelty of a philosophy that is part and parcel of the cruel fallen world to which it belongs. When Montaigne evokes the atrocities committed during the Wars of Religion solely for the sake of enjoying the pleasurable sight—"jouïr du plaisant spectacle"—of a tortured victim dying in anguish, he casts in retrospect a startling light on Cato's suicide and on that *virtuous* pleasure, that "esjouissance de son ame . . . plaisir extraordinaire . . . volupté virile," that the essay has attributed a few pages earlier to the Stoic hero as he watched his own "beautiful," self-inflicted death. Cato was just such a man dying in gruesome anguish, and the philosopher's pleasure as he admires his own act of virtue—and the pleasure of later spectators who behold his beautiful act again in artistic or literary representations—may now seem to bear a disturbing resemblance to the sadistic visual pleasures of cruelty.[11] Such virtue is obtained through the struggle of opposing drives—"le combat des appetits contraires (424;

308)—particularly of reason against the appetites of the body: Cato's suicide might be read as the emblematic display of philosophical disdain for the body, ripped apart by the sage's own hands. Admirable as this self-mastery may be, Montaigne suggests that it comes at the price of committing cruelty, particularly physical cruelty, against one's nature, to the point where the philosopher's virtue may become the mirror of the vice it represses. Even the long-since-perfected virtue of Socrates and Cato may be suspect. The reflective pleasure that both took in their suicides is a reminder that such virtue, effortless now, once had to struggle with a vice that has long since been stamped out in their natures. The cruelty of that struggle seems once again to resurface into view in the tableau of Cato's death: for what Cato did to himself, according to the terms of the essay's ensuing discussion of cruelty, shouldn't be done to a dog—or to any living being.

We may thus read the whole essay of "De la cruauté" as a steady retreat from the cruelty of virtue. It becomes clear why Montaigne should have revised his view of how to represent Cato's death, shifting from the spectacular scene of disembowelment to the uneventful vigil on the night preceding the suicide. It likewise becomes clear why he preferred the relaxed death-scene of Socrates to Cato's high tragedy. And the parts of the essay fit together as well; for the shift from Cato to Socrates is one emblematic step in the shift in the essay's argument from an initial admiration of embattled virtue to the self-portrait of Montaigne's own effortless goodness. The stages of the argument can be traced as follows: (1) virtue as defined by Stoic and Epicurean thought as the struggle to overcome vice is superseded by (2) an effortless, perfected virtue, embodied by Cato and Socrates, that has removed all occasions of vice; as figures of that higher virtue, Montaigne prefers (3) the death of Socrates over that of Cato because it appears more effortless; but such effortless philosophical virtue, because it is the product of a former struggle with the sage's nature, is (4) less easy—less natural, more cruel—than Montaigne's good-natured disposition. Thus, while the essayist may disparage his mere goodness, we are nonetheless left to feel how much saner we would be to embrace our own good nature, not to foster internal quarrels and conflicts within ourselves, rather than to pursue a virtue that would denature us. And how much better for society, particularly for Montaigne's France, itself prey to the internal divisions of civil war, which are the correlative of the self-divisions inculcated by the heroic virtues of Stoicism and of Cato and Socrates. The essay links an absence of cruelty toward oneself with Montaigne's lack of cruelty toward other creatures. And the converse, as we saw in the previous chapter may also apply: those who cannot forgive themselves—particularly those that cannot forgive their own bodies that doom them to mortality—will not be apt to show clemency toward others.

The Nature of Nobility

By the end of "De la cruauté," Montaigne has thus questioned and reversed the essay's opening proposition, its apparent valorization of virtue over mere goodness.

> Il me semble que la vertu est chose autre et plus noble que les inclinations à la bonté qui naissent en nous. Les ames reglées d'elles mesmes et bien nées, elles suyvent mesme train, et representent en leurs actions mesme visage que les vertueuses. Mais la vertu sonne je ne sçay quoy de plus grand et plus actif que de se laisser, par une heureuse complexion, doucement et paisiblement conduire à la suite de la raison. (422)

> It seems to me that virtue is something other and nobler than the inclinations towards goodness that are born in us. Souls naturally regulated and wellborn follow the same path, and show the same countenance in their actions, as virtuous ones. But virtue means something greater and more active than letting oneself, by a happy disposition, be led gently and peacefully in the footsteps of reason. (306)

The ensuing argument of the essay suggests that a docile goodness may not only for all practical purposes resemble, but even be preferable to, a willful and strenuous virtue. This goodness is at peace with itself rather than engaged in moral warfare. At the same time, Montaigne questions whether virtue is in fact *nobler* than a goodness that comes naturally to the wellborn. The ambiguity of "bien nées"—does it mean those naturally good or those of noble descent, or are the two the same?—allows us to read the essay within an age-old debate about the nature of aristocracy: is nobility the product of lineage or of personal virtue?[12]

When Montaigne later speaks of his own good nature, he describes this lucky accident of birth—"le sort de ma naissance"—as a class attribute. The affability and whatever moral goodness he finds in himself are due less to reason than to Fortune.

> Elle m'a faict naistre du'une race fameuse en preud'homie et d'un tres-bon pere: je ne sçay s'il a escoulé en moy partie de ses humeurs, ou bien si les exemples domesticques et la bonne institution de mon enfance y ont insensiblment aydé; ou si je suis autrement ainsi nay . . . (427)

> She had me born of a race famous for integrity, and of a very good father. I do not know whether he infused into me a part of his humors, or else whether the home examples and the good education of my childhood insensibly contributed to it, or whether for some other reason I was born so: . . . (311)

Montaigne's explanation of his goodness appears to waver between nature and nurture as he describes his upbringing in his father's noble house: but if nurture played a part, it did so *insensibly*—not through conscious philosophical discipline. He similarly speaks of an "instinct and impression that I brought away from my nurse"—"instinct et impression que j'en ay apporté de la nourrice" (428; 312)—to suggest just how *natural*, unstudied, and uniquely his own is the hatred of vice that he has carried with him all of his life. His birth and ancestry appear decisive: like father, like son.[13]

Montaigne thus appears to embrace a traditional and socially conservative viewpoint that grants to the nobly born a special disposition to goodness. Gordon Braden and Alban Forcione have shown how Erasmus, Rabelais, and Cervantes could turn this mystified notion of an innate aristocratic probity into a quasi-Pelagian defense of the potential goodness of human nature and—against Lutheran tenets—of the freedom of the will.[14] The aristocratic denizens of Rabelais' Abbey of Theleme can act according to their own wills ("Faictz ce que vouldras"),

> par ce que gents liberes, bien nez et bien instruictz, conversans en compaignies honestes, ont par nature un instinct et aguillon, qui tousjours les pousse à faictz vertueux et retire de vice, lequel ilz nommoient honneur.[15]
>
> because people who are free, well born and well educated, conversant with honest company, have by nature an instinct and spur, which always push them towards virtuous acts and draw them back from vice, and which they call honor.

The self-determining Thelemites resemble those "ames reglées d'elles mesmes et bien nées" whom Montaigne invokes at the beginning of his essay and among whom he would include himself. Like the essayist, they possess a natural instinct to ethical integrity that Rabelais identifies as a specifically aristocratic sense of honor. Montaigne places noticeably less emphasis on the importance of education—the Thelemites are not only "bien nées" but "bien instruictz" and the products of a humanist education—and his essay, in its quarrel with a learned, philosophical virtue, stresses the lack of effort and study with which he conducts his moral behavior. And if the name of Theleme indicates that it is the realm of the perfected will, Montaigne's equally easy, instinctive goodness seems to require little or no willpower at all.

This ease is itself an early modern aristocratic pose. The claim that noble birth produces a natural goodness can only be affirmed if such goodness appears to be spontaneous. The self-presentation of the aristocrat, now increasingly codified in sixteenth-century handbooks of courtesy and manners, demanded a conspicuous carelessness. Frank Whigham writes of the problem of performing an

> ascriptive identity, an identity that by definition cannot be achieved by human effort. As a result there arose a basic governing principle of the display of *effortlessness*, Castiglione's *sprezzatura*, designed to imply the natural or given

status of one's social identity and to deny any earned character, any labor or arrival from a social elsewhere.[16]

Montaigne thus doubly affirms his noble caste when he tells us that he comes by his goodness naturally from the "race" of his forefathers and when he asserts that this hereditary goodness has spared him the pains of philosophical discipline. His claim to an easy native goodness as opposed to a virtue that requires struggle can thus be read as an expression of aristocratic hauteur and *sprezzatura* comparable to the disdain for pedants and professional writers against whose carefully structured and argued works he pointedly opposes the apparently—and one must, of course, emphasize "apparently"—impromptu and dilettantish jottings of the *Essais*. The very style of the essays that Montaigne describes with two adjectives that translate the idea of Castiglione's *sprezzatura*—"desdaigneux" (638; 483) and "mesprisant" (172; 127)—mimes a kind of natural effortlessness that, in turn, proclaims the nobility of the writer.[17]

The same disdainful *sprezzatura*, finally, distinguishes the ethical stance of Plutarch from that of Seneca in Montaigne's comparison of his two favorite authors in "Des livres" (2:10), a comparison that could be seen to restate in little the issues of "De la cruauté."

> Cettuy-cy [Seneca] se peine, se roidit et se tend pour armer la vertu contre la foiblesse, la crainte et les vitieux appetits; l'autre [Plutarch] semble n'estimer pas tant leur effort, et desdaigner d'en haster son pas et se mettre sur sa targue. (413)

> Seneca labors, strains, and tenses himself to arm virtue against weakness, fear, and vicious appetites; Plutarch seems not to esteem their power so much, and to disdain to hurry his step or stand on guard for them. (300)

Plutarch stands at ease in the battle of virtue, a battle he does not even acknowledge. He neither regards the effort of vice, nor is willing to exert effort against it; he cannot be bothered. Unlike the Stoic Seneca, tensed for moral warfare, the ethical attitude of Plutarch, Montaigne remarks when he returns to the same comparison in "De la phisionomie" (3:12), is "plus desdaigneuse et plus destendue" (1040)—"more disdainful and less tense" (795). Montaigne makes this Plutarch a version of the moral alternative to Stoic virtue that he himself represents in his own unstudied and native goodness. Plutarch's disdain and ease are forms of a distinctively aristocratic nonchalance, and so, we may conclude, is the ethical behavior of the wellborn Montaigne, behavior that comes naturally—or at least appears to do so.

The claim to noble birth and to a long-established lineage—a "race"—asserted here and in other passages in the *Essais* particularly struck and drew the scorn of Montaigne's first readers.[18] They knew that Montaigne's family had indeed come from a "social elsewhere," that his merchant great-grandfather had bought the chateau of Montaigne, and that the essayist was the first of his line to drop the family name of Eyquem and to call himself after the property. They knew that Montaigne and his father before him had assumed, as mayors of Bordeaux, the adminstrative functions associated with the *noblesse de robe*, the aristocracy of office-holding bureaucrats and magistrates, normally of recent ennoblement, who were not to be confused with a warrior and time-honored *noblesse d'épée*. We, looking back from our century, should recognize that the cultures of the robe and the sword often overlapped.[19] Montaigne's father had been a soldier in his youth, fighting in Italy under Lautrec; Montaigne himself accompanied the court of Charles IX to the siege of Rouen in 1562, though it is uncertain how much fighting he saw on that or any other occasion. Whatever its military attainments, however, the family did not have a long history of noble elevation, and Montaigne may have been quite aware of how silly his snobbish pretensions made him look. In "De l'art de conferer," he pokes fun at noblemen who boast of mostly falsified family genealogies (929; 709), and the anecdote may carry a personal reference in an essay so much concerned with knowing oneself.

Montaigne, however, is not merely engaged in social climbing in "De la cruauté" when he takes the apparently conservative social position of insisting on the importance of birth—as opposed to a virtue that the essay has largely discredited—as the criterion of nobility. He assumes membership in the *noblesse d'épée* with its feudal and martial traditions in order to teach that class a new morality that properly defines nobility. By linking good birth with a natural disposition to leniency and a hatred of cruelty, Montaigne can criticize the behavior of his aristocratic contemporaries for being insufficiently *noble*.

The attack on hunting in "De la cruauté" is the locus for this argument against the cruelty and bloodthirstiness of aristocratic culture. For the hunt was the peculiar pursuit and exclusive privilege of the nobility. So the Duke in the second part of *Don Quixote* informs the dubious Sancho Panza.

> The chase is the image of war; it has its stratagems, wiles, and ambushes, by which one can overcome the enemy in safety; in it we have to bear extreme cold and intolerable heat; indolence and sleep are scorned; bodily strength is invigorated; the limbs of one who takes part in it are made supple; indeed, it is an exercise that can be taken without harm to anyone and with pleasure to many. And the best point about it is that it is not for everybody, as other kinds of sports are, except hawking, which is also reserved for kings and great lords.[20] (Chapter 34)

The Duke's defense of the chase is traditional and owes much to the *Cynegeticus* of Xenophon. The twelfth chapter of Xenophon's treatise offered an ideological justification of hunting as an aristocratic preserve: the hunt not only prepared young men for the hardships of war, but offered them a training in virtue that would turn them into true nobles. In the sixteenth century, however, Erasmus satirized precisely these links among hunting, nobility, and war. In *The Praise of Folly*, the goddess Folly lists among her fools those noble huntsmen who delude themselves into thinking that they are living like kings while they pursue the chase: "Cutting up bulls and oxen is properly given over to the humble plebeian, but it is a crime for game to be slaughtered except by a gentleman." In fact, Folly observes, while her cultivated humanist author takes aim at an uneducated, uncouth aristocracy pursuing its traditional pastime, they have degenerated not only to the ranks of common butchers, but into brute animals themselves.[21] In his famous pacifist commentary on the adage "Dulce bellum inexpertis," Erasmus argues that killing animals in hunting was the first step toward killing men in warfare in the history of primitive humanity.[22]

Thomas More takes up the arguments of Erasmus and gives them a further ethical turn in the greatest Renaissance polemic against aristocratic society, the *Utopia*. In their model commonwealth, the Utopians relegate "the whole activity of hunting, as unworthy of free men, upon their butchers—a craft, as I explained before, they exercise through their slaves." They do so, More's narrator comments in the same passage, because they hold the chief pleasure of the hunt to lie in the spectacle of slaughter.

> But if you are attracted by the hope of slaughter and the expectation of a creature being mangled under your eyes [*sub oculis*], it ought rather to inspire pity [*misericordiam*] when you behold a weak, fugitive, timid, and innocent [*innoxium*] little hare torn to pieces by a strong, fierce, and cruel dog [*a crudeli discerptum*] . . . the hunter seeks nothing but pleasure [*voluptatem*] from the killing and mangling of a poor animal. Even in the case of brute beasts, this desire of looking on bloodshed [*spectandae necis libidinem*], in their estimation, either arises from a cruel disposition or degenerates finally into cruelty through the constant practice of such brutal pleasure [*aut ab animi crudelis affectu censent exoriri, aut in crudelitatem denique, assiduo tam efferae voluptatis usu defluere.*][23]

Hunting, for More, is an act of cruelty, the taking of pleasure in beholding the killing of an innocent, a sight that should rather inspire pity. Like Erasmus, More suggests that the hunters—whose sport causes them repeatedly to look upon bloodshed—have sunk to the level of beasts of prey, and here he may additionally recall Seneca's argument in the *De Clementia* that the practitioners of cruelty who delight in blood and gore have changed into wild creatures of the woods. Such cruelty, the *Utopia* further implies, may be a class attribute of the nobility back in Europe who indulge in hunting as their exclusive pastime.

This humanist condemnation of the cruelty of the hunt lies behind Cervantes's fiction and Sancho Panza's rebuke to the Duke and Duchess—those representatives of the aristocracy in *Don Quixote* whom Cervantes consistently depicts as sadists and as torturers both of Sancho and of Don Quixote himself. Sancho objects to the nobility pursuing the hunt "for the sake of a pleasure that, in my opinion, should not be one at all, for it consists in killing an animal that has committed no crime."[24]

Sancho could almost be citing the Montaigne of "De la cruauté," the Montaigne who cannot bear to hear the cries of a hare in his dogs' teeth and who further notes, just after he has commented on the new and unheard of cruelties of the civil wars:

> De moy, je n'ay pas sceu voir seulement sans desplasir poursuivre et tuer une beste innocente, qui est sans deffence et de qui nous ne recevons aucune offense. Et, comme il advient communement que le cerf, se sentant hors d'alaine et de force, n'ayant plus autre remede, se rejette et rend à nous mesmes qui le poursuivons, nous demandant mercy par ses larmes,
>
> > [B] quaestuque, cruentus
> > Atque imploranti similis,
>
> [A] ce m'a tousjours semblé un spectacle tres desplaisant.
> [B] Je ne prens guiere beste en vie à qui je ne redonne les champs. (432-33)

> For myself, I have not even been able without distress to see pursued and killed an innocent animal which is defenseless and which does us no harm. And as it commmonly happens that the stag, feeling himself out of breath and strength, having no other remedy left, throws himself back and surrenders to ourselves who are pursuing him, asking for our mercy by his tears,
>
> > [B] Bleeding with moans
> > Like some imploring creature,
> >
> > > (Virgil)
>
> [A] that has always seemed to me a very unpleasant spectacle.
> [B] I hardly take any animal alive that I do not give it back the freedom of the fields. (316)

The essayist has projected the innocence that he claims for himself upon the hunted animals whose deaths he cannot bear to hear or see.[25] His attitude is easily placed within an Erasmian tradition critical of the hunt: in particular, the link that the larger argument of "De la cruauté" draws between cruelty and spectacle is epitomized in More's insistence in the *Utopia* upon the ocular pleasure of cruelty that lies at the center of the chase and that brutalizes the hunter. Montaigne's description of the scene of the hunt, however, takes on the peculiar inflection of the larger *Essais*: the encounter between hunter and cornered stag joins the many similar scenes in Montaigne's book that take place between a conqueror and the vanquished adversary who lies in his power. The anthropomorphized weeping deer surrenders itself and supplicates the victorious hunter for clemency: this return to the martial showdown that opens the *Essais* takes seriously the traditional analogy between hunting and warfare, but only to criticize the sportsman for reproducing in the fields the unbelievable cruelty of the civil wars that Montaigne has just finished mentioning. The quotation from the *Aeneid* (7.501–2) inserted in the B text deepens the resonance of the analogy, describing as it does Silvia's pet deer—already half-anthropomorphized—whom Ascanius wounds during the hunt of Book Seven and thereby instigates the war of the second half of the Virgil's epic. Montaigne almost always frees the beasts he captures alive: he is like his warrior hero Epaminondas, who never killed those he vanquished in battle.

We should, in fact, pause at this point to note the resemblance between the essayist's self-portrait of a "nature facile et debonnaire," and the figure of the Theban Epaminondas whom, we saw at the end of the previous chapter, the *Essais* celebrate as the most excellent of men and their highest moral exemplar. According to "De l"utile et de l'honneste" (3:1), Epaminondas possessed an extreme "debonnaireté de complexion" and "la facilité des meurs les plus molles [C] et la pure innocence" (801; 609); he was the paragon of clemency. It is worthwhile here to recall the chronology of the *Essais* and to remember that this figure of the merciful, innocent Epaminondas is a product of the 1588 version of the *Essais*, but the self-portrait of the cruelty-hating Montaigne is already in place in the 1580 A text. If Montaigne may appear to imitate the model Epaminondas, we should rather perceive that idealized Epaminondas as a *post facto* projection of the moral qualites that the essayist discovers to inhere *naturally* in himself as a kind of instinct he has retained unchanged from his nurse and infancy. The relationship of the modern "moi" of the *Essais* to the ancient Epaminondas is symptomatic of the argument and structure of "De la cruauté" itself, where Montaigne's discussion of his own moral disposition eventually takes over the essay: to the point where the essayist implicitly holds himself up as an ethical model, displacing the essay's earlier classical exemplars of Cato and Socrates. Montaigne's natural disposition leads him to the course of clemency in the hunt, and that good nature is the sign and product of his good birth, his nobility.

As a hunter who hates hunting, the parvenu Montaigne manages to have it both ways. He follows the pastime that defines his membership in a traditional nobility—the *noblesse d'epée* with its martial ethos—and yet suggests that his true nobility is measured by his very aversion to the blood sport in which that ethos found expression.[26] Montaigne adds his voice to an Erasmian polemic against hunting that indicts a more comprehensive cruelty of aristocratic culture. In a fundamental discussion of "De la cruauté," Philip Hallie concludes that "the power that Montaigne wants to restrain is the power of the strong to torture the weak. Every cruel being is in a position of superior strength with regard to his victim . . ."[27] "De la cruauté" and the larger *Essais* are particularly directed to the moral reform of an aristocratic ruling class, a class that needs to be taught what it means to be "well-born" and to be "naturally" noble. According to the logic of the essay, the accident of birth that makes one noble is not merely a question of lineage; the nobility of the lineage itself is attested to by the native, instinctual disposition to goodness ("bonté")—the opposite of cruelty—handed down to its heirs, and Montaigne is one such lucky heir. Conversely a cruel nobleman is no nobleman at all. Montaigne's aristocratic pretensions that raised the eyebrows of early readers of the *Essais* are in this respect as strategic as they are snobbish. The essayist speaks as a *noble d'épée* in order to inculcate new values in the powerful, to persuade them to act more like the noblemen they claim to be; foremost among these values is the refusal to use power cruelly against others, particularly when one has "vengeance in hand."

"COUARDISE MERE DE LA CRUAUTÉ"

The place of the nobility is clearly defined vis-à-vis the act of vengeance in Montaigne's second essay on cruelty; the attitude that the nobleman takes toward revenge differentiates him from members of other classes.[28] The A-text version of "Couardise mere de la cruauté" begins by recalling and apparently reversing the terms of the first essay, "Par divers moyens." We are once again in the situation of war and the treatment of the defeated by their victors. Valor, Montaigne asserts, causes its possessor to continue fighting only where he meets resistance, and to draw back when he sees the enemy at his mercy. It is rather cowardice that lies behind massacres of the vanquished, and the common people, "cette canaille du vulgaire" (694; 524), who carry them out and commit unheard-of cruelties—"cruautez inouies" (693; 524)—since they have no other notion of valor except killing. Montaigne compares them to craven dogs who bite at the carcasses of the dead beasts whom they did not dare to attack in the field, and thus continues the linking of hunting, war, and cruelty of "De la cruauté."

In "Par divers moyens" Montaigne opined differently, at least in the A-text version of his opening essay. There, we recall, a masculine virtue yielded only at the sight of a similar virtue exhibited in the resistance of the cornered enemy: it was rather the common people, women, and the essayist himself whose "mollesse" caused them to commiserate with, and grant mercy to, the vanquished. The B-text addition that Montaigne places toward the very beginning of "Couardise mere de la cruauté" carries the reversal of the first essay further. Experience has shown him, he notes, that harsh and inhuman behavior is customarily accompanied by a "mollesse feminine," and he cites the example of Alexander, tyrant of Pherae, who cruelly murdered so many of the citizens under his rule and yet wept at theatrical performances. "Mollesse," that Senecan term of disparagement that Montaigne has morally rehabilitated in "Par divers moyens" and in other essays, reappears here with all of its original negative force.

Montaigne, as we have seen, is capable of contradicting himself at his pleasure, and such contradictions are built into the skeptical argument of the *Essais*. Each time he looks at the central question of cruelty, revenge, and clemency, his perspective shifts and a different account emerges. What does not change, however, is the moral imperative of which Montaigne attempts to convince his reader, and we may regard the reversals of "Couardise mere de la cruauté" part as much of a strategy of persuasion as of a blanket skepticism. If in the first essay of the collection we should be *more* like common people and women, it is so that we will pardon the defeated; here we should be *less* like common people and women—and less like tyrants such as Alexander—so that we will pardon the defeated. The "we" in question is the noble class to which Montaigne belongs, and the B-text addition at the opening of the essay already indicates the structure of the essay's argument and its attempt to locate an ethics for a nobility that lies between the lower classes on the one hand and the tyrannical monarch on the other. Both the commoner and the tyrant are cowards and both are cruel killers. "Vaillance" belongs to the aristocrat, who should show his bravery by sparing his enemies.

The brief first, A-text version of the essay, a couple of pages long, spells out its argument in a single paradox. The reason why we should not kill those on whom we seek revenge is that dead men cannot feel our vengeance.

> Chacun sent bien qu'il y a plus de braverie et desdain à battre son ennemy qu'à l'achever, et de le faire bouquer que de le faire mourir. D'avantage que l'appetit de vengeance s'en assouvit et contente mieux, car elle ne vise qu'à donner ressentiment de soy.... Et de tuer un homme c'est le mettre à l'abry de nostre offense. (694)

> Every man clearly feels that there is more defiance and disdain in beating his enemy than in finishing him off, and in making him lick the dust than in making him die. Moreover, the appetite for vengeance is thereby better assuaged and contented, for it aims only at making itself felt.... And to kill a man is to put him in shelter from our harm. (524)

Just as Montaigne redefines the nature of nobility and valor, here he redefines revenge from its usual practice as a blood vendetta to the simple humiliation of the enemy: he covers over the radical nature of this redefinition with the assertion that it is a universally held commonplace that everybody feels. We want the victims of our vengeance to feel it, to receive its "ressentiment," and, Montaigne goes on to argue, to repent their acts against us—to make some acknowledgment of our power over them. But if we shoot them in the head, he wryly notes, they will just die making a defiant face at us as they fall—"il nous faict la mouë en tombant" (694; 524). Since we will get no satisfaction by killing them, all that we would prove by doing so is that we are afraid that they might live on to kill us.

> nous quittons par là et la vraye fin de la vengeance, et le soing de nostre reputation: nous craignons, s'il demeure en vie, qu'il nous recharge d'une pareille. (695)

> we abandon both the true end of vengeance and the care of our reputation. We fear that if he remains alive, he may renew the attack.

We wish, Montaigne says, to conquer more safely than honorably—"plus surement que honorablement" (695; 525)—and thus show ourselves to be cowards like the common people who commit massacres and cruelties after victories have been won on the battlefield.

But now the essay discovers a hole in its argument. Sparing one's victims may not, in fact, be the only way to make them feel one's vengeance. Tyrants, whose bloody behavior is due to similar, cowardly fears for their safety—"le soing de leur seurté" (699; 529)—kill their suspected enemies, but do so slowly through protracted torture.

> Les tyrans pour faire tous le deux ensemble, et tuer et faire sentir leur colere, ils ont employé toute leur suffisance à trouver moyen d'alonger la mort. Ils veulent que leurs ennemis s'en aillent, mais non pas si viste qu'ils n'ayent loisir de savourer leur vengeance. Là dessus ils sont en grand peine: car, si les torments sont violents, il sont courts; s'ils sont longs, ils ne sont pas assez douloureux à leur gré: les voylà à dispenser leur engins. (700)

> Tyrants, in order to do both things together, both to kill and to make their anger felt, have used all their ingenuity to find a way to prolong death. They want their enemies to be gone, but not so fast that they may not have leisure to savor their vengeance. Thereupon they are in great perplexity; for if the tortures are violent, they are short; if they are long, they are not painful enough to suit them. So they go dispensing their instruments of torture. (529)

The essay offers a still further explanation for the cruel torments that the tyrannical Alexander the Great inflicts upon Betis in the first essay of Montaigne's book. The tyrant's physical cruelty is an extension of his cowardice: afraid to let those he has vanquished live on to be a potential threat to him, yet unwilling to forgo vengeance by killing them outright, he turns to torture. The passage also glosses the unheard-of atrocities that, according to "De la cruauté," have become everyday practice in Montaigne's war-torn France: the sadistic pleasure of watching men dying in anguish is the coward's version of revenge. Montaigne goes on to repeat verbatim his condemnation voiced in "De la cruauté" of the use of torture in criminal executions: "Tout ce qui est au delà de la mort simple me semble pure cruauté" (700; 530; see "De la cruauté" 431; 314). The state justice that breaks criminals on the wheel partakes in the pure cruelty of tyranny. These passages were found to be objectionable by the papal censor who reviewed the *Essais* in 1581, but Montaigne did not omit them from the subsequent editions of his book.[29]

Between a cowardly common people who cruelly kill the vanquished and thereby defeat the purpose of revenge and tyrants who kill *and* avenge themselves through torture, the highest form of cruelty, stand the essayist and his audience: neither plebeians nor rulers, they are perforce aristocrats. As noblemen, they will know what is the nobler and courageous course to follow, and they will seek a bloodless revenge, showing clemency to the enemies who lie at their mercy.[30]

Or so they ought to do. The critical force of Montaigne's identification with the old nobility emerges when he complains that his noble contemporaries are failing to live up to the traditional standards of behavior of their class. Three times in the essay, twice in the A-text version and once in a B-text addition, Montaigne recalls an earlier, more humane generation of noblemen, "nos peres."

[A] là où nos peres avoient quelque degré de vengeance, nous commençons à cette heure par le dernier, et ne se parle d'arrivée que de tuer: qu'est-ce, si ce n'est couardise?(694)

[A] Nos peres se contentoient de revencher une injure par un démenti, un démenti par un coup, et ainsi par ordre. Ils estoient assez valeureux pour ne craindre pas leur ennemy vivant et outragé. (695)

[B] Les butes, les tournois, les barrieres, l'image des combats guerriers estoient l'exercise de nos peres: cet autre excercise est d'autant moins noble qu'il ne regarde qu'une fin privée, qui nous apprend à nous entreruiner, contre les loix et la justice, et qui en toute façon produict tousjours des effects dommageables. (698)

[A] why, whereas our fathers recognized some degrees in revenge, do we nowadays begin with the ultimate, and from the outset speak of nothing but killing? (524)

[A] Our fathers contented themselves with avenging an insult by giving the lie, the lie by a blow, and so in order. They were valorous enough not to fear their enemy, living and outraged. (525)

[B] Shooting at the butts, tournaments, tiltings, practice at warlike combats were the exercise of our fathers. This other exercise [fencing] is all the less noble as it regards only a private end, which teaches us to destroy one another, contrary to the laws and justice and in every way always produces harmful results. (527)

By invoking the usage of noble ancestors, the *mos maiorum*, Montaigne here, too, lays claim to a noble caste: he *has* noble ancestors to invoke—although Joseph Scaliger disparagingly objected that Montaigne's father (in reality, or closer to it, the essayist's great-grandfather) was a "seller of herring."[31] But if Montaigne includes himself in the "we" of the French aristocracy, he thereby obtains the authority to criticize from within the ethical degeneracy of his class. The nobles of earlier times carried out their vendettas among themselves without feeling obliged by fear to kill a fallen enemy who might recover and come back to attack them anew. But the nobles of the present day have lost the bravery of their ancestors: they no longer behave nobly.

The case in point, Montaigne goes on assert in a B-text addition that is as long as the original version of the essay, is the new habit of fighting alongside seconds, thirds, and fourths that has crept into the French duel. If "De la cruauté" castigates hunting, the favorite pastime of the aristocracy, "Couardise mere de la cruauté" voices its critique of noble culture by condemning one of its other defining—and no less bloody—rituals, the duel.[32] Montaigne's disapproval partly echoes the standard complaints that the governments of early modern states expressed in their edicts forbidding dueling; the civil authorities sought to achieve a "monopoly of violence," as Lawrence Stone has observed, and to prevent noblemen from taking the law into their own hands.[33] In the passage cited above Montaigne notes that fencing, newly come into vogue from Italy, serves only for private duels and bears no relationship to the training in arms needed for fighting in real battle, the kind of military exercise practiced by "our fathers,"—the kind, as the essay goes on to document, sponsored by the well-run states of antiquity whose political thinkers either looked down upon or prohibited the teaching of other martial arts (698–99; 527–28). The subject of the state, noble or not, owes his physical prowess and his very life to the purpose of defending the state and is not entitled to risk them to vindicate his own individual honor.[34] Instead of engaging a foreign enemy, Montaigne remarks, dueling has taught us to destroy one another—"nous entreruyner": the reflexive and reciprocal verb suggests that the duel is another form of the civil war that wracks his French society.

Montaigne observes that the duel is "contrary to the laws and justice," and he thereby reveals his *politique* sympathies for a strong royal government and for the rule of law itself. He also seems momentarily to take the viewpoint of the *noblesse de robe*, that new class of lawyers and jurists whose emergence in a France where judicial offices and justice itself are for sale he describes with some disgust in "De la coustume" (1:23). There, in fact, Montaigne describes the reluctance to fight duels and to become a law unto oneself as the definining difference between the office-holding *robins* and the traditional nobility.

> lequel estat, ayant la charge des loix et souveraine authorité des biens et des vies, face un corps à part de celuy de la noblesse; d'où il avienne qu'il ayt doubles loix, celles de l'honneur et celles de la justice, en plusieures choses fort contraires (aussi rigoureusement condamnent celles-là un démanti souffert, comme celles cy un démanti revanché); par le devoir des armes, celuy-là soit degradé d'honneur et de noblesse qui souffre un'injure, et, par le devoir civil,celuy qui s'en venge, encoure une peine capitale (qui s'addresse aux loix, pour avoir raison d'une offence faite à son honneur, il se deshonnore, et qui ne s'y addresse, il en est puny et chastié par les loix); et, de ces deux pieces si diverses se raportant toutesfois à un seul chef, ceux-là ayent la paix, ceux-cy la guerre en charge; ceux-là ayent le gaing, ceux-cy l'honneur; ceux-là le sçavoir, ceux-cy la vertu; ceux-là la parole, ceux-cy l'action; ceux-là la justice, ceux-cy la vaillance; ceux-là la raison, ceux-cy la force; ceux-là la robbe longue, ceux-cy la courte en partage? (118)

> which estate, having charge of the laws and the sovereign authority over property and life, forms a body apart from that of the nobility. (Whence it comes about that there are two sets of laws, those of honor and those of justice, in many matters quite opposed. The former condemn as rigorously a man's enduring being given the lie as the latter condemn his avenging it.) What could be more barbarous than that by the code of arms the man who endures an insult should be degraded from honor and nobility, and by the civil code he who avenges an insult should incur capital punishment? (He who appeals to the laws to get satisfaction for an offense to his honor dishonors himself; and he who does not appeal to them is therefore punished and chastised by the laws.) And that of these two bodies, so different but nevertheless joined to a single head, one should have charge of peace, the other of war; one should have gain as its share, the other honor; one knowledge, the other virtue; one words, the other action; one justice, the other valor; one reason, the other force; one the long robe, the other the short? (85)

It is to the new legal class that, as we have seen, Montaigne, the magistrate from a recently ennobled family, might himself be suspected to belong, however much he may deplore its venality, its preference for gain over honor. He presumably identified with the *robe* values of peace, learning, and justice rather than with the martial valor that has become, to his evident impatience, the exclusive measure of nobility in France. The final opposition in the passage, between reason and force, tilts decisively in favor of the *robins*, and suggests that the essayist may all along prefer the rule of law over the code of private honor and violence incarnated in the duel. Yet the overall tenor of the passage nevertheless sides with the old nobility against the upstart lawyers: Montaigne assumes the voice of a *noble d'épée* complaining about the state to which France has come when a gentleman given the lie cannot defend his honor with his sword without the risk of punishment.

Montaigne takes on a similar voice in "Couardise mere de la cruauté" when he attacks the duel by appealing not to the logic of the state from whose jurisdiction the dueling nobleman quite knowingly and willfully declares his exemption in questions of honor, but, on much less conventional grounds, to the nobleman's sense of honor and fair play itself. While their noble forefathers may have conducted affairs of honor by degree and in ordered stages—insult, giving the lie, a blow—that allowed for mediation and reconciliation at each step, the duelists of today pursue each other to the death, afraid of future vengeance. Moreover the duel has degenerated by the custom of including other parties, and Montaigne should know since his brother, the sieur de Mattecolom, was involved as a second fighting beside his principal in a duel in Rome. The inventors of this practice must have feared fighting alone—"la solitude faisoit peur" (695; 525)—yet self-reliance is the truest form of courage, the kind of courage one might suppose the duel to have been instituted to display.

> Outre l'injustice d'une telle action, et vilenie, d'engager à la protection de vostre honneur autre valeur et force que la vostre, je trouve du desadvantage à un homme de bien et qui pleinement se fie de soy, d'aller mesler sa fortune à celle d'un second. (696)

> Besides the injustice and baseness of such an action, engaging another valor and strength than your own in protection of your honor, I find it a disadvantage to a nobleman who trusts fully in himself, to go and involve his fortune with that of a second. (525)

The language has become Stoic, recalling the early essay "De la solitude," where Montaigne advocates that we make our happiness depend on ourselves and that we remove ourselves from ties that bind us to others—"faisons que nostre contentement despende de nous; desprenons nous de toutes les liaisons qui nous attachent à autruy" (240; 177). Such Stoic self-sufficiency is easily aligned with the ideals of aristocratic autonomy, personal bravery and political independence—in short, of "honor"—that inform the duel. But modern duelists fall short of these ideals: they do not behave as a nobleman, an "homme de bien," should. Paradoxically, they assert their right to settle their private scores as individuals and summon others to their defense. Along the same lines, Montaigne objects to the new art of fencing.

> mais ce n'est pas proprement vertu, puis qu'elle tire son appuy de l'addresse et qu'elle prend autre fondement que de soy-mesme. L'honneur des combats consiste en la jalousie du courage, non de la science . . . et, en mon enfance, la noblesse fuyoit la reputation de bon escrimeur comme injurieuse, et se desroboit pour l'apprendre, comme un mestier de subtilité, desrogeant à la vraye et naifve vertu. (697)
>
> But this is not properly valor, since it draws its support from skill and has its basis in something other than itself. The honor of combat consists in the jealousy of courage, not of craft. . . . And in my childhood the nobility avoided the reputation of good fencers as insulting, and learned it furtively, as a cunning trade, derogating from true and natural valor. (527)

Skill in fencing is like the second or third you take along with you to the duel, an external supplement to your own valor, and thus a witness to your fear. The new swordsmanship comes from Italy and thus carries with it overtones of a new court culture: something that could be learned and not inherited as "natural valor" through blood lineage. Montaigne once again invokes an earlier, more virtuous nobility that acquired the new fencing art, but at least was ashamed of doing so. (There may be some irony attached to the fact that they learned fencing in secret, mimicking and entering into the very duplicity or "subtilité" of the art itself and acting like one of Castiglione's courtly noblemen attempting through *sprezzatura* to treat an acquired skill as a natural endowment.)

If the duelist no longer relies on his courage alone, the second, committed to the honor of another, may find himself acting in equally cowardly, ignoble fashion. The duel with seconds is like warfare. If you defeat your own adversary, you must join your companion against his foe. Such ganging up is "supercherie," (696; 526) a translation of the Italian "soverchieria," which theorists of the duel used to describe fighting with unfair odds and trickery against a foe unable to defend himself; Montaigne compares it to an armed man attacking an opponent whose sword is broken or who is already badly wounded. Such outrageous behavior was supposed to be the *cause* for fighting a duel, not part of the duel itself.[35] But because you are obliged as a second to your principal, you cannot meet your obligation to behave becomingly as an "homme de bien."

> La courtoisie que vous pouvez et certes devés faire à vostre ennemy, quand vous l'avez reduict en mauvais termes et à quelque grand desadvantage, je ne vois pas comment vous la puissiez faire, quand il va de l'interest d'autruy, où vous n'estes que suivant, où la dispute n'est pas vostre. Il ne pouvoit estre ny juste, ny courtois, au hazard de celuy auquel il s'estoit presté. (697)
>
> The courtesy that you can and indeed should offer to your enemy when you have reduced him to bad terms and some great disadvantage, I do not see how

you can offer it when the interest of another is at stake, where you are only an assistant, where the dispute is not your own. He [Montaigne's brother] could be neither just nor courteous at the risk of the man to whom he had lent himself. (526)

Sparing the defeated now becomes a gesture of courtesy, the courtesy that you are obliged to show—"vous devés faire"—to your fallen opponent. *Noblesse oblige*: the language and argument have shifted from Stoic self-sufficiency to old-fashioned chivalry. "Courtoisie" is a word that appears infrequently in the *Essais*; for our purposes, it is a notable attribute of the paragon Epaminondas in "De l'utile et de l'honneste," who, in his mildness toward the very enemies against whom he waged war, responded to the call of "pure courtoisie" (802; 609). In the present case, the term retains some of its technical meaning from the literature of dueling; one may extend to one's adversary the *courtesy* of mending his armor or of replacing a broken sword as well as sparing his life.[36] It is a question of maintaining a fair fight. But courtesy also conveys a larger sense of the shows of respect, deference, and favor that were exchanged among noblemen and were the cement of aristocratic society. Kirsten Neuschel writes that the "exchange of courtesy which abounds in nobles' correspondence, then, was an expression of the need continually to be acknowledged as honorable by fellow nobles."[37] Montaigne appeals to this code of behavior by which he and his fellow noblemen sought mutual recognition in order to argue that the contemporary duel betrays their own standards of honor and nobility. The duel has become cowardly—and hence cruel: fought to the death, it does not allow for the act of clemency by which the courteous nobleman would make his noble identity known.

By the same argument cruelty is ignoble, behavior that should be reserved, according to "Couardise mere de la cruauté," to the plebeians subject beneath and the tyrants ruling above the aristocracy. But the examples of dueling in this essay and of hunting in "De la cruauté" show the aristocracy not only capable of cruelty but incorporating it into its own hallowed institutions. Montaigne speaks as a *noble d'épée* so that he may show the traditional military nobility its shortcomings and teach it a milder ethos: perhaps the ethos of the more pacific, law-abiding *noblesse de robe*. In what may reflect a real split in the essayist's class identification, he presents clemency and a vengeance that stops short of death *not* as the softhearted values of a new legal aristocracy looked down upon by the hereditary nobility, but rather as that soldierly nobility's truest expression of honor and valor. The gentleness that marks the gentleman is innate and effortless, the sign that blood will tell; it is the behavior of noble forefathers, deviation from which attests to present-day degeneracy. The conservative tenor of Montaigne's argument does not conceal a radical criticism of the noble class to which he aspires to belong.

It is a notable feature of the two essays on cruelty that Montaigne nowhere makes an argument against vengeance on Christian grounds. In fact, the appeal to aristocratic honor might be felt to be the opposite of the Christian doctrine of meekness and turning the other cheek—we have seen Montaigne explicitly reject the idea of teaching such doctrine to a "young prince" in "De la diversion." The ethical arguments of the *Essais* proceed typically in purely secular terms, a reflection of Montaigne's humanist tastes; perhaps, too, he recognized that the conflict between Catholics and Protestants in his France made the evocation of Christian tenets a risky proposition. The extent of the secular nature of his ethics is measured in the original A-text ending of "Couardise mere de la cruauté" where Montaigne voices his disapproval of the use of torture in capital executions. He thinks of crucifixion.

> Josephe recite que, pendant les guerres des Romains en Judée, passant où l'on avoit crucifié quelques Juifs, il y avoit trois jours, reconneut trois de ses amis, et obtint de les oster de là; les deux moururent, dit-il, l'autre vescut encore depuis. (701)

> Josephus relates that during the wars of the Romans in Judea, passing a place where they had crucified some Jews three days before, he recognized three of his friends and obtained leave to remove them from there. Two died, he says; the other lived on after. (530)

One cannot but think of another crucifixion in Judea where, after three days, one of three crucified men lived on.[38] The C-text addition closes the final version of the essay with an anecdote that beneath its ghastly details also sounds Christological; the horrible execution of George Sechel, whose blood and flesh were fed to his followers in a kind of demonic parody of the mass, while Sechel himself prayed for the "salut" of his beloved brother and drew "on himself all the hatred for their misdeeds"—"tirant sur soy toute l'envie de leurs meffaicts" (701; 530). But the attention in both cases is not upon a divine sacrifice but the horror of a human cruelty that exceeds "la mort simple." For Montaigne the message of this crucifixion is that one should not crucify people.

Chapter Three

THE CULTURE THAT CANNOT PARDON:
"DES CANNIBALES" IN THE LARGER *ESSAIS*

AT A FAIRLY early point in "Des cannibales"(1:31) Montaigne placed a passage that has greatly contributed to the idea of the noble savage, and that has caused the essay to be read as an encomium of the natural way of life enjoyed by the inhabitants of the New World. It is the passage cited and imitated by Shakespeare in *The Tempest* (2.1.143–64), when the old courtier Gonzalo envisions the utopian commonwealth he would build if he could rule Prospero's island. Montaigne asserts that the existence of the Brazilian cannibals surpasses in happiness not only the mythical Golden Age but the ideal polities projected by Lycurgus and Plato, who were unable to imagine maintaining a society "with so little artifice and human solder"—"avec si peu d'artifice et de soudeure humaine" (206; 153), that is, without the intervention of culture. The essayist goes on to define this state of nature by listing the cultural institutions it lacks: it has no trade, no writing or arithmetic, no juridical or political offices, no servitude or class division between rich and poor, no business or testamentary settlements, no kinship relations, no agriculture or metallurgy. This impressive chain of privatives reaches its rhetorical climax as the cannibals' language itself proves devoid of the terms of a European culture that lacks their simplicity:

> Les paroles mesmes qui signifient le mensonge, la trahison, la dissimulation, l'avarice, l'envie, la detraction, le pardon, inouies. (206)

> The very words that signify lying, treachery, dissimulation, avarice, envy, belittling, pardon—unheard of. (153)

These terms suggest that what the cannibal lacks, above all, is the self-consciousness and self-division of the European. The perception of the "primitive" or the "natural" human being is shaped by a dialectic—*they* are what *we* are not—that will become a constituent feature of romanticism and of Rousseau's noble savage two centuries later. The cannibal cannot tell a lie, not knowing what one is, or betray, or dissemble, and the integrity and single-mindedness of his contented existence is witnessed by his lack of desire of more for himself or of less for others: envy is here a middle term between avarice and detraction.

So far so good, but it is the last not-so-innocent term, "pardon," that should give us pause. "*In cauda venenum*," "the sting is in the tail," or, as Montaigne himself in "Des livres" (2:10) describes the technique of the epigram that ends with a reversal of what has preceded it, "the stings with which Martial sharpens the tail"—"les esguillons dequoy Martial esguise la queuë" (412; 299). The whole essay of "Des cannibales" ends with a spectacular instance of this technique: "They do not wear breeches," says the essayist, seemingly dismissing the whole subject. But here the unsettling final term, "pardon," already anticipates the ensuing description of the central, repeatedly staged event of the cannibals' culture: the confrontation of the victorious cannibal with a defeated enemy who lies at his mercy. The cannibals do not pardon their captives, but eat them instead "to betoken an extreme revenge"—"pour representer une extreme vengeance" (209; 155).[1] In this case the cannibals' single-mindedness, which prevents any deviation from their goal of vengeance, becomes bloody-mindedness.[2]

The showdown between victor and victim is by now familiar to us, placed front and center in Montaigne's book by its opening essay. Far from describing a utopian New World distinct from the mores and ethical issues of Europe, "Des cannibales" occupies a cardinal position in the reflections on clemency and revenge, Stoic virtue, noble valor, and cruelty that we have traced through a series of interrelated essays of Montaigne's book, and we shall see that it textually echoes those essays and repeats their concerns. Despite the disavowals of the above passage, the cannibal culture is not characterized just by negation, but by its own peculiar—and horrific—institutions. It is indeed a culture that has been simplified and stripped down, but it thereby allows Montaigne to depict all the more clearly a whole society based on vengeance and warfare, a society where everyone displays valor and everyone possesses unbending Stoic resolve. The result is a society at war with itself, if only half-knowingly—and it is all too similar to Montaigne's France. It is, in fact, in his examination of the Brazilians and of another culture of military virtue, the gladiatorial Roman society in "Des mauvais moyens employez à bonne fin" (2:23), that Montaigne can fully extend the political implications of his ethical thought, and it is, perhaps paradoxically, in these societies, geographically and historically distant, that he constructs dark models for his present-day France, torn apart by the Wars of Religion. The Stoic resolve of the undaunted cannibal captive facing his or her fate in the cooking pots finds, in fact, a further analogue in Montaigne's disapproving portraits of religious martyrs, both ancient and contemporary, who not only allow but positively invite their enemies to roast them alive. His calamitous historical situation of civil war and religious fanaticism on the part of both Catholics and Protestants, in which no side is willing to give an inch—to bestow or ask for pardon—governs the parallels that Montaigne finds among refractory French noblemen, intransigent religious zealots, Roman gladiators, and Brazilian cannibals.

Cosmographers and Topographers

"Des cannibales" has in recent years become the widest read and best known of Montaigne's essays, the one essay that many people know if they know no other.[3] Anthologized and studied alongside other early European responses to the New World, it has often been understood outside of the context of the *Essais* themselves. My argument embeds the essay once again in that context and contends that Montaigne's discussion of the cannibals turns out more than casually to refer to his own France and that the terms with which it discusses the Brazilian natives are deeply rooted in his own historical and political preoccupations. This reading runs counter to a traditional and still prevalent reception of "Des cannibales." Criticism has congratulated Montaigne for his freedom from ethnocentric prejudice. The essayist does famously declare that "each man calls barbarism whatever is not his own practice"—"chacun appelle barbarie ce qui n'est pas de son usage" (205; 152)—an authentic early formulation of an attitude of cultural relativism that can be glimpsed as well in "De la coustume" (1:23), where cannibalism is again a test case.[4] He further asserts his preference for the unbiased, objective ethnographic detailing of *topographers* over the interpretative reporting of *cosmographers* who always add something of their own in the telling, and he insists that he has received his information about the cannibals from an eyewitness, a servant of his who had spent some time among them.[5]

Gérard Defaux, in an important polemical article, has suggested the extent to which this version of Montaigne as proto-anthropologist is untenable. He doubts the very existence of the servant and points out that all of Montaigne's descriptions of the cannibals derive from the works of those cosmographers he professes not to have consulted. Moreover, he notes how Montaigne himself interprets the cannibals and shapes his description of their culture according to preexisting European typologies; for instance, he connects the passage I began with to conventional Ovidian descriptions of the Golden Age, the same Golden Age that the cannibals are said to surpass. Defaux concludes that the essay ends in an aporia; its true subject is not an escape from ethnocentrism but rather just the opposite: the impossibility of ever acknowledging—achieving knowledge of—the foreign other because the would-be knower cannot escape the terms of his own language and culture.[6]

As helpful as Defaux's arguments are in demystifying the claims of the essay to an impartial, factual account of the cannibals and their society, his conclusions are unnecessarily drastic. The ideal of an objective or transparent reporting of the practices of an alien culture—just the facts, please—is indeed utopian. There are no "facts" without interpretation, since "facts" are constituted by the language that describes them, in this case the language and cultural codes of the European observer of the New World peoples. But it does not follow that everything gets lost in the translation, that *nothing* of the cannibals' culture can get through the interpretative accounts made of it both by the cosmographers and by Montaigne himself, however distorting those accounts may be. Even the most confirmed structuralist is conscious that alien cultures do communicate with each other, with greater and lesser degrees of understanding and accommodation of their discursive systems to the challenge of the new—just as the individual discursive systems of a given culture change and develop across time and become capable of expressing new concepts and ideas.

Even if Montaigne's essay may not tell us much about the Brazilian cannibals—and it may tell us more than Defaux is inclined to think—it can tell us something about Montaigne's France, at least as seen through the essayist's eyes.[7] *Des cannibales* invites this comparative and self-reflexive approach, for at the celebrated moral high point at the center of essay, Montaigne declares of the Brazilians' cannibalism,

> Je ne suis pas marry que nous remerquons l'horreur barbaresque qu'il y a en une telle action, mais ouy bien dequoy, jugeans bien de leurs fautes, nous soyons si aveuglez aux nostres. Je pense qu'il y a plus de barbarie à manger un homme vivant qu'à le manger mort, . . . (209)

> I am not sorry that we notice the barbarous horror of such acts, but I am heartily sorry that, judging their faults rightly, we should be so blind to our own. I think there is more barbarity in eating a man alive than in eating him dead; . . . (155)

and goes on to condemn the European use of torture, especially that which he and his fellow Frenchmen have recently seen for themselves during the Wars of Religion. Those wars pursue Montaigne's thought no matter how far geographically or historically afield it goes. By the same token, it is a humanistic article of belief that one studies other cultures partly in order to understand something about one's own. It should come as little surprise if the cannibal society that Montaigne's essay describes should serve as a model—even, as it does in this passage, as a kind of ethical yardstick—for the situation in his France.

For the cannibal society to do so, however, its barbaric horror needs to be noticed. The customary reading of "Des cannibales" that praises Montaigne's impartial objectivity toward the New World peoples is tacitly based on the approval of them he voices in such passages as the comparison to the Golden Age—as if objectivity and approval were the same, as if the recognition of cultural difference and relativity precluded moral judgment, and as if it were impossible for a European to disapprove of the cannibalism of non-Europeans without revealing an incurable ethnocentrism or, even worse, a colonialist mentality.[8] The ideological stakes that may lie behind this reading need not concern us, but in its perpetuation of the idea of the noble savage, it reverses Montaigne's concern. It recognizes all too well the barbarity of the European while being blind to that of the cannibal. This selective vision is not the essay's fault, for while Montaigne continues to praise the virtue and abilities of the Brazilians throughout *Des cannibales*, its second half draws the reader ever closer to the war and cannibalism in which such virtue results, from the initial image of an age of gold to images of dismembered limbs and roasted flesh.

Cannibal Cruelty

The cannibals, according to the essay, fight their wars merely for glory and to demonstrate their superiority in valor over their enemies—the cannibals from the other side of their mountains. They practice cannibalism not from any dietary necessity but only for the sake of revenge. They are, it seems, willing to spare and set free the prisoners they take in battle, a pardon of sorts, providing that they confess and acknowledge their defeat—"la confession et recognoissance d'estre vaincus" (210; 156). They threaten the prisoners with torture and dismemberment and remind them of the feast that will made of their flesh.

> pour cette seule fin d'arracher de leur bouche quelque parole molle ou rabaissée, ou de leur donner envie de s'en fuyr, pour gaigner cet avantage de les avoir espouvantez, et d'avoir faict force à leur constance. (210–11)

> for the sole purpose of wringing from their lips some weak or base word, or making them want to flee, so as to gain the advantage of having terrified them and broken down their firmness. (156)

The cannibals attempt to break down the constancy of their adversaries and make them say uncle; when that fails, as it almost always does for reasons that will be examined below, they eat them.

The ritual scenario of Brazilian cannibalism picks up echoes of other passages on torture, revenge, and cruelty from the *Essais* that we have already looked at in the last two chapters. Let us return still once more to the confrontation of Alexander and Betis in the 1588 B-text addition to "Par divers moyens on arrive a pareille fin."

> Tu ne mourras pas comme tu as voulu, Betis; fais estat qu'il te faut souffrir toutes les sortes de tourmens qui se pourront inventer contre un captif. L'autre, d'une mine non seulement asseurée, mais rogue et altière, se tint sans mot dire à ces menaces. Lors Alexandre, voyant son fier et obstiné silence: A-il flechi un genouil? lui est-il eschappé quelque voix suppliante? Vrayment je vainqueray ta taciturnité; et si je n'en puis arracher parole, j'en arracheray au moins du gemissement. Et tournant sa cholere en rage, commanda qu'on luy

perçast les talons, et le fit ainsi trainer tout vif, deschirer et desmembrer au cul d'une charrette. (9)

"You shall not die as you wanted, Betis: prepare yourself to suffer every kind of torment that can be invented against a captive." The other, with a look not only confident, but insolent and haughty, stood without saying a word to these threats. Then Alexander, seeing his proud and obstinate silence: "Has he bent a knee? Has any suppliant cry escaped him? I'll conquer your muteness yet, and if I cannot wring a word from it, at least I'll wring a groan." And turning his anger into rage, he ordered Betis' heels to be pierced through and had him thus dragged, alive, torn and dismembered, behind a cart. (5)

This addition to the first essay—which now, however, sets the tone and scene for the entire *Essais* that follow it—clearly echoes "Des cannibales": the conqueror's exasperated, vain effort to wring a word ("arracher parole") of supplication from his imperturbable captive leads to his vindictive dismemberment of the captive's body.

It makes a difference that the body in this case is still alive, and the language—"tout vif, deschirer et desmembrer"—is also reminiscent of the already cited condemnation of modern European torture in "Des cannibales," particularly of the atrocities practiced in the name of religion by the Catholic and Huguenot zealots in the French civil wars.[9]

Je pense qu'il y a plus de barbarie à manger un homme vivant qu'à le manger mort, à deschirer, par tourmens et par geénes, un corps encore plein de sentiment, le faire rostir par le menu, le faire mordre et meurtrir aux chiens et aux pourceaux (comme nous l'avons, non seulement leu, mais veu de fresche memoire, non entres des ennemis anciens, mais entre des voisins et concitoyens, et, qui pis est, sous pretexte de pieté et de religion), que de le rostir et manger apres qu'il est trespassé. (209)

I think that there is more barbarity in eating a man alive than in eating him dead; and in tearing by tortures and the rack a body still full of feeling, in roasting a man bit by bit, in having him bitten and mangled by dogs and swine (as we have not only read but seen within fresh memory, not among ancient enemies, but among neighbors and fellow citizens, and what is worse, on the pretext of piety and religion) than in roasting and eating him after he is dead. (155)

Montaigne makes the same distinction between mutilating a dead and a sentient body in his repeated polemic against execution-by-torture in "De la cruauté" and "Couardise mere de la cruauté": any execution that goes beyond simple killing is cruelty. In the former essay, he is appalled by those who, through the license of the civil wars in France, take pleasure in dismembering their victims—"hacher et détrencher les membres d'autruy" (432)—and he invokes there by contrast the New World cannibals who only cut up and eat their captives *after* they have killed them.

> Les sauvages ne m'offensent pas tant de rostir et manger les corps des trespassez que ceux qui les tourmentent et persecutent vivans. (430)
>
> Savages do not shock me as much by roasting and eating the bodies of the dead as do those who torment and persecute them living. (314)

Such cruelties practiced on living and feeling victims find their perhaps most horrific version in the *Essais* in the C-text conclusion of "Couardise mere de la cruauté," in a scene we have discussed: the cannibalism performed on the living body of George Sechel, whose followers and brother are forced to eat his flesh and drink his blood. The anecdote depicts the extremes reached by the cowardly cruelty examined in that essay, the cruelty of the tyrant. By operating upon live victims, the torturers of the Old World, where, according to "Des cannibales," tyranny and cruelty are ordinary vices—"la tyrannie, la cruauté . . . nos fautes ordinaires" (210; 156)—outdo in cruelty the cannibalism of the New World, which is by contrast the product of a warfare that is described as wholly noble and aristocratic—"toute noble et genereuse" (210; 156). Yet the Brazilian cannibals are cruel nonetheless; they have readily adopted the more sadistic methods of executing prisoners taught them by the Portuguese conquistadors as an even better form of vengeance than their own (209; 155). And their customary behavior, too, is implicated in Montaigne's reflections on cruelty and revenge, for it is with the promise of similar torture and dismemberment—"des tourmens . . . du detranchement de leurs membres" (210; 156)—that they try to break the will of their captive foes.

In trying to force a confession of defeat from their prisoners, the cannibals follow—up to a point—the practice of revenge that Montaigne recommends to a nobleman in "Couardise mere de la cruauté." There, as we have seen, the essayist declares that the object of vengeance should be to make itself felt on the enemy, to make him yield in humiliation—"bouquer" (694; 524)—and repent of his offense. Killing him will only defeat one's purpose.

> Il s'en repentira, disons nous. Et, pour luy avoir donné d'une pistolade en la teste, estimons nous qu'il s'en repente? Au rebours, si nous nous en prenons garde, nous trouverons qu'il nous faict la mouë en tombant: il ne nous en sçait pas seulement mauvais gré, c'est bien loing de s'en repentir. (694)
>
> "He will repent it," we say. And because we have given him a pistol shot in the head, do we think that he repents it? On the contrary, if we consider it, we will find that he makes a face at us as he falls. He does not even hold it against us, so far is he from repenting. (524)

Villey's dating suggests that this passage was written in the same period as an analogous scene in "Des cannibales," describing the final moments of the captive cannibal before his enemies kill and eat him as a sign of extreme vengeance.

> Ceux qui les peignent mourans, et qui representent cette action quand on les assomme, ils peignent le prisonnier crachant au visage de ceux qui le tuent et leur faisant la mouë. De vray, ils ne cessent jusques au dernier souspir de les braver et deffier de parole et de contenance. Sans mentir, au pris de nous, voilà des hommes bien sauvages; car, ou il faut qu'ils le soyent bien à bon escient, ou que nous le soyons: il y a une merveilleuse distance entre leur forme et la nostre. (212)

> Those that paint these people dying, and who show the execution, portray the prisoner spitting in the face of his slayers and making a face at them. Indeed to the last gasp they never stop braving and defying their enemies by word and look. Truly here are real savages by our standards; for either they must be thoroughly so, or we must be; there is an amazing distance between their character and ours. (158)

The repentance of the victim sought by the avenger in "Couardise mere de la cruauté" is closely related to the acknowledgment of having been vanquished sought by the cannibals and by Alexander from the captive Betis, but no such admission is forthcoming in any of these cases. The defiance of the cannibal, sticking out his tongue at his conquerors at the instant of his death, is thus not so unique as *Des cannibales* here proclaims it to be, although it is exemplary of the emptiness of a vengeance that rarely brings any satisfaction to the avenger—and may, for that very reason, turn all the more lethal. However noble the aims of their revenge, the cannibals end up killing their victims. But the behavior of the cannibals seems purer—more natural—because it is so deeply inculcated by their culture, because, knowing "how to enjoy their condition happily and be content with it"—"sçavoir heureusement jouyr de leur condition et s'en contenter" (210; 156)—the cannibals cannot imagine behaving otherwise. It is they rather than the European observers, castigated earlier in the essay for judging according to the standards of their own countries, who are truly caught up in—we might say are the victims of—their ethnocentrism.[10]

Cannibal Culture

The essay repeatedly emphasizes the fertility of the cannibals' region, which abounds in fish and flesh (207; 153), and their contentment with the necessities of nature: "anything beyond that is superfluous to them"—"tout ce qui est au delà, est superflu pour eux" (210; 156). Spending their whole day dancing (207; 154), the cannibals live in a land of Cockaigne—and they certainly do not need to eat each other to make up a protein deficiency in their diets.[11] Their cannibalism and the warfare that literally feeds it are superfluous, a product of a culture, not of nature, however close to nature the Brazilians may appear to be. This culture, however simplified, possesses its own logic. Its essentials, which are twofold, are stated twice in a short space of the essay:

> Il ne leur recommande que deux choses: la vaillance contre les ennemis et l'amitié à leur femmes.
> ... toute leur science ethique ne contient que ces deux articles, de la resolution à la guerre et affection à leurs femmes. (208)

> He [the cannibal prophet] recommends to them only two things: valor against the enemy and love for their wives.
> ... their whole ethical science contains only these two articles: resoluteness in war and affection for their wives. (154)

These two injunctions of cannibal ethics turn out to be related, for in this polygamous culture a warrior with a higher reputation for valor will have more wives than another—"en ont d'autant plus grand nombre qu'ils sont en meilleure reputation de vaillance" (212; 158). By their number, the wives become the badge of their husbands valor, and the "jealousy" with which they contend to obtain more companions for the "honor" of their spouse mirrors the "jealousy in valor"—"jalousie de la vertu" (210; 156)—that is the sole basis of the cannibals' warfare with their neighbors.

For otherwise, the cannibals have little way of telling one another apart. In a passage that appears to owe more to Plato's *Republic* than to his ethnographic sources, Montaigne relates that "They generally call those of the same age, brothers; those who are younger, children; and the old men are fathers to all the others"—"Ils s'entr'appellent generalement, ceux de mesme aage, freres; enfans, ceux qui sont au dessoubs; et les vieillards sont peres à tous les autres" (210; 156)—and they leave their property to all in common.[12] In a society where all are alike, martial valor becomes the only mark of identity, and the invincible courage of the cannibal warrior is perhaps less to be marveled at when it and it alone defines who he is. Cannibal society thus appears intensely competitive: all the more so because there is but one focus of competition and because the cannibals are so identical one with another. Their striving one and all to distinguish themselves in battle in the same culturally prescribed manner only makes them seem more alike.

Here, then, is an example, at the level of a whole society, of that crisis of likeness that René Girard has described as the crisis of culture itself and the source of its violence.[13] Among the cannibals this violence is apparently displaced from within the society of similar males—competing to establish their dissimilarity—onto the foreign enemy, but the pattern of likeness only reinstates itself when the enemy turns out to be another cannibal tribe with an identical culture from the other side of the mountains. The reciprocity is spelled out by the essayist's laconic sentence: "These on this side, do the same in their turn"—"Autant en font ceux-cy à leur tour" (210; 156)—and, most remarkably, in the song of the cannibal captive before he is executed and devoured.

> J'ay une chanson faicte par un prisonnier, où il y a ce traict: qu'ils viennent hardiment trétous et s'assemblent pour disner de luy: car ils mangeront quant et quant leurs peres et leurs ayeux, qui ont servy d'aliment et de nourriture à son corps. Ces muscles, dit-il, cette cher et ces veines, ce sont les vostres, pauvres fols que vous estes; vous ne recognoissez pas que la substance des membres de vos ancestres s'y tient encore: savourez les bien, vous y trouverez le goust de vostre propre chair. (212)

> I have a song composed by a prisoner which contains this challenge, that they should all come boldly and gather to dine off him, for they will be eating at the same time their own fathers and grandfathers, who have served to feed and nourish his body. "These muscles," he says, "this flesh and these veins are your own, poor fools that you are. You do not recognize that the substance of your ancestors' limbs is still contained in them. Savor them well; you will find in them the taste of your own flesh." (158)

"An invention that certainly does not smack of barbarity"—"Invention qui ne sent aucunement la barbarie"—Montaigne immediately comments, playing in this gustatory context on the connotation of *sent* and, perhaps of the *essai* itself, as a kind of tasting. Wit aside, Montaigne might well congratulate the invention of the cannibal's song, *because it is his own*, as a comparison to his source in André Thevet's *Les Singularitez de la France antarctique* demonstrates. There the cannibal captive sings:

> Les Margageas noz amis sont gens de bien, forts & puissans en guerre, ils ont pris & mangé grand nombre de noz ennemis, aussi me mangeront ils quelque iour quand il leur plaira: mais de moy, j'ay tué & mangé des parens et amis de celuy qui me tient prisonnier: avec plusieurs semblables paroles.[14]

> The Margageas our friends are valiant, strong, and powerful in war, they have taken and eaten a great number of our enemies, just as these enemies will eat me, too, some day when it will please them to do so: but for my part, I have killed and eaten the relatives and friends of him who holds me prisoner: with many similar words.

The inventive essayist has supplied the other similar words the cosmographer has left out—much as we have seen him improve upon his ancient sources and invent an anecdote about Epaminondas that they omitted. He should be credited for the alimentary conceit—not at all barbarous—that the cannibals are eating not only the flesh of their fathers and grandfathers that has gone into nourishing the captive they eat in turn, but, as the captive says, *their own flesh*.

Montaigne, that is, deliberately revises Thevet's account in order to depict a cannibal society and larger culture that, even as it directs its violence outwards in war against its enemy, is literally devouring itself. Not only is the enemy another identical cannibal, not only does the perfect reciprocity of vengeance between the two enemy tribes reinforce their similarity and promise an unending chain of violence that turns the victory of today into tomorrow's defeat. More, the competition of valor *within* the society fuels the warfare in the first place and, even as it seeks to differentiate one cannibal from another, leads them all to the same end: killed or eaten by an enemy who will be killed or eaten in turn. At the end of the essay, Montaigne asks a cannibal who has been brought to France, a cannibal captain or king, one who had thus succeeded in distinguishing himself in an otherwise egalitarian and virtually anonymous culture, what advantage he gained from his superior position. "He told me that it was to march foremost in war"—"il me dict que c'estoit marcher le premier à la guerre"] (214; 159): designated the first in bravery, but also the first to be killed.

A Roman Analogue

The cannibal culture, in which we may now discern as many dystopian as utopian features, is not an isolated case in the *Essais*. Some of its patterns, in particular its emphasis on military prowess and valor, its collapse of difference between foreign war and intrasocietal competition and violence, its ultimately self-defeating and self-consuming mechanisms, are found in Montaigne's analysis of ancient Rome in the short essay, "Des mauvais moyens employez à bonne fin" (2:23). The title of the essay suggests its link with the opening essay, "Par divers moyens on arrive à pareille fin," and the Roman gladiators who will be its central focus are, like the cannibalism of the New World natives, cited in "De la cruauté" as instances of institutionalized cruelty (433; 316); like "Des Cannibales," "Des mauvais moyens" belongs to a whole cluster of interrelated essays.

The evil means of the essay's title are twofold—the foreign wars the Romans fought and the gladiatorial games they held in their arenas—and these are interrelated. The essay begins with the conceit of the body politic, whose superabundance of health needs on occasion to be purged by a bloodletting: by sending out a part of the population to conquer new territory, as the ancient Franks first came to France or as the Romans founded their colonies. The conceit shifts its meaning as Montaigne describes a second Roman strategy.

> Par fois aussi ils ont à escient nourry des guerres avec aucuns, leurs ennemis, non seulement pour tenir leurs hommes en haleine, de peur que l'oysiveté, mere de corruption, ne leur apportast quelque pire incovenient,
>
> > *Et patimur longae pacis mala; saevior armis,*
> > *Luxuria incumbit,*

mais aussi pour servir de saignée à leur Republique et esvanter un peu la chaleur trop vehemente de leur jeunesse, escourter et esclaircir le branchage de ce tige foisonnant en trop de gaillardise: à cet effet se sont ils autrefois servis de la guerre contre les Cartaginois. (683)

Sometimes also they deliberately fostered wars with certain of their enemies, not only to keep their men in condition, for fear that idleness, mother of corruption, might bring them to some worse mischief—

> We bear the evils of long peace; fiercer than war,
> Luxury weighs us down
>
> (Juvenal)

—but also to serve as a bloodletting for their republic and to cool off a bit the too vehement heat of their young men, to prune and clear the branches of that too lustily proliferating stock. (517)

Here the metaphor of bloodletting becomes literalized in a sinister way, for the hot-blooded valorous Roman youth who threaten the republic and who are purged from its body in fact shed their own blood on enemy soil. The overly healthy and abundant population of Rome is kept in check by periodic wars, and the essay goes on to acknowledge, as Montaigne thinks of his contemporary France, that a foreign war is a lesser evil than a civil one (683; 518). Yet the Roman wars are also said to keep the young men of the city "in condition" ("en haleine"), and the same metaphor of military or athletic training crops up when the essay turns explicitly to its titular subject of means and ends and describes how "the Romans trained the people to valor and contempt for dangers and death by those furious spectacles of gladiators"—"les Romans dressoient le peuple à la vaillance et au mespris des dangiers et de la mort par ces furieux spectacles de gladiateurs" (684; 518). The chicken-and-egg paradox of the essay lies in the question of whether the military virtue and prowess instilled by the gladiatorial games was the response to or the cause of Rome's foreign wars: whether those wars required a hot-blooded citizenry trained up in valor or whether the games created the hot-blood in Rome's youth that then required war in order to be purged in foreign climes. The distinction of means and ends collapses in any event, for both the wars and gladiatorial games are means supposedly conducive to the same end, which is the health of the Roman republic, but, in fact they feed off of one another in an endless cycle. Even the distinction between the gladiators and the citizenry collapses by the end of the essay:

Les premiers Romains employoient à cet exemple les criminels; mais dépuis on y employa des serfs innocens, et des libres mesmes qui se vendoyent pour cet effect; [B] jusques à des Senateurs et Chevaliers Romains, et encore des femmes: . . . (685)

The early Romans used criminals for such examples; but later they used innocent slaves, and even freemen who sold themselves for this purpose; [B] finally Roman senators and knights, and even women ... (519)

Thus the potential civil violence that Rome tried to avoid by fighting wars against external enemies returns—as a kind of double—in the combat of the arena, which, with the 1588 B addition to the essay, finally includes all sectors of the population. Even Rome's foreign wars were partly directed at her own citizens, and here the society trained up in military valor is seen manifestly warring against itself.

In their brave composure the gladiators, whose behavior educated the Romans in valor, closely resemble the cannibals. Verbal echoes further link the descriptions of these similar self-destructive cultures.

> C'estoit, à la verité, un merveilleux exemple, et de tres-grand fruict pour l'institution du peuple, de voir tous les jours en sa presence cent, deux cens, et mille couples d'hommes, armez les uns contre les autres, se hacher en pieces avecques une si extreme fermeté de courage qu'on ne leur vist lácher une parolle de foiblesse ou commiseration, jamais tourner le dos, ny faire seulement un mouvement lâche pour gauchir au coup de leur adversaire, ains tendre le col à son espée et se presenter au coup. (684)

> It was in truth an admirable example, and very fruitful for the education of the people, to see every day before their eyes a hundred, two hundred, even a thousand pairs of men, armed against one another, hack each other to pieces with such extreme firmness of courage that they were observed never to let slip a word of weakness or commiseration, never to turn their back or make even a cowardly movement to avoid their adversary's blow, but rather to extend their neck to his sword and offer themselves to the blow. (518)

Montaigne prefaces this combat in which the gladiators cut each other to pieces with an implicit comparison to the ancient practice of allowing the vivisection of criminals. The fate of the victims, "cut up alive"—"déchirez tout vifs" (664; 518)—links "Des mauvais moyens" both to the condemnation of torture in "Des cannibales" and to Alexander's treatment of Betis ("tout vif, deschirer") in "Par divers moyens." The marvelous, instructive example of the gladiators' firmness of courage is like the firmness of the cannibals' warfare—"C'est chose emerveillable que de la fermeté de leurs combats" (209; 155)—in which retreat and fear are unknown. And whereas both the cannibals and Alexander sought in vain to wring suppliant words from their captives—"quelque parolle molle ou rabaissée" as "Des cannibales (210) has it—the gladiators will not let a word of weakness escape their lips. Similarly, Montaigne writes of the cannibal captives.

> il ne s'en trouve pas un, en tout un siecle, qui n'ayme mieux la mort que de relascher, ny par contenance, ny de parole, un seul point d'une grandeur de courage invincible: ...(210)

there is not one in a whole century who does not choose to die rather than to relax a single bit, by word or look, from the grandeur of an invincible courage; ... (156)

At the center of both the Brazilian and Roman cultures is a ritualized spectacle of bravery—is it the means or the end, the true raison d'être, of their warfare? The defeated cannibal and gladiator demonstrate their refusal to give in to their conquerors or to the prospect of death. Their stubborn silence and unmoved countenances are the signs of a rigid virtue that will not unbend—compare "relascher ... de parole" and "lácher une parolle"—unless, in the case of one cannibal captive, to sing a song of defiance or, of another, to make a face at his captors. In both cultures, this unyielding valor—which in Rome the gladiatorial spectacle is supposed deliberately to inculcate upon the citizenry—produces a state of permanent warfare, both without and, as it turns out, within the society.

The Cannibals and France: Noble Stoics

"Des mauvais moyens" ends with a second evocation of the civil wars in the France of Montaigne's day. In a final ironic twist of the essay's terms, France has become a kind of fighting arena and a dumping ground where other countries can send *their* excess of hot-blooded young soldiers to do combat as mercenaries, i.e., gladiators (685; 519). For if the cannibal culture that consumes itself finds an analogy in the equally self-destructive mechanisms of Roman culture, both, in turn, are looked at as models for France. At the end of "Des cannibales" the cannibals who have been brought to France express their wonder at the class hierarchy of its society, having noticed "that there were among us men full and gorged with all sorts of good things, and that their other halves were beggars at their doors, emaciated with hunger and poverty"—"qu'ils avoyent aperçeu qu'il y avoit parmy nous des hommes pleins et gorgez de toutes sortes de commoditez, et que leurs moitiez estoient mendians à leurs portes, décharnez de faim et de pauvreté" (214; 159). But for all the difference that the cannibals see between French society and their own, the wording suggests instead the *similarity* between the two. In France the rich are eating off the poor, literally stripping their flesh away ("décharnez") by starving them. It is a more mediated kind of cannibalism, but cannibalism nonetheless. The cannibal visitors express surprise that the poor do not strike back. But peasant revolts and class warfare were, in fact, endemic to sixteenth-century French society.[15] And, as both the closing remark of "Des mauvais moyens" and the condemnation of cruel religious strife at the center of "Des cannibales" attest, the Roman and cannibal societies, societies where foreign war collapses into internecine war, point specifically to Montaigne's contemporary France, gripped by the Wars of Religion.

The warring cannibals hold up a dark mirror to the belligerents in France, in particular to the embattled French aristocracy, with whom they share a similar heroic ethos that combines emulative martial valor with a kind of Stoic constancy—that combination which we have seen Montaigne refer to, only to discount, as "virtue," and from which he declares his own ethical distance. In a shrewd observation upon "Des cannibales," Michel de Certeau asked, "Does not this detour into the New World reconnect with a medieval model that was then in the process of disappearing?"—the model of a feudal warrior society, where, as de Certeau puts it, "speech and weaponry coincided in 'honor.'"[16] I would suggest, where de Certeau probably would not, that this model could not disappear fast enough for Montaigne, the royalist *politique*. We have seen his critique of an all-too-prevalent culture of aristocratic violence and vendetta in his two essays on cruelty. In "Des cannibales" Montaigne further demonstrates the wider political consequences of this culture by attributing its Stoic postures and martial values to the cannibals and by observing how they turn the cannibals' otherwise idyllic existence into a constant state of warfare and revenge.

Montaigne depicts the cannibals as perfect Stoics, so perfect that they call Stoicism itself into question. After he has described the "invincible courage" with which the cannibal captives face their death and foil all the attempts of their captors to break their "constancy" (210–11; 156), the essayist comments

> c'est un tour d'art et de science, et qui peut tomber en une personne lâche et de neant, d'estre suffisant à l'escrime. L'estimation et le pris d'un homme consiste au coeur et en la volonté; c'est là où gist son vray honneur; la vaillance, c'est la fermeté, non pas des jambes et des bras, mais du courage et de l'ame; elle ne consiste pas en la valeur de nostre cheval, ny de nos armes, mais en la nostre. Celuy qui tombe obstiné en son courage [C] "*si succederit, de genu pugnat*". [A] Qui pour quelque dangier de la mort voisine ne relasche aucun point de son asseurance; qui regarde encores, en rendant l'ame, son ennemy d'une veuë ferme et desdaigneuse, il est battu, non pas de nous, mais de la fortune; il est tué, non pas vaincu. (211)

> it is a trick of art and technique, which may be found in a worthless coward, to be an able fencer. The worth and value of a man is in his heart and his will; there lies his real honor. Valor is the firmness, not of legs and arms, but of heart and soul; it consists not in the worth of our horse or our weapons, but in our own. He who falls obstinate in his courage [C] *if he has fallen, he fights on his knees* [Seneca]. [A] He who relaxes none of his assurance, no matter how great the danger of imminent death; who, giving up his soul, still looks firmly and scornfully at his enemy—he is beaten not by us, but by fortune; he is killed, not conquered. (157)

The citation from Seneca's *De Providentia* added in the C edition is inserted into a passage that already recalls Seneca's *De Constantia* and is an inventory of Stoic commonplaces. One thinks of Seneca's vanquished, but defiant Stilbo, who "wrested the victory from the conqueror." In a world of never-say-die Stoics, there can be no surrender, for no one is ever defeated. The Stoic morality in this respect hardly differs from that of the cannibals. If the aim of revenge, according to "Couardise mere de la cruauté," was to force an admission of defeat and repentance from the enemy, to be a Stoic or a cannibal means never having to say you're sorry.

The remark about fencing that opens this Senecan passage in "Des cannibales" ties such Stoic virtue to the traditional ethos of the European martial aristocracy. For, as we have already noted in the previous chapter, Montaigne similarly derogates fencing in a passage in the B text of "Couardise mere de la cruauté;" he describes such swordsmanship as a new Italian art—an acquired art and not the inheritance of noble birth—and thus tied to an emerging court culture.[17] Such martial skill actually detracts from the valor of the warrior noble.

> mais ce n'est pas proprement vertu, puis qu'elle tire son appuy de l'addresse et qu'elle prend autre fondement que de soy-mesme. L'honneur des combats consiste en la jalousie du courage, non de la science; et pourtant ay-je veu quelqu'un de mes amis, renommé pour grand maistre en cet exercice, choisir en ses querelles des armes qui luy ostassent le moyen de cet advantage, et lesquelles dépendoient entierement de la fortune et de l'asseurance, affin qu'on n'attribuast sa victoire plustost à son escrime qu'à sa valeur; et, en mon enfance, la noblesse fuyoit la reputation de bon escrimeur comme injurieuse, et se desroboit pour l'apprendre, commme un mestier desrogeant à la vraye et naifve vertu. (697)

> But this [fencing] is not properly valor, since it draws its support from skill and has its basis in something other than itself.
> The honor of the combat consists in the jealousy of courage, not of craft. And therefore I have observed a friend of mine, renowned as a grand master in this exercise, to choose in his quarrels weapons that deprived him of the means of this advantage, and which depended entirely on fortune and assurance, so that his victory should not be attributed to his fencing skill rather than his valor. And in my childhood the nobility avoided the reputation of good fencers as insulting, and learned it furtively, as a cunning trade, derogating from true and natural valor. (527)

With its appeal to noble forefathers, this passage describes the "natural valor" of the aristocracy—a class attribute that one is born with and that cannot be taught—in Stoic terms of a reliance on "soy-mesme" or, as "Des cannibales" puts it, on "la nostre." The friend of Montaigne who forgoes the advantage of his fencing skill seeks to depend on fortune and assurance ("asseurance"), or, again to compare the way the same terms are used in the passage of "Des cannibales," on an assurance that will acknowledge only fortune as its conqueror. The observation that the honor of combat consists in a "jalousie de courage" recalls the warfare of the cannibals, whose only basis is a "jalousie de la vertu," and is paralleled in turn by still another passage of "Des cannibales," this a later C-text addition: "The role of true victory is in fighting, not in coming off safely; and the honor of valor consists in combat, not in victory"—"Le vray vaincre a pour son roolle l'estour, non pas le salut; et consiste l'honneur de la vertu à combattre, non à battre" (212; 157). The idea of a natural or native valor ("naifve vertu") further links the old European warrior aristocracy to the New World natives, whose own culture of martial valor is, at least initially, declared by "Des cannibales" to be so close to an "original naturalness"—"naifveté originelle"(206; 153).

The cannibals still seem to embody a heroic virtue that is natural and unspoiled, unlike the contemporary French nobility of "Couardise mere de la cruauté," whose taking up of fencing is just one instance that essay cites of their failure to live up to the traditional values of their class. The Brazilians are noble savages, indeed, and may be bathed, as de Certeau, suggests in the nostalgic afterglow of a feudal order and warrior culture now waning in Europe. The warfare the cannibals practice is wholly "noble et genereuse"—we might say that it is warfare with class. Waged for the sake of martial valor itself, it possesses for that reason a kind of beauty that to some degree excuses what the essayist recognizes is a human disease— "et a autant d'excuse et de beauté que cette maladie humaine en peut recevoir" (210; 156). This aesthetic admiration which we have seen Montaigne profess for an aristocratic, Stoically inflected heroism that he simultaneously mistrusts and even deplores—that "reverence" produced, according to his opening essay, by the "saincte image de la vertu"—runs through "Des cannibales" and helps to account for the peculiar tone of the essay.[18] Montaigne, who normally dwells skeptically on the "inconstance de nos actions," cannot but admire and marvel at the consistency of a culture so committed to martial virtue and to bravery, a consistency so similar to the constancy sought by Stoicism. Such virtue is *naive*—the cannibals neither know nor are able conceive of any other behavior than what their culture teaches them—and it may owe its consistency to that very cause. Those heroic individuals Cato and Socrates, according to "De la cruauté," made a perfected habit of virtue but only after long philosophical training and struggle against vice; the valor and constancy of the entire cannibal society is second nature to it.

Yet there is also something bordering on satire in Montaigne's admiring description of the cannibals as the perfect upholders of the Stoic bravery to which the French nobility aspires—and one remembers his complaint in "Des récompenses d'honneur" that his nation gives to valor the highest rank among the virtues and that the only and essential form of nobility in France is the profession of arms (384; 277). The most valorous nobleman, the most rigid Stoic are no better than cannibals. For it is the attempt of Montaigne's contemporary aristocrats to perpetuate the traditional military ethos of the *noblesse d'epée* and atavistically to make a virtue of fighting that has plunged France into a civil war of even more terrible cruelty than the retaliatory warfare and cannibalism that wracks the Brazilians' society.

Perfect valor, moreover, to judge from the cannibals, only makes the warring antagonists the more unyielding and vindictive, willing neither to admit defeat nor to spare the defeated—the word "pardon" is not in the cannibals' vocabulary. The ritual of the cannibal and his victim that returns us to the showdown situation of "Par divers moyens" belies that essay's opening proposal—the opening proposal of the *Essais* themselves—that the victorious captor will be deterred from killing his foe by some reverence he might be supposed to feel for the image of virtue in another. Nor is the virtuous cannibal moved by a pity for his fellow man that is condemned by Stoicism as vicious weakness; the equally Stoic captive, his courage invincible to the end, feels no pity for himself. One begins to suspect, as the collapsing of means and ends suggests in the parallel case of the Roman gladiatorial games in "Des mauvais moyens," that the ritual vengeance of cannibalism is as much the cause as the result—at least it is the mirror image—of the Brazilian's wholly noble warfare. Montaigne's most original insight is to suggest that the victor's vengeful killing of his defeated enemy grows logically out of a warrior culture of emulation in which every individual strives to outdo rivals in valor, seeing in every enemy a rival, in every rival an enemy to be overcome. The Wars of Religion in France, his analogy to the cannibals implies, have provided the occasion for a similar culture, the culture of aristocratic competition, to break into open conflict.[19] The Stoic language of personal autonomy easily overlaps with an aristocratic language of honor that describes the nobleman's desire to preserve—and willingness to fight for—local independence and feudal prerogatives against all comers. At the national scale the murderous clash of indomitable individual wills has been converted into the intransigence of the warring factions, whose reluctance to give in or to compromise is a matter of honor as well as religion. "Des cannibales," that is, may not so much create the figure of the noble savage as disclose the savagery of the nobility.

The Cannibals and France: Stoic Martyrs

Montaigne recognized, of course, that the stubbornness of the antagonists of the civil wars was bolstered by their religious faith; the obstinacy of the Protestants was met by the inflexibility of the Catholic League. It was nonetheless the Huguenots who most explicitly identified their "constancy" in the face of persecution as a superior form of Seneca's Stoic "constantia." In *Feux*, the middle book of his epic poem *Les Tragiques*, Agrippa d'Aubigné, the Huguenot poet and Montaigne's contemporary, describes the tortures and martyrdom to which his coreligionists were subjected and the resolution they displayed, a "constance" that, he concludes at the end of the book, was a God-given sign of their election.[20] One of the Huguenot martyrs, Richard de Gastines, a precocious child and a "fair mirror of constancy" ["beau mirouer de constance"] (722), gives a long speech in which he cites Seneca and the ancient Stoics as models from whom a contempt for death can be learned (789–810); when he sheds natural tears at the sight of his father condemned with him on the scaffold, Richard nonetheless declares that his soul remains unmoved ["pas esmeuë"] (937). And d'Aubigné includes another anecdote about two girls tortured by their Catholic aunt and uncle who try to turn them back to the worship of "idols": "for thirty days these girls, torn by whips and hot irons, retain their assurance."

> Par trente jours entiers ces filles, deschirees
> De verges et fers chauds, demeurent asseurees; . . . (1013–14)

Obstinacy against torture and death becomes in this Protestant vision a divinely inspired religious experience that is to be aligned with the martyrdom of the saints of the early church. And it has a direct political application, encouraging other Huguenots in their intransigence.

Montaigne takes a dim view of such behavior. In the essay, "Defence de Seneque et de Plutarque" (2:32), he notes that if one asked the participants "in these civil wars, there will be found acts of patience, obstinacy and stubbornness in this miserable age of ours and amid this rabble"—"en ces guerres civiles, il se trouvera des effets de patience, d'obstination et d'opiniatreté par-my nos miserables siecles et en cette tourbe molle" (724; 547)—equal to the examples of antiquity.

> Combien en a l'on veu se laisser patiemment brusler et rotir pour des opinions empruntées d'autruy, ignorées et inconnues! (724–25)

> How many of them have been seen patiently letting themselves be burned and roasted for opinions borrowed from others, unknown and not understood. (548)

The peasants being roasted for religious tenets they do not comprehend are less constant than merely stubborn. Where Montaigne in "Des cannibales" condemned the use of torture, of roasting victims bit by bit, especially under the pretext of piety and religion, he here looks with no less disapproval at the other side, the victims' own behavior. The peasants are dying for *opinions*—this is the usual term used in polemical literature to attack Huguenot beliefs—and thus are examples of their "opiniastreté," a kind of blind obstinacy.²¹ The B-text addition to the essay goes on to compare their conduct to the storied stubbornness of women. "And stubbornness," it concludes, "is the sister of constancy, at least in vigor and firmness"—"Et est l'opinastreté soeur de la constance, au moins en vigueur et fermeté" (725; 548). The sister is the inferior female version or false double of constancy: Montaigne seems concerned to discredit religious obstinacy by differentiating it from Stoic firmness. The suspicion remains, however, that he sees both kinds of inflexibility as self-destructive. The unwillingness to relent and compromise—as Montaigne has now repeatedly shown in examples ranging from the behavior of Betis before Alexander to the commander whose "opiniastreté" caused him to hold out in his fortress against the enemy in "On est puny pour s'opiniastreter a une place sans raison"—is an exasperating provocation, inviting from the wielders of power the violence and cruelty they are only too willing to deal out. Like d'Aubigné's witnesses to their faith, these peasants seek out martyrdom, and martyrdom is what they get. But, in the process, they have engulfed France in civil war.

The moderate Catholic Montaigne distrusts religious fanaticism on either side of the Wars of Religion. He nonetheless appears especially critical of a Huguenot intransigence that has appropriated the language and gestures of Stoicism. His aversion to such obstinate faith and its political consequences lies behind one final set of passages from the *Essais* that I want to juxtapose with "Des cannibales." In "De l'yvrongnerie" (2:2) Montaigne questions to the point of condemning the behavior of the early martyrs of the faith themselves. This essay moves from its ostensible subject of drunkenness to an attack on the idea of Stoic constancy. Even the sage has to blink at a threatening blow, the essayist remarks with some satisfaction, and he concludes that "all actions outside the ordinary limits are subject to sinister interpretation"—"Toutes actions hors les bornes ordinaires sont subjectes à sinistre interpretation" (346; 250). The 1580 A text goes immediately on to illustrate the point.

> quand nous oyons nos martyrs crier au Tyran au milieu de la flamme: C'est assez rosti de ce costé là, hache le, mange le, il est cuit, recommance de l'autre; quant nous oyons en Josephe cet enfant tout deschiré des tenailles mordantes et persé des aleines d'Antiochus, le deffier encore, criant d'une voix ferme et asseurée: Tyran, tu pers temps, me voicy tousjours à mon aise; où est cette douleur, où sont ces tourmens, dequoy tu me menassois? n'y sçais tu que cecy? ma constance te donne plus de peine que je n'en sens de ta cruauté; ô lâche belistre, tu te rens, et je me renforce; fay moy pleindre, fay moy flechir, fay moy rendre, si tu peux; donne courage à tes satellites et à tes bourreaux: les

voylà defaillis de coeur, ils n'en peuvent plus; arme les, acharne les:—certes il faut confesser qu'en ces ames là il y a quelque alteration et quelque fureur, tant sainte soit elle. (347)

Our martyrs were heard crying out to the tyrant in the midst of the flame: "It's roasted enough on that side, chop it up, eat it, it's cooked, start on the other side!" And that child in Josephus, all torn by biting pincers and pierced by the awls of Antiochus, still defied him, crying out with a firm and steady voice: "Tyrant, you're wasting your time, here I am still at ease; where is that pain, where are those torments, with which you were threatening me? Is this all you know how to do? My constancy gives you more pain than I feel from your cruelty. O cowardly wretch, you are giving up, and I am growing stronger; make me complain, make me bend, make me yield, if you can; give your satellites and your executioners courage; see, they have lost heart, they can do no more; arm them, goad them!" When we hear such defiance, surely we must confess that in these souls there is some alteration, some frenzy, however holy it be. (250)

Here are two further scenes of torture, two more confrontations between vindictive powers and defiant victims: the unshakeable constancy of the latter is in these cases the testimony of their sanctity. It is a coincidence, though I think a telling one, that d'Aubigné's rhyme words, "deschiree" and "asseuree," reappear in Montaigne's quite free adaptation of a passage from *On the Martyrdom of the Maccabees* (8–16) attributed to Josephus, itself an elaboration of the famous story of the martyrdom of the seven brothers in 2 Maccabees 7. In the scriptural version, the first of these brothers, all of whom affirm their faith in God and defiance of Antiochus Epiphanes, is, at the tyrant's orders, cooked alive in a frying pan (4–5), linking these Jewish witnesses to "our [i.e., Christian] martyrs," in this case Saint Lawrence, martyred on the grill, whose words are reported by Prudentius in the second hymn (401–8) of the *Book of Crowns* (*Peristephanon*). Both of these culinary martyrdoms, of course, evoke the vengeful rites performed by the New World cannibals—and the modern-day French practice of roasting the living flesh of religious enemies. The defiant words of the martyrs to their tyrannical persecutors match the song of the cannibal prisoner toward his captors: all exhibit the highest Stoic virtues of firmness, assurance, constancy. The Jewish child of Maccabees explicitly reveals the element of aggression in this constancy: it is meant to cause pain in the tyrant Antiochus, to reciprocate his cruelty.

But it also summons that cruelty into action. The child literally asks for it—make me bend, make me yield—just as the "mine . . . asseurée" of the captive Betis makes his conqueror Alexander ask "has he bent a knee?"— "A-il flechi un genouil" and to tear Betis limb from limb—"deschirer et desmembrer"—behind his chariot. Montaigne labels the behavior of the martyrs, as well as the "Stoic sallies"—"saillies Stoïques" (347; 251)—that immediately follow them in "De l'ivrongnerie," as forms of frenzy. It is a holy madness, but nonetheless madness: in relationship to the larger essay it is a deeper and more vicious form of drunkenness than the mere consumption of wine.[22] He remarks at the original end of the essay that it "transcends our own judgment and reason; inasmuch as wisdom is an orderly management of our soul, which she conducts with measure and proportion and is responsible for"—"surpasse nostre propre jugement et discours. D'autant que la sagesse c'est un maniment reglé de nostre ame, et qu'elle conduit avec mesure et proportion, et s'en respond" (348; 251). Montaigne wants none of it: this religious conviction that is so easily confused with opinionated stubbornness, this passive-aggression that makes the martyr complicit with his own torture and turns a Stoic contempt for the body into cruelty against one's own limbs. The trouble with would-be martyrs, and Montaigne doubtless has in mind their modern French counterparts—primarily Huguenots, but surely Catholics as well—is that they will not listen to reason and that they positively demand to be killed: their constancy becomes interchangeable with the cruelty with which it is met. As interchangeable as a cannibal prisoner from one identical tribe defying his cannibal captors from another, all of them one flesh.

Religious extremism is linked explicitly to New World cruelty in a B-text passage that Montaigne added to the ending of "De la moderation" (1:30), the essay that directly precedes "Des cannibales." This new ending to the essay in the 1588 edition of Montaigne's book now becomes, as Claude Rawson has pointed out, a kind of prologue to, as well as Montaigne's further gloss on, "Des cannibales."[23] "De la moderation" is already linked to the discussion of excessive virtue in "De l'yvrongnerie" by its opening citation of Paul in Romans 12:3, a sentence that Montaigne had also spelled out in Latin on the wall of his celebrated library:

> Ne soyez pas plus sages qu'il ne faut, mais soyez sobrement sages. (197)

> Be not wiser than you should, but be soberly wise. (146)

The beginning of the essay pleads for the sobriety of moderation versus the drunkenness of virtue carried to unwholesome extremes, an immoderate virtue which, a C-text addition twice asserts, makes a man "sauvage" (198; 146).[24] The B-text conclusion remarks on the excesses committed in the name of religion, a religion which not only inspires martyrs to stand up to torture, as in "De l'yvrongnerie," but motivates the torturers themselves.

> Cette impression se raporte aucunement à cette autre si ancienne, de penser gratifier au Ciel et à la nature par nostre massacre et homicide, qui fut universellement embrassée en toutes religions. . . . Et en ces nouvelles terres,

descouvertes en nostre aage, pures encores et vierges au pris des nostres, l'usage en est aucunement receu par tout: toutes leurs Idoles s'abreuvent de sang humain, non san divers exemples d'horrible cruauté. On les brule vifs, et, demy rotis, on les retire du brasier pout leur arracher le coeur et les entrailles. A d'autres, voire aux femmes, on les escorche vifves, et de leur peau ainsi sanglante en revest on et masque d'autres. Et non moins d'exemples de constance et resolution. Car ces pauvres gens sacrifiables, viellars, femmes, enfans, vont, quelques jours avant, questant eux mesmes les aumosnes pour l'offrande de leur sacrifice, et se presentent à la boucherie chantans et dançans avec les assistans. Les ambassadeurs du Roy de Mexico, faisant entendre à Fernand Cortez la grandeur de leur maistre, apres luy avoir dict quil avoit trente vassaux, desquels chacun pouvoit assembler cent milles combatans, et qu'il se tenoit en la plus belle et forte ville qui fut soubs le ciel, luy adjousterent qu'il avoit à sacrifier aux Dieux cinquante milles hommes par an. De vray, ils disent qu'il nourissoit la guerre avec certains grands peuples voisins, non seulement pour l'exercise de la jeunesse du païs, mais principallement pour avoir dequoy fournir à ses sacrifices par des prisonniers de guerre. (201)

This idea has some relation to that other very ancient one, which consists of thinking that we gratify heaven and nature by our massacre and homicide, a belief universally embraced in all religions. . . . And in these new lands discovered in our time, still pure and virgin compared with ours, this practice is to some extent accepted everywhere: all their idols are drenched with human blood, not without various examples of horrible cruelty. They burn the victims alive, and take them out of the brazier half-roasted to tear their heart and entrails out. Others, even women, are flayed alive, and with their bloody skins they dress and disguise others. And there are no fewer examples of constancy and resolution. For these poor people that are to be sacrificed, old men, women, children, themselves go about, some days before, begging alms for the offering at their sacrifice, and present themselves to the slaughter singing and dancing with the spectators.

The ambassadors of the king of Mexico, to give Hernand Cortez an idea of the greatness of their master, after having told him that he had thirty vassals, each of whom could assemble a hundred thousand fighting men, and that he lived in the most beautiful and strongest city under heaven, added that he had fifty thousand men a year to sacrifice to the god. Indeed, they say he fostered war with certain great neighboring peoples, not only to exercise the youth of his country, but principally to have enough prisoners of war to supply his sacrifices. (149)

The passage begins by speaking of "our" massacre, a prudently oblique reference to the killings of Saint Bartholomew's Day that turns the particularly French instance into a universal religious habit, belonging to the "we" of humanity. With equal prudence, it then quickly turns to cruelties similarly perpetuated for the sake of religion in the New World. Here the distinction disappears between committing atrocities on dead or living bodies, central in "Des cannibales" to declaring the Brazilians less cruel than the French protagonists of the Wars of Religion who roast their enemies bit by bit under the pretext of piety. "On les brule vifs . . . on les escorche vifves": in their zeal to please their god the Aztecs practice their cruelty on living and sentient sacrificial victims. In "Des cannibales" we may be led to wonder whether the cannibalism practiced by the Brazilians is not simply the ritual by-product of a wholly noble warfare carried out for its own sake but rather the vengeful motor that in fact drives that warfare. In the case of the Aztecs sacrifice and the enormous numbers of victims it requires is the explicit motive of their wars. The Mexican king fosters conflicts with his neighbors not only to exercise his country's youth, verbally recalling the practice of the Romans of "Des mauvais moyens employez à bonne fin," who similarly fostered foreign wars ("nourry des guerres") to keep their overly vehement youth in fighting trim ("en haleine"). His primary aim is the acquisition of prisoners for immolation.

And the prisoners meet the horrible cruelty inflicted upon them with a corresponding constancy and resolution, just as the two are rhetorically balanced in Montaigne's prose. The sacrificial victims go beyond a defiance that invites cruelty actually to collaborate in their own torture and death. The songs they sing on the way to their ghastly fates may be reminiscent of the psalms and hymns that Huguenot hagiography ascribed to constant, even joyful and ecstatic Protestant martyrs led to the scaffolds by their Catholic enemies.[25] But the Mexicans, both the victims and their executioners, appear here to share the *same* faith, a religion whose fanaticism demands a constancy no less cruel, no less part of the cruelty it enshrines as holy.

Placed directly before "Des cannibales," this darker version of New World culture at the end of "De la moderation" suggests that the self-consuming society of the Brazilian cannibals is, as I have argued, the product of a virtue carried to excess—a virtue that makes them "savages" in an ethical sense. It reinforces, furthermore, the analogy between the reciprocal cruelty of the cannibals' continual, unyielding warfare and the civil wars in France, where religious zeal only intensifies the brutality and stiffens the defiance of the warring parties. The individual cannibal's killing and eating of his single captive now finds its equivalent in the Mexican sacrifice of thousands of prisoners—a practice that Montaigne, from his sources, would have known included the eating of the victims' flesh. Yet this torture and slaughter that has become the all-consuming end of Aztec culture is but one version of the massacre and killing embraced by all religions. Montaigne never names the Saint Bartholomew's Day Massacre in the *Essais*, but he may confront that traumatic event most directly—and unexpectedly—here: projected across the Atlantic in the Aztecs' spectacular rituals of murder.

Montaigne the Cosmographer

Montaigne declares of his use of citation that he speaks the words of other writers only so much the more to speak himself—"Je ne dis les autres, sinon pour d'autant plus me dire" (148; 108). In a similar way, he discusses other societies in order to lay bare the workings of his own. In its treatment of the Brazilian natives, "Des cannibales" rehearses and verbally recalls the obsessive topics of Montaigne's opening essay, of his essays on cruelty, of his parallel discussions of gladiators and martyrs: and all of these are addressed to the situation of his embattled France. France, too, is turning into a society of obstinate valor. At the end of "De la praesumption" (2:17), Montaigne comments with bitter irony that in his country's civil wars, valor has become so "populaire," so widespread and distributed among all classes of society, that it is impossible to choose among so many examples of perfect constancy—"il se trouve parmy nous des ames fermes jusques à la perfection, et en grand nombre, si que le triage en est impossible à faire" (662; 502). As is the case with the cannibals, all of them perfectly and identically courageous, it becomes impossible to distinguish one Frenchman from another on the basis of valor, a valor that is, he implies in the essay's next and final sentence, no longer uncommon—"non commune." In "Des cannibales" and throughout the *Essais* Montaigne treats this valor as a logical outgrowth as much as a perverse form of Stoic virtue, in particular the virtue of constancy: whether it is the martial valor and honor to which the French aristocracy is devoted, whether it is the stubbornness of religious fanaticism, whether, in most cases, it is a combination of the two. The refusal to yield by one side is matched by, and indeed elicits the refusal to relent by the other and the unheard-of cruelties of the Wars of Religion. The opening sentence of the *Essais* had asserted that the most *common* way of dealing with a vindictive enemy was to practice submission and to evoke pity. But in the cannibals' society it is the other way around: the uncommon, extraordinary gesture of valorous defiance has become the ordinary, unfailing norm and, as a result, they eat one another. And it is increasingly so in France as well. One of Montaigne's projects in the *Essais* is to persuade his countrymen to return to the most common, hence most sane, course of submission and, as we shall see in our next chapter, to teach them an ethics of yielding that may lead them out of their political crisis. The Brazilian cannibals may win the essayist's admiration for their indomitable valor, but the society without pardon or pity that this valor creates provides an admonitory object lesson for Montaigne's contemporary France.

But if the account of the Brazilian culture in "Des cannibales" is directed toward and shaped by the current distress of France, if the cannibals' society holds up a not-so-distortedt mirror to Montaigne's own, what happens to his claims to present the New World natives on their own terms? These terms seem to belong less to the cannibals than to recurring preoccupations of the *Essais* that tell us about the essayist and his response to the specific historical circumstances of the French civil wars.

And yet, it may be precisely because Montaigne sees the cannibals through the terms of the crisis of his own society that he may come to understand something central about their culture.[26] The Tupinamba of Brazil were, of course, far removed culturally from the Aztecs and it may not be legitimate to compare or link the two—although we may at least have Montaigne's warrant to do so from the passage on the Aztecs he inserted at the close of "De la moderation," juxtaposed as it is with "Des cannibales" that follows directly upon it. The Aztecs produced written records that preserve some of the rituals of their warrior culture. In a magnificent reconstruction of this culture, Inga Clendinnen has argued that the Aztec warrior had to "strive to desire, or at least to embrace" not only the idea of capturing prisoners for sacrifice—and cannibalism—but also the prospect that he would himself be captured, sacrificed, and eaten by his enemies in turn. That is, the warrior and his captive were finally interchangeable: dying in the correct sacrificial way was as much a test and expected part of the warrior's bravery as his prowess on the battlefield. As Clendinnen describes the elaborate ritual of the feast of Xipe Totec, the captor of the chief sacrificial victim

> was given the cane and a bowl of blood which he carried throughout the city, daubing the blood on the mouths of the stone idols in all the temples. The circuit completed, he went to Moctezuma's palace to return the magnificent regalia of he who offers a victim at the gladiatorial stone, and from there went back to his local temple to flay and dismember his captive's body. And then, later in the day, he watched his lamenting kin eat the maize stew and the flesh of his captive, while they wept for their own young warrior. He did not participate, saying "Shall I perchance eat my very self?" . . .
> Behind the desperate excitements of battle lay the shadow of the killing stone, and a lonely death among strangers. This is why the captor, in the midst of the adulation accorded him for having taken a victim for the sun, wore at the cannibal feast of his kin the chalk and down of the victim; why the kin lamented; why he could not eat of what was indeed his "own flesh", for he too, ideally, would die on the stone, and his flesh be eaten in another city.[27]

Here, if Clendinnen's compelling analysis is correct, was another cannibalistic New World society that ate its own flesh—and acknowledged as much. But we should recall that the "invention" of the cannibal's defiant song in Montaigne's essay, the song where he tells his captors that they will be enjoying the taste of their own flesh when they feast off his own, belonged to Montaigne himself, the humanist sitting in his study, not to the eyewitness testimony of his ethnographic sources. It may be nothing more than coincidence, but this juxtaposition of the sixteenth-century essayist and the modern scholar suggest a pleasing paradox: perhaps only by confronting the New World culture from the vantage point and preoccupations of his own could Montaigne put the right words in the mouth of his valiant cannibal.

Chapter Four

AN ETHICS OF YIELDING: "DE L'ART DE CONFERER" AND "DE LA PHISIONOMIE"

HERE IS ONE more gloss that the wider *Essais* offer on "Des cannibales." About one third of the way into his long exploration of skepticism in the "Apologie de Raimond Sebond," Montaigne sums up his argument and declares its apologetic moral.

> J'en diray seulement encore cela, que c'est la seule humilité et submission qui peut effectuer un homme de bien. Il ne faut pas laisser au jugement de chacun la cognoissance de son devoir; il le luy faut prescrire, non pas le laisser choisir à son discours: autrement, selon l'imbecilité et varieté infinie de nos raisons et opinions, nous nous forgerions en fin des devoirs qui nous mettroient à nous manger les uns les autres, comme dit Epicurus. (488)
>
> I will add only this, that humility and submission alone can make a good man. The knowledge of his duty should not be left to each man's judgment; it should be prescribed to him, not left to the choice of his reason. Otherwise, judging by the imbecility and infinite variety of our reasons and opinions, we should finally forge for ourselves duties that would set us to eating one another, as Epicurus says. (359)

The passage suggests that the retaliatory revenge and cannibalism of the Brazilians of "Des cannibales" is the result of a culture in which no one ever submits (and hence no one ever pardons). The cannibals in that essay never yield to the demand of their captors—the demand simply that they yield—and they are amazed, when they come to France, to see the Swiss guards of Charles IX submitting—"se soubmissent à obeyr" (213; 159)—in obedience to the child king. (Here, too, the cannibals reveal that they are just as ethnocentric as any European observer of *their* Brazilian culture.) But it is in fact just such *political* obedience, this passage in the "Apologie" implies, that offers a way out of the present civil strife in France: an obedience to religious and civic authorities, perhaps above all to the French monarchy, however weak its present king may be. The terms "humilité et submission" in the passage are a C-text replacement for the single word "obedience" in the editions of the *Essais* prior to 1595, and, for Montaigne, the ethical posture of submission is virtually synonymous with and inseparable from the political imperative of obedience. In the very next sentence Montaigne adds that the first law that God gave to humanity was the law of "pure obedience." This recollection of Adam and Eve is further glossed in a C-text assertion that "From obeying and yielding spring every other virtue"—"De l'obeir et ceder naist toute autre vertue." Morality begins with obedience, but obedience to what or whom? In the context of the "Apologie," Montaigne must primarily urge submission to the teachings of Roman Catholicism and a rejection of the "opinions" of Protestantism. Yet yielding to religious authority cannot be easily separated from other forms of political obedience: in "De la coustume ou de ne changer aisément une loy receüe" (1:23), Montaigne remarks, with Machiavellian accents, that the most apparent sign of the justice and utility of Christianity itself is its "precise recommendation of obedience to the magistrate and maintenance of the government"—"exacte recommandation de l'obéissance du Magistrat, et manutention des polices" (120; 87–88). Similarly, the aim of submission in this passage is not the salvation of souls but political peace: how not to end up as cannibals.

The morality that begins with obedience and yielding thus has a political end; in a time of civil war Montaigne has made virtue out of political necessity. This excerpt from the "Apologie" glosses not only "Des cannibales," but all the life-and-death showdowns between vindictive victors and defiant vanquished that have reappeared in the *Essais* from "Par divers moyens on arrive a pareille fin" and its opening sentence that posed the choice of submission or resistance to those who have us in their power. Montaigne, we have seen in our last chapter, persuades against the latter course of resistance. He mistrusts and condemns, even as he may admire the bravery of, those who stand up to their conquerors—and provoke the conquerors to kill them. In all of the cases he cites, whether the victims are New World cannibals, citizens of defeated cities, indomitable gladiators, or religious martyrs, Montaigne is thinking about the antagonists of the Wars of Religion in France. He thinks of the obstinacy of the Huguenots and the equally fanatic Catholics of the League. He thinks about the factious French nobility, Catholic and Protestant, whose intransigence and refusal to follow the lead of the crown is a matter of noble honor and independence—and self-interest—as much as sectarian zeal. By the same token, Montaigne still has France in mind when he advocates the first course of submission, more common if less glamorous and heroic. His French readers, especially his noble readers, should learn to behave more like commoners, to acknowledge and learn to yield to a higher authority, an authority that Montaigne locates in a central monarchy strong enough to sort out religious disputes, to guarantee the rule of law, and to put an end to aristocratic anarchy. This is the *politique* solution to the French crisis that the historical Montaigne upheld when he sided against the League in the 1580s and when, after the death of the duke of Anjou in 1584, he acted as an intermediary between

Henri III and his legitimate heir and successor, the then Protestant Henri of Navarre.[1] The national settlement that Montaigne hoped to see put in place called for a new morality, the politically inflected morality that the *Essais* provide when they explore an ethics of submission: how one can yield *and* still retain a sense of honor and personal integrity.

Montaigne's insistence on bowing to the powers placed above one has an authoritarian character. He speaks constantly against innovation, though it should be emphasized that he *always* refers primarily to Protestantism when he does so. He has accordingly been called a "conservative," though the label is somewhat anachronistic and misleading.[2] In the political discourse of the sixteenth century—and with few exceptions the practice has continued to our present day—all factions, even the most radical, claimed to seek the conservation and restoration of traditional rights and forms of government. In Montaigne's historical context, his advocacy of strong monarchy can in fact look progressive, part of the building of the new nation-state; the alternative claims of local autonomy and noble prerogative preached by sixteenth-century monarchomachs, first Protestant, then Catholic, suggest a backwards turn toward feudalism and the past.[3] However some ideas of the monarchomachs may have contributed to subsequent republican and anti-absolutist thought, it was *their* opposition to royal authority and to an absolutism yet to emerge that partook of a distinctly conservative aristocratic nostalgia. Montaigne was himself not immune from such nostalgia—the sentiment of a conservatism rather different from that normally attributed to him—even as he promoted obedience to monarchical and ecclesiastic authority.

Some of this ambivalence is visible in another passage in which Montaigne spells out the imperative of obedience, at the end "De l'amitié" (1:28), where he puts words into the mouth of his beloved dead friend Estienne de la Boétie. In fact, Montaigne deliberately rewrites and sanitizes the political thought of La Boétie, who in his youth had composed a tract, *De la servitude volontaire*, that objected to the willing obedience of subjects to the power of a single ruler.[4] Montaigne tells us that the reprinting of this work by Huguenot propagandists to aid their arguments against submission to regal authority had caused him to give up his own plans to include it, as an example of La Boétie's own essay writing—"Il l'escrivit par maniere d'essay . . . " (183–84; 135)—with pride of place at the center of the first book of the *Essais*. Montaigne attempts here to set the record straight about La Boétie's political beliefs.

> Je ne fay nul doubte qu'il ne creust ce qu'il escrivoit, car il estoit assez conscientieux pour ne mentir pas mesmes en se jouant. Et sçay d'avantage que, s'il eust eu à choisir, il eut mieux aimé estre nay à Venise qu'à Sarlac: et avec raison. Mais il avoit un'autre maxime souverainement empreinte en son ame,

> d'obeyr et de se soubmettre tres-religieusement aux loix sous lesquelles il estoit nay. Il ne fut jamais un meilleur citoyen, ny plus affectionné au repos de son païs, ny plus ennemy des remuements et nouvelletez de son temps. (194)
>
> I have no doubt that he believed what he wrote, for he was so conscientious as not to lie even in jest. And I know further that if he had had the choice, he would rather have been born in Venice than in Sarlat, and with reason. But he had another maxim sovereignly imprinted in his soul, to obey and submit most religiously to the laws under which he was born. There never was a better citizen, or one more devoted to the tranquillity of his country, or more hostile to the commotions and innovations of his time. (144)

In this passage, too, the line between obedience to political and religious authority is hard to draw. Montaigne suggests their potential identity by his choice of the punning adverb, "religeusement," that describes the scrupulous submission of La Boétie to the laws—and traditional royal government—of his native country. And such "laws" may themselves include or even primarily designate the dictates of Catholic faith, as they do in the title of "De la coustume," an essay whose condemnation of innovation in the body-politic—both of the introduction of religious reform and of the challenge to monarchy posed alike by Huguenots and by the Catholic extremists of the League—this La Boétie appears to echo.

Yet, at the same time, Montaigne acknowledges that La Boétie meant what he said in the antimonarchical *De la servitude volontaire*. Given a choice, he would have been born a citizen of the republic of Venice. Sixteenth-century aristocrats looked longingly to the freedom of Venice, where patrician nobles governed themselves and where the head of state, the doge, was limited in power and consigned to a largely ceremonial role; they did so, even as they looked down on the Venetian patricians as insufficiently noble merchants. Montaigne cannot resist the usual joking reference to the Venetian's lack of horsemanship—the perennial badge of nobility—in "De l'art de conferer" (922; 703), but here he seconds La Boétie's opinion ("et avec raison"). Outside the *Essais*, the historical Montaigne promised in 1588 to accompany Jacques de Thou should the latter accept the French ambassadorship to Venice.[5] The notion of retirement in Venice turns up in "De la vanité" (3.9) when Montaigne discusses the idea of dying away from home and family: "Je me conseillerois volontiers Venise pour la retraicte d'une telle condition et foiblesse de vie" (982; 750). Montaigne can imagine enjoying the liberty that Venice has to offer, but he can do so only as a final retreat from the political world and as a form of death, the ultimate liberation. Like the La Boétie whom he portrays, Montaigne acknowledges that there is no escape from the political obligations and arrangements of the France in which he was born. And these entail bowing before the authority of king and church.

The admiration for Venetian freedom that Montaigne shares with his beloved La Boétie should alert us to the particular application to the aristocracy of his argument for obedience. To return to the passage from the "Apologie" where Montaigne asserts that only humility and submission can produce an "homme de bien," we should note the primary sixteenth-century connotation of this term as "nobleman," even as the essayist plays on the idea that a good man—i.e., an obedient one—possesses a kind of nobility. Montaigne's prescription about what it takes to make a nobleman is very close to the one that his contemporary Torquato Tasso was formulating shortly before Montaigne visited him during his imprisonment in Ferrara in 1580. In his dialogue on nobility, *Il Forno*, Tasso writes of the noblemen of the Duchy of Ferrara who acknowledge the "absolute or almost absolute power and similar to that of kings" of the Este dukes.

> They can demonstrate no greater sign of nobility than the servitude, obedience, and loyalty they have demonstrated to your princes [*la servitù co'vostri principi e l'ubbedienza e la fedeltà dimostrata*], for which they have been worthy of all those ranks and those titles that are fitting to most noble gentlemen.[6]

Here, indeed, is a voluntary servitude to princely power, one that, according to Tasso, defines the very nature of nobility. In exchange, princely favor confers upon the obedient nobleman his noble status and honors. This blueprint for an absolutism that in the sixteenth century was still a project and idea rather than an achieved political reality suggests what might be at stake for Montaigne's "homme de bien." The aristocrat was to submit to the throne not only his political agency, but the very determination of his noble identity, which would cease to be the self-authenticating property of his lineage and local power.[7]

Tasso's treatise spells out the emerging relationship between prince and noble that lies behind Montaigne's call for obedience; it also suggests why such a call might expect to meet resistance from the essayist's noble contemporaries. For in France, Montaigne notes in "De l'inéqualité qui est entre nous" (1:42), the aristocracy, particularly the provincial grandees, were accustomed to living like so many little kings—"Roytelets"—on their estates, where they were scarcely touched two times in their lives by the weight of royal sovereignty, and lived as free as the Venetian doge—"il est aussi libre que le Duc de Venise." Only courtiers, seeking honors and rewards by their service to the crown, experience an essential and real subjection: "La subjection essentielle et effectuelle ne regarde d'entre nous que ceux qui s'y convient et qui ayment à s'honnorer et enrichir par tel service" (266; 195). The obedience that Montaigne advocates would now extend this subjection—a servitude that had been indeed voluntary, a kind of career choice for the ambitious noble—and enforce it upon the aristocracy at large. It is no wonder that many noblemen balked at the wholesale transformation of their class into courtly servants: they understood their refusal to yield to royal authority as a defense of their traditional prerogatives and independence, even of their conception of their nobility itself. Why would the noble have to pine, as Montaigne and his La Boétie do, for the liberty of Venice, if he did not relinquish in the first place a freedom that was both Venetian (aristocratic) and even itself royal (Doge-like) in its autonomy from the crown?

The obedience that Montaigne makes the cornerstone of his political morality was thus not without tensions and contradictions. He was outlining the morality of the new royal servant, and I have earlier identified it with the morality of the law-abiding (and lawgiving) *noblesse de robe*. The alternative of quasi-feudal independence, he knew, led to anarchy, to so many noble warlords waging private wars against the crown and among themselves: without a single authority to prescribe their duties, men would devour one another. Montaigne criticizes the aristocratic culture of violence and vendetta; he urges clemency and an avoidance of cruelty as the true indices—and as an alternative ethos—of nobility. This moral reform of the aristocracy boils down to the choice that the French nobleman had to make of submission rather than resistance to his king. The choice entailed giving up habits of unyielding honor and militancy in order to become a good subject.

Yet those noble habits died hard. Montaigne, who preferred to pose as a member of the *noblesse d'épée*, professes reverence "for the sacred image of valor." He expresses admiration for those very noble gestures of heroic intransigence and Stoic autonomy whose shortcomings and dangers for the French social order he exposes and denounces. A persistent cross-current appears to run against the ethical positions staked out by the *Essais*: a residual longing for an aristocratic life answerable only to itself. Like the noblemen of his period whom he describes, Montaigne feels himself pulled in two directions, and these may be felt in the contrast between the Montaigne we know from the historical record, a counselor and servant to both Henri III and Henri IV, and the idealized self-image of the *Essais*, the Montaigne who lives in splendid noble isolation and freedom on his estate and in his beloved library. In "De trois commerces" (3:3), which includes his description of the library, Montaigne explains that his solitude primarily allows him to escape "servitude et l'obligation" (823; 625): he claims to live himself like a little king instead of in servitude to monarchy.

But Montaigne did not simply look back with nostalgia on those noble habits of independence and self-definition that, in a new political climate, appeared to be incompatible with loyal obedience to royal authority. He also tried to recuperate and internalize them by describing an honorable kind of submission that is the result of free individual choice. This was the course that in our first chapter we saw Montaigne himself take when, in the episode from his mayoralty in Bordeaux described in "Divers evenemens de mesme conseil," he faced down his potentially mutinous troops by freely submitting and entrusting his safety to them. In two essays of the Book Three, written in the same period as that B-text anecdote of "Divers evenemens," Montaigne similarly offers himself as a model in the ethics of giving in, and these essays return in other guises to the showdown between vindictive foes that opens the *Essais*. In "De l'art de conferer" (3:8) Montaigne discusses how a skeptic's awareness of the imperfection of human understanding teaches him to yield in verbal disputes and to divert the quest for truth into a pursuit of self-knowledge and self-mastery; the essay further suggests how its context of personal conversation can be expanded to wider, national debates. "De la phisionomie" (3:12) takes up again the opposition of natural behavior to philosophical virtue already explored in "De la cruauté" in order to describe a trusting submission to others as part of human nature itself. Montaigne recounts how on two different occasions during the civil wars the course of submission saved him when he was in the hands of political enemies. At the same time, Montaigne explores the limits of the ethical position he embodies by contrasting his salvation with the fate of Socrates, who heroically defied his fellow Athenian citizens and died a martyr for justice and philosophical truth: here is one last instance, and a powerfully persuasive one at that, of the value, if not the efficacy, of resistance. The two essays begin from very different premises—the negative skepticism of "De l'art de conferer," the positive naturalism of "De la phisionomie"—but these two sides of Montaigne's thought converge in their shared moral conclusion: in the *choice* that Montaigne makes to yield to others. The political implications of his ethical model are clear: for, against the argument and title of La Boétie's treatise, Montaigne upholds a servitude that would preserve human dignity—and a sense of noble honor—just because it is voluntary.

Talking Things Out

That the confrontation between warring adversaries of Montaigne's opening essay should be reimagined in "De l'art de conferer" as a confrontation between two partners in a conversation, each of them eager to win his point, already tells half the story. If only, Montaigne suggests, his countrymen would talk, rather than fight out their differences, they would take a large step toward peace. Moreover, with its models in the Italian treatises on aristocratic comportment, della Casa's *Galateo* and Guazzo's *La civil conversazione*, to which Montaigne alludes at the beginning of the essay (922–23; 704), this conversation might be emblematic of that pacification and ethical reform of the nobility that the essayist seeks to effect. By the next century, in fact, through a process at once political and cultural that

Norbert Elias has described, the class identity of the nobleman would depend less on military prowess than on civility, as the nobleman also adapted himself to the role of courtier and princely servant.[8] Civil conversation, which Montaigne in "Des trois commerces" (3:3), describes as the realm of the "honnête homme" (824; 625)—anticipating another cultural ideal of the following century—is a training ground in the good manners and self-restraint required of the noble subject of absolutism. It is so not least because it teaches him how to yield.

Montaigne's essay on the art of conversation acknowleges the importance of contending for mastery with one's interlocutor even as it suggests that the conversationalist's final aim is self-mastery. This agonistic model of conversation in "De l'art de conferer" similarly wavers between a two-way exchange of knowledge and a self-reflection undertaken separately by each partner of the discussion: the former easily turns into the latter where the knowledge one gains is specifically knowledge of oneself. Self-awareness and the self-control that comes with it are repeatedly the ends achieved by Montaigne's talking with others.[9]

At the opening of the essay Montaigne asserts that the knowledge that he can communicate—to his reader, to his interlocutor—is exclusively negative: what not to do. It is a kind of admonition or "advertissement" (921; 703). By publishing his own "imperfections" (922; 703) he assures that others will learn to fear them *in themselves*: just as, the essayist says, he is every day warned and advised by the foolish countenance put up by another—"Tous les jours la sotte contenance d'un autre m'advertit et m'advise" (922; 703). Yet the essay goes on to describe a positive form of "advertissement" that one speaker can extend to the other in conversation, the kind of criticism and advice that can cause some speakers to be offended if you do not take it to heart—"j'en cognoy quelqu'un qui plaint son advertissement, s'il n'en est creu" (925; 705). Because of the reflexive and inherently contentious nature of conversation, one is apt to throw such criticism back on the other who gave it: the kettle returns the compliment to the pot. Montaigne does not outright reject this impulse, but he does not let it prevent the criticism from sinking in.

> Ny ne me semble responce à propos à celuy qui m'advertit de ma faute, dire qu'elle est aussi en luy. Quoy pour cela? Tousjours l'advertissement est vray et utile. (930)

> Nor does it seem to me an appropriate reply to someone who warns me of my fault, to say that it is also in him. What of it? The warning is still true and useful. (710)

By the same token, our own possession of a vice should not stop us from the charitable good deed of admonishing others who also have it. But,

Montaigne says, we are not spared an "internal jurisdiction," and in the very act of giving our "advertissement" we should repeat what is his free adaptation of the words that Plutarch ascribes to Plato.

> Ne suis-je pas moy mesmes en coulpe? mon advertissement se peut-il pas renverser contre moy? Sage et divin refrein, qui fouete la plus universelle et commune erreur des hommes. (929)

> "Am I not myself at fault? May not my admonition be turned around against me?" A wise and divine refrain, which scourges the most universal and common error of mankind. (709)

All conversational gambits thus tend to the one goal of self-knowledge. The participant as speaker or as listener, as taker or giver of an admonition that is either negative ("This is what is wrong with me") or positive ("This is what is wrong with you"), turns the exchange back on himself and to a recognition of his "imperfections." Montaigne assists this process by anticipating and helping on the conclusions of a strong debater—"contre un homme vigoureux je me plais d'anticiper ses conclusions" (936; 715)—while he allows weaker opponents to get mired and stuck in their arguments so that at last they may recognize themselves: "qu'en fin ils se recognoissent" (937; 716).

In this last respect, Montaigne acts like Socrates, who, he notes in a C-text addition placed earlier in the essay, disputed more in favor of the disputants than of the dispute in order to lead Euthydemus and Protagoras to the knowledge of their "impertinence" (927; 708): their inability to speak pertinently about their subject that is, in Montaigne's wordplay, the mark of their presumptuousness in claiming to be able to do so. Indeed, the conversation that Montaigne describes seems to be an exercise in Socratic ignorance: the Socrates who knows nothing showing others that they know no more than he does. For the self-knowledge that is at stake is closely related to the question of whether one has any knowledge at all, the famous "Que sçay-je" that accompanied a pair of scales as Montaigne's device, as he tells us in the "Apologie de Raimond Sebond" (527; 393)—and we seem to have entered into that essay's vast domain of skepticism.

The imperfection that one acknowledges is thus the limit of one's own "suffisance," another key word of "De l'art de conferer" that colors a primary sense of "capacity of intellectual judgment" with the ethically charged notion of self-sufficiency. An earlier essay of Montaigne's book argues, as its title stipulates, that it is folly to measure the true and false by our own individual, human capacity—"C'est folie de rapporter le vray et le faux à nostre suffisance" (1:27)—and defends the miracles witnessed by Saint Augustine and other saints of the early church. The essay concludes, like the "Apologie," by enjoining entire submission to the authority of our

(Catholic) ecclesiastical polity: "Ou il faut se submettre du tout à l'authorité de nostre police ecclesiastique ou du tout s'en dispenser" (182; 134). The target here is obviously the Protestant attack on ecclesiatical tradition and emphasis on the spiritual inspiration of the individual believer, but Montaigne also accuses himself, for his earlier mistaken use of the liberty of choice and personal selection—"cette liberté de mon chois et triage particulier" (182; 134) to decide which church doctrines to accept or reject. At the end of "De l'art de conferer," he takes up a secular version of the same argument when, in considering the doubtful miracles recounted by Tacitus, he says that he has made it his custom to bow before the authority of such great witnesses—"J'ay accoustumé en telles choses de plier soubs l'authorité de si grand tesmoings" (942). To assert a knowledge sufficient to judge on one's own, without deference to outside authority, is presumptuous and impertinent—as well as a challenge to religious and political order.

Conversation naturally tests and breaks down such illusory ideas of selfsufficiency, the more so when it is practiced acccording to Montaigne's reflexive model. The beginning of "De l'art de conferer" contrasts the lively engagement with a speaker who can answer you back and challenge you with the less intense activity of reading books—though the essay ends by extending the model of conversation to Montaigne's study of Tacitus and, by a further implicit extension, to his reader's study of the *Essais*.

> L'estude des livres, c'est un mouvement languissant et foible qui n'eschauffe poinct: là où la conference apprend et exerce en un coup. Si je confere avec une ame forte et un roide jousteur, il me presse les flancs, me picque à gauche et à dextre, ses imaginations eslancent les miennes. La jalousie, la gloire, la contention, me poussent et rehaussent au dessus de moy-mesmes. Et l'unisson est qualité du tout ennuyeuse en la conference. (923)

> The study of books is a languishing and feeble activity that gives no heat, whereas discussion teaches and exercises us at the same time. If I discuss with a strong mind and a stiff jouster, he presses on my flanks, prods me right and left; his ideas launch mine. Rivalry, glory, competition push me and lift me above myself. And unison is an altogether boring quality in discussion. (704)

The passage introduces the metaphors of combat that run through the essay to describe contentious conversation. Montaigne specifically has the joust in mind—he later borrows an image from tilting at the ring (928; 708)—even if toward the essay's end, he declares his mortal hatred for real jousting that has often, notably in the case of the death of King Henri II, resulted in bloodshed: it is ugly to fight in play—"Il faict laid se battre s'esbatant" (939; 717), he affirms in a punning epigram added to the C text. Conversation is thus doubly distanced from physical combat: it is the talky and genuinely bloodless version of the tournament, itself a form of play war, and it similarly keeps conflict within ceremonial containment. But by the same token, Montaigne expresses his preference for a no-holds-barred discussion, which he compares to a rough lovemaking whose scratches and bites pleasurably, draw blood—"comme l'amour, és morsures et egratigneures sanglantes" (924; 705).[10] Conversation is a combative love, a loving combat. By unspoken convention the parties have agreed in advance to disagree, and to enjoy a playful game of verbal sparring. For contention and emulation, the attempt to outdo and defeat the other, bring out the best of their abilities, even abilities that they did not know they had: in the heat of argument Montaigne surpasses himself.

Yet these very qualities of contradiction and rivalry that, Montaigne goes on to say, arouse and exercise him—"m'esveillent . . . et m'exercent" (924; 704)—are likely to produce violent reactions that exceed the agreed-upon bounds of conversation. Montaigne adds a passage on contradiction into the C text that seems itself to contradict what has gone before.

> Noz disputes devoient estre defendues et punies comme d'autres crimes verbaux. Quel vice n'esveillent elles et n'amoncellent, tousjours regies et commandées par la cholere! Nous entrons en inimitié, premierement contre les raisons, et puis contre les hommes. Nous n'aprenons à disputer que pour contredire, et, chascun contredisant et estant contredict, il en advient que le fruit du disputer c'est perdre et aneantir la verité. (926)

> Our disputes ought to be forbidden and punished like other verbal crimes. What vice do they not stir and heap up, being always governed and commanded by anger? We feel hostility first against the reasons, and then against the men. We learn to argue only in order to contradict; and with each man contradicting and being contradicted, it turns out that the fruit of the argument is to ruin and annihilate the truth. (706)

Civil discussion soon collapses when you cannot bear to be opposed and take the game of conversation personally.[11] For we want to win the game. The desire to defeat our rival that sharpens and exercises our faculties turns to anger and enmity when it is thwarted. The implications for public debates are clear; Montaigne comments in a related passage in "Des boyteux" (3:11) that "there is nothing on which men are more intent than on making a way for their opinions. Where the ordinary means fail us, we add command, force, fire, and the sword"—"Il n'est rien à quoi communement les hommes soient plus tendus qu'à donner voye à leurs opinions: où le moyen ordinaire nous fault, nous y adjoustons le commandement, la force, le fer, et le feu" (1028; 786). France's recent troubles appear here as the result of the breakdown of a political conversation where the desire for domination by the parties in the discussion has replaced the questing after truth, and where talking has been succeeded by violence. The telltale term "opinions" evokes the new Protestant doctrines and the stubborn "opiniastreté" of their adherents. In "De l'art de conferer," Montaigne has blushingly acknowledged that something similar happens to him in private discussion when the conversation loses its orderly thread.

> Il me chaut peu de la matiere, et me sont les opinions unes, et la victoire du subject à peu près indifferente. Tout un jour je contesteray paisiblement, si la conduicte du debat se suit avec ordre. . . . Mais quand la dispute est trouble et des-reglée, je quitte la chose et m'attache à la forme avec despit et indiscretion, et me jette à une façon de debattre testue, malicieuse, imperieuse, de-quoy j'ay à rougir apres. (925)

> I care little about the subject matter, opinions are all one to me, and I am almost indifferent about which opinion wins. I will argue peaceably a whole day if the debate is conducted with order. . . . But when the argument is confused and disorderly, I give up the substance and attach myself angrily and indiscriminately to the form, and throw myself into a headstrong, malicious, and imperious way of arguing, which I have to blush for afterward. (706)

Once the rules of conversation are broken, it loses its gamelike nature, and each angry speaker seeks only to have his own way. Or conversely, anger and the pursuit of victory cause orderly argument to swerve from the point and to deteriorate into random bickering and name-calling.

Montaigne, however, does not merely explore the paradox that the contention necessary for productive conversation can also be responsible for its collapse. The peaceable discussion that he says he can carry out all day appears to depend on the conditions that he spells out in the preceding sentence. The topic must be something he cares little about and about which he can entertain all opinions; he must be nearly indifferent to which side wins: in other words, as long as the matter of discussion is something which he does not take seriously, he can spin out the conversational game indefinitely—and it is the orderly conduct of the game by its rules that he *does* take seriously. This order, like the larger social order for which it seems to serve as a model, becomes an end in itself. It depends on the rational capacities of the speakers to keep discussion on track and to the point, but even more on their mutual commitment to preserve the form of conversation over and above its matter and the positions they defend.

We have to ask, in this case: what happens to the "truth" ("verité") that the essay variously invokes as the goal of conversation—a truth that risks being lost and annhilated when order fails and the speakers lose their composure and fall into obstinacy and rage? Montaigne hedges on this issue, but the general answer is skeptical. At times, he acknowledges that truths can emerge from discussion, and, as we shall see, he gladly surrenders to them when they do. But he notes that while everyone can speak truthfully, few indeed can speak with order, prudence, and *sufficiency*—"Tout homme peut dire veritablement; mais dire ordonnéement, prudemment, et suffisamment, peu d'hommes le peuvent" (928; 708). That is, we seldom can explain with ordered reason, or even understand, why the truths that we utter are true: we cannot judge the true and false by our own "suffisance." Viewed in this light, there is *no* topic that Montaigne takes seriously, that he can seriously expect to lead to truth, not even—or especially—disputes over religious truth.

The stakes of discussion are thus reduced, and reduce discussion itself, to a playful exercise or pastime; a few pages later Montaigne compares it to the hunt.

> L'agitation et la chasse est proprement de nostre gibier: nous ne sommes pas excusables de la conduire mal et impertinemment; de faillir à la prise, c'est autre chose. Car nous sommes nais à quester la verité; il appartient de la posseder à une plus grande puissance. (928)

> Agitation and the chase are properly our quarry: we are not excusable if we conduct it badly and impertinently; to fail in the catch is another thing. For we are born to quest after truth; to possess it belongs to a greater power. (708)

Like the conversation as joust, this hunt is conceived as a violent exercise that never comes to the moment of the kill: and so it answers to the critique of hunting that we have seen in "De la cruauté" where Montaigne tells us that he almost always lets his captured quarry go free.[12] In both of these figures for conversation, joust and hunt, Montaigne has reimagined aristocratic blood sports without the blood; he is once again teaching his noble contemporaries a more civil and pacific pursuit. Conversation is peaceable, however, and, as a kind of intellectual workout, its own reward, just because the quarry truth is ever elusive and belongs to a higher, divine power: and in this sense the "truth" that may be available to the human parties in discussion is simply that truth lies beyond them—though they also achieve a salutarily humbling self-knowledge by owning up to their lack of *suffisance*. Because neither party can reach the truth, neither can overcome the other. What both can do is to conduct the hunt after truth in a seemly way that avoids impertinence—that is, with *order*—and this amounts to giving up not the search but the end, not the competition with one's interlocutor, but the possibility of victory. When the goal of the conversation becomes open-ended and the two speakers remove the further objective of victory that is the cause of anger and hostility, the discussion can go on peaceably all day long.[13]

Montaigne's skepticism is here easily aligned with an ethical disposition. Those of us, he has earlier asserted in the essay, who deprive our judgment of the right to make decisions, look mildly on opinions that differ from ours—"Nous autres, qui privons nostre jugement du droict de faire des arrests, regardons mollement les opinions diverses." For the same reason Montaigne enters into discussions with great freedom and ease: "liberté et facilité" (923; 704). That same "mollesse," the "mollitia" condemned by the Stoics that the soft-hearted and easygoing Montaigne reclaims as his own good nature, is enabled by his skeptical suspension of judgment. But conversely and perhaps more importantly, Montaigne's easy, yielding behavior makes possible his skeptical position: so long as his pride were to insist on winning a victory at all costs over the interlocutor whom he casts as his rival and opponent, he could not acknowledge the insufficiency of his own understanding and achieve thereby the *advertissement* of self-knowledge. This skeptical knowledge is thus inseparable from a kind of self-mastery, which becomes possible only once it has been detached from the will to master others.

Montaigne thus enters the arena of conversation both to compete and to yield. In "De l'art de conferer," the repeated figures of combat show Montaigne in the posture of surrender, whether to "truth" or to his conversational adversary.

> Je festoye et caresse la verité en quelque main que je la trouve, et m'y rends alaigrement, et luy tend mes armes vaincues, de loing que je la vois approcher. [C] Et, pourveu, qu'on ny procede d'une troigne trop imperieuse et magistrale, je presente l'espaule aux reprehensions que l'on faict en mes escrits; et les ay souvent changez plus par raison de civilité que par raision d'amendement: aymant à gratifier et nourrir la liberté de m'advertir par la facilité de ceder; ouy, à mes despans. (924)

> I give a warm welcome to truth in whatever hand I find it, and cheerfully surrender to it and extend my conquered arms, from as far off as I see it approach. [C] And provided they do not go about with too imperious and magisterial a frown, I lend a hand to the criticism people make of my writings, and have often changed them more out of civility than to improve them, loving to gratify and foster my critics' freedom to admonish me by the ease with which I yield—yes, even at my own expense. (705)

The turn here from the first version of the essay to the C-text addition is telling and captures the double logic of Montaigne's model of conversation. In the first instance, he yields happily for the sake of a truth that disarms him at once when he sees it coming; in the second he yields for the sake of yielding. Even when the critics of the *Essais* give him bad advice, he makes the revisions they suggest, if only to encourage more criticism and the possibility of *advertissement*. The facility and liberty that he brings to conversation are now divided between himself and his interlocutors. His ease is an ease of yielding that ensures their freedom to criticize, and indeed it is the free and equal terms of their exchange—the form rather than the truth of the matter—that are at stake. Montaigne finds it hard to take criticism that seeks to dominate him with a show of power ("impérieuse") or professional authority ("magistrale"); it gets his back up.

Yet conversation is nonetheless a mock-combat in which the attempted domination of one's interlocutor is always a component, and Montaigne has contended that it is a necessary component for the discussion to have any life in it and to give full exercise to one's wits. The trick is learning how to place the objective of victory elsewhere.

> Je me sens bien plus fier de la victoire que je gaigne sur moy quand, en l'ardeur mesme du combat, je me faict plier soubs la force de la raison de mon adversaire, que je me sens gré de la victoire que je gaigne sur luy par sa foiblesse. (925)

> I feel much prouder of the victory I win over myself when, in the very heat of battle, I make myself bow beneath the force of my adversary's reason, than I feel gratified by the victory I win over him through his weakness. (706)

> Quelle plus grande victoire attendez vous, que d'apprendre à vostre ennemy qu'il ne vous peut combatre? Quand vous gaignez l'avantage de vostre proposition, c'est la verité qui gaigne; quand vous gaignez l'avantage de l'ordre et de la conduite, c'est vous qui gaignez. (927)

> What greater victory do you expect than to teach your enemy that he is no match for you? When you win the advantage because of your proposition, it is truth that wins; when you win the advantage because of order and method, it is you who win. (708)

In both of these passages, too, the truth that emerges from the discussion, whether wielded by Montaigne or his interlocutor, is relegated to secondary importance. In the first, Montaigne masters his own will to master his conversational adversary: it is not so much the adversary's superior arguments or the superior adversary himself who wins as it is Montaigne, who, by the very act of yielding and acknowledging his defeat, has won a victory over himself. The second passage frankly acknowledges the competitive dimension of conversation: we want nothing more than to dominate our fellow speaker, who has now become explicitly our "enemy." When it is Montaigne's own turn to prevail, however, he can only take the credit for doing so from the order of his argument, not from its substance. The possession of a stronger case is not one's own achievement, but rather how one lays it out and explains it: to do so better than one's opponent is the measure of one's superiority and a true personal victory. But, as we have already seen, the commitment to order and logic also entails curbing the very drive for victory and the effort to dominate, as it were, the conversation. You win, Montaigne says, but it is once again a victory over yourself.

The paradoxes here—that one wins even when one yields, that one wins by not trying to win—suggest a certain smugness that is not unrelated to the no-lose position of Stoicism: inner self-mastery becomes a more than adequate compensation for curbing one's outward will to power over others. That aggression toward others, however, takes another form in the second half of "De l'art de conferer." The essay takes a satiric turn as it exposes the lack of *suffisance* of other speakers whose seeming authority depends on their claims to experience; on their rank and offices and the external pomp that comes with them; on a prudence falsely attributed to them by the outcome of events over which fortune, not they, had control; on arguments they have merely borrowed from others. The section extends the Socratic logic of the larger essay—that one reveals the ignorance of others only after acknowledging one's own, that one turns such instances of *advertissement* back upon oneself—and at the same time exceeds it, suggesting the satisfaction that comes from seeing through appearances.

Its centerpiece is Montaigne's vision of the king and his court.

> Ce que j'adore moy-mesmes aus Roys, c'est la foule de leurs adorateurs. Toute l'inclination et soubmission leur est deuë, sauf celle de l'entendement. Ma raison n'est pas duite à se courber et flechir, ce sont mes genoux. (935)

> What I myself adore in kings is the crowd of their adorers. All deference and submission is due to them except that of our understanding. My reason is not trained to bend and bow, it is my knees. (714)

The emperor has no clothes, or perhaps only consists in his clothes, in his royal trappings and entourage that impress us as do theater costumes, the "masque des grandeurs" (935; 714) that players put on stage.[14] A successful reign is no proof of the king's capacity: given the vagaries of fortune, Montaigne wryly notes, kingdoms have been as well ruled by children, women, and madmen as by the most "suffisans Princes" (934; 713).

Montaigne nonetheless reaffirms his total outward submission to his king. His bowing and bending to the monarch transports to the political realm his pliant bending before his conversational rival ("je me faict plier") and is a version, as well, of his bending before the authority of great witnesses, secular and sacred ("de plier soubs l'authorité de si grands tesmoings")—whether or not he quite believes in the miraculous events they report. For Montaigne reserves to himself an inner realm of understanding and reason, from which he can judge with hardheaded skepticism the abilities of the king whom he chooses to obey. His submission is thus a knowing choice and, in this respect, a free one. As in his conversation, Montaigne does not so much bow to a superior as to the preservation of the order—here quite explicitly the political order of France—that such submission upholds. At the same time, since the skepticism directed at the king reflexively applies to his own imperfections—is Montaigne any wiser, could he govern any better?—he recasts his yielding to external power as an inner-directed act of will, an overcoming of the self and its presumption.

In one respect, Montaigne does claim if not exactly superiority, at least to have an advantage over the king whom he serves. He may be no wiser than his ruler but, like Socrates, he knows that he is no wiser, and it is this self-knowledge that is unavailable to the great. Montaigne has just explored this disadvantage of greatness in the essay of that name, "De l'incommodité de la grandeur" (3:7), which has immediately preceded "De l'art de conferer," and which is closely tied to it.[15] Princes, he states there, are excluded from the kind of friendly competition and rivalry of which conversation is one form.

> Or l'incommodité de la grandeur, que j'ay pris icy à remarquer par quelque occasion qui vient de m'en advertir, est cette cy. Il n'est à l'avanture rien plus plaisant au commerce des hommes que les essays que nous faisons les uns contre les autres, par jalousie d'honneur et de valeur, soit aux exercises du corps, ou de l'esprit, ausquels la grandeur souveraine n'a aucune vraye part. A la verité, il m'a semblé souvent qu'à force de respect on y traicte les Princes desdaigneusement et injurieusement. . . . Si on recognoist qu'ils ayent tant soit peu d'affection à la victoire, il n'est celuy qui ne se traivalle à la leur prester, et qui n'aime mieux trahir sa gloire que d'offenser la leur: on n'y employe qu'autant d'effort qu'il en faut pour servir à leur honneur. (918)

> Now the disadvantage of greatness, which I have chosen to comment on here because of an occasion that has just called my attention to it, is this. There is perhaps nothing more pleasant in association with men than the trials of strength we have with one another, in rivalry of honor and worth, whether in exercise of the body or of the mind, and in these sovereigns have no real share. In truth, it has often seemed to me that by force of respect princes are treated disdainfully and insultingly in these matters. . . . If people recognize that princes have the slightest desire for victory, there is no one who will not labor to give it to them and who will not rather betray his own glory than offend theirs, everyone exerts only as much effort as is needed to serve their honor. (701)

The king has no one to play with, no one, that is, who will compete seriously with him: and Montaigne recalls his own frustration as a child with those who refused to treat him as a worthy opponent. The king has no way to test his own strength against others, whether in jousting where, Montaigne remarks, the king looks as if he is wearing enchanted armor since no one will oppose him (918; 701) or in debate, where even fools can claim that they have allowed themselves to be defeated (919; 702). The loaded term here is "essays," which includes Montaigne's own self-reflexive writing as a similar trial of strength that leads, in his case, to the generally skeptical discovery of his weakness. Because of the submission due to them, kings have no way to know their own abilities, and especially their limitations and imperfections by which they might receive such a salutary *advertissement*. Montaigne comments in a passage of "De l'experience" that looks back on both "De l'art de conferer" and "De l'incommodité de la grandeur" that no class of men has more need than kings of such true and frank admonition—"Or il n'est aucune condition d'hommes qui ayt si grand besoing que ceux-là de vrays et libres advertissemens" (1078; 826)—and here he announces in the last essay of his book that his true metier would be to advise his king as a nonflattering counselor: and by implication this would be the proper role of the *Essais* themselves, teaching as they do, the trial, but especially the error, of human understanding.

Montaigne thus assumes a privileged position vis-à-vis his king at the same time that he bows before him. He is not taken in by the impression that the king may give of possessing a superior understanding to his own. On the contrary, he sees the king lacking the self-knowledge—and the possibility of ever attaining it—that he, Montaigne, receives by submitting to his ruler. And he claims this perhaps self-gratifying knowledge as the product of a mental space whose thought and reason remain free and do not bow to power and authority. This space is related to the "arriere-boutique toute nostre" (241; 177), that back of the shop of Stoic autonomy that Montaigne famously described in "De la solitude" (1:39) as the site of our true freedom. Montaigne has politically rehabilitated the Stoic independence and self-mastery he admires in his earliest essays by giving them a skeptical inflection: we are free to criticize and to doubt, especially to refocus such criticism and doubt back on ourselves and thus to master our own presumption and our impulse to lord it over others that comes with it. By defining this freedom as private and ultimately self-directed, Montaigne attempts to remove from it any suggestions of political opposition. More pertinently, Montaigne insists that the self-knowledge to which the free understanding arrives, a knowledge of its own lack of *suffisance*, leads it to self-mastery and to submission to external authority. The opposite is also true in an argument that reveals its quasi-circular nature: submission to the monarch already entails the self-mastery that enables a true and free understanding.

Montaigne thus comes close (while he does it one better) to the spirit of Seneca's contention in Epistle 73, that the sage philosopher, far from being contumacious or refractory toward his ruler, is instead grateful to the political power that preserves the peace and liberty he enjoys. Montaigne has ceased to profess Stoicism if he ever in fact did. His notion of self-mastery, the acknowledgment of one's human weakness, is almost the opposite of the Stoic sage's superhuman self-control; he rejects the Stoics' treatment of the body, their condemnation of pity, above all those moments in Seneca where intransigent virtue appears to be aligned not with yielding but with resistance to power. But his thought retains enough Stoic elements, especially the tradeoff he proposes of outward compliance for inner sovereignty, to have affinities with the contemporary neostoicism of Lipsius that, Gerhard Oestreich has argued, was designed for the subject of the new absolutist state.[16] Montaigne undertakes a political project similar to that of Lipsius: he seeks to persuade potentially refractory subjects (nobles, Huguenots, Ligueurs) to become philosophers, that is, to accept philosophically—in the name of, and in exchange for, philosophical freedom—their servitude to their king. (We may wonder how convincing this argument would be to a sixteenth-century magnate worried about losing personal and local power, though implicit in the argument is the idea that the crown and the order it will impose on a present state of anarchy may be the best guarantee of noble privilege in the long run.[17]) The subject is made to feel more fortunate than and a little sorry for the lonely king who, in another rendering of this argument in "De l'inequalité qui est entre nous" (1:42), is said to be deprived of the mutual friendship and society with others—"amitié et societé mutuelle" (266; 195)—in which consists the most perfect and sweetest fruit of human existence. Without such mutuality there can be no self-knowledge; without self-knowledge no self-mastery. The suggestion, which takes up another classical commonplace, is that the subject can enjoy a truer kingship over himself than his king, for all his power, possesses. The subject, particularly the noble subject, becomes once again a "Roytelet," reigning over an inner domain of his own.[18]

Just what the king is missing emerges toward the end of "De l'art de conferer," where Montaigne presents one more version, a utopian one, of conversation—and of the larger social relations for which such conversation might provide a model. He thinks of a social gathering of private friends, teasing and teaching one another.

> Pouvons nous pas mesler au tiltre de la conference et communication les devis pointus et coupez que l'alegresse et la privauté introduict entre les amis, gossans et gaudissants plaisamment et vifvement les uns les autres? . . . Pour mon regard, j'y apporte plus de liberté que d'esprit, et y ay plus d'heur que d'invention; mais je suis parfaict en la souffrance, car j'endure la revenche, non seulement aspre, mais indiscrete aussi, sans alteration. Et à la charge qu'on me faict, si je n'ay dequoy repartir brusquement sur le champ, je ne vay pas m'amusant à suivre cette pointe, d'une contestation ennuyeuse et lasche, tirant à l'opiniastreté: je la laisse passer et, baissant joyeusement les oreilles, remets d'en avoir

ma raison à quelque heure meilleure. N'est pas marchant qui tousjours gaigne. La plus part changent de visage et de voix où la force leur faut, et par une importune cholere, au lieu de se venger, accusent leur foiblesse ensemble et leur impatience. En cette gaillardise nous pinçons par fois des cordes secrettes de nos imperfections, lesquelles, rassis, nous ne pouvons toucher sans offence; et nous entre-advertissons utillement de nos deffauts. (938–39)

> May we not include under the title of discussion and communication the sharp, abrupt repartee which good spirits and familiarity introduce among friends, bantering and joking wittily and keenly with one another? . . . For my part, I bring to it more freedom than wit, and have more luck at it than inventiveness. But I am perfect in forbearance, for I endure retaliation, not only sharp but even indiscreet, without being disturbed. And when a sally is made against me, if I have no brisk retort to make on the spot, I don't go wasting my time, pursuing the point with a boring and lax argumentativeness bordering on obstinacy; I let it pass, and cheerfully lowering my ears, put off getting my revenge until a better time. There is no merchant who always gains. Most men change their countenance and their voice when strength fails them and, by an ill-timed anger, instead of getting revenge, reveal their weakness and their impatience at the same time. In this gay mood we sometimes pluck the secret strings of each other's imperfections, which when we are calm, we cannot touch without offense, and we profitably give one another an admonition of each other's defects. (717)

In this summing up of the concerns of the essay, conversation has become a slinging of barbs and insults, but all in good fun. If Montaigne yields before the point scored by his interlocutor, their exchange nonetheless remains open and competitive—a testing ground of their wit—and he waits for a future occasion to get back at him. But yield he does, bowing his ears and doing so joyfully rather than break the spirit of the repartee, a spirit of playfulness and of *liberty*. To be discountenanced by anger or to fall into opinionated stubbornness, it is a sign of weakness. By yielding Montaigne instead demonstrates his strength, not so much of wit as of character, his ability to master his own self-love. And such self-mastery is the means to self-knowledge. For what we can say in jest to one another without taking offense, in a freedom that is near to complete, can disclose otherwise unsayable truths—*advertissements*—about our imperfections. As the reflexive "entre-advertissons" suggests, such admonishment can be perfectly mutual, a give and take. The proverbial wisdom taken from the marketplace shifts the essay's terms of analogy from the battlefield to a world of peaceful exchange and mutual profit.

Can't you take a joke? There may be no subject of discussion that Montaigne can take seriously, but this scene of reciprocal banter threatens to trivialize the idea of conversation, especially if we want to see in it the model for a national discussion in the essayist's strife-torn France. Insults that could kill—antichrist, heretic, tyrant, politique (this last could be a term of abuse)—were no matter for jest when leveled by and at the parties to this national discussion, nor were the religious causes they upheld as final truths. Montaigne nonetheless wants to suggest that if the warring antagonists would take *themselves* less seriously, they might learn to bend if not entirely to bow, and that this flexibility might make possible a real conversation among them, the basis of negotiation and reconciliation. The skeptical, easygoing selfhood that Montaigne espouses is both this conversation's condition and its desired product. If he sees an ideal model of conversation in the teasing intimacy of friends, it is because the best conversation, by its freedom, order, and absence of anger, should promote friendship—a sense of trust and equal footing—among its speakers. So long as they master their drive for mastery and learn to submit, not so much to each other as to the order and decorum of discussion—the "art" of the essay's title—these speakers, friends or not, can keep on talking, instead of fighting, until the end of time.

Putting Up a Good Front

The effect of the conversation described by "De l'art de conferer" is to transform a potentially adversarial confrontation between parties struggling for dominance into an irenic exchange between equals. Montaigne obtained a similar outcome in the two vignettes he recounts of his experience in the Civil Wars in "De la phisionomie" (3:12), the penultimate essay of his book. Here, however, were no mannerly discussions mimicking more deadly conflicts, but the real thing: twice fallen into the hands of vengeful enemies, Montaigne not only escaped to tell about it, but achieved a relationship of understanding and trust with his erstwhile foes. These stories at the end of "De la phisionomie" are the culmination of the series of showdowns that the *Essais* depict between defiant or submissive captives and their merciless or clement captors, and they constitute an ethical and political conclusion to Montaigne's book. We may feel that these moments of separate peace that Montaigne achieved in the midst of civil strife are what the *Essais*, or at least that particular strain of thought in the *Essais* that I have traced in this study, have been leading up to, moments that vindicate the moral posture for which Montaigne has argued all along and which he has exemplified in his self-portrait. The easygoing, natural, unheroic Montaigne triumphs over the forces of violence and hatred around him and even—to a certain extent—converts their protagonists to his humane outlook and behavior.

But, as usual for the reader of Montaigne, it is not so simple. "De la phisionomie" suggests that there is indeed something courageous, even heroic in Montaigne's own way of yielding to those who hold him in their power—it is not simple submission, by any means. But the essay also proffers the contrasting example of Socrates standing up for justice before his judges among the Athenian people—it is not simple defiant heroism or aggressive self-assertion. The two men, Montaigne and Socrates, approach one another as mirror figures, but their respective conduct nonetheless diverges in what Montaigne, referring to Socrates' trial, will call their loftiest "essay" (1054; 807). Socrates, witness to philosophical truth, presents the best case possible for resistance to power even if it leads to martyrdom—the martyrdom that we have seen Montaigne condemn in "De l'ivrognerie" even among the saints of the early Church themselves. If Montaigne can show a better way, and even suggest that it represents a way out of France's civil wars, he does so by acknowledging just how powerful and attractive is the alternative of Socrates' heroism that he has given up. Montaigne's ethical thought here reveals its own self-knowledge, its awareness of the limits of what it can and cannot achieve.

"De la phisionomie," in fact, begins by evoking the figure of Socrates who has come down to us through the authority of ancient authors; one does best, Montaigne suggests, to look for moral teaching in an age other than his own war-torn, ethically weak era.

> Quasi toutes les opinions que nous avons sont prinses par authorité et à credit. Il n'y a point de mal: nous ne sçaurions pirement choisir que par nous, en un siecle si foible. Cette image des discours de Socrates que ses amys nous ont laissée nous ne l'approuvons que pour la reverence de l'approbation publique; ce n'est pas par nostre cognoissance: ils ne sont pas selon nostre usage. S'il naissoit à cette heure quelque chose de pareil, il est peu d'hommes qui le prisassent. (1037)

> Almost all the opinions we have are taken on authority and on credit. There is no harm in this: we could not make a worse choice than our own in so feeble an age. The version of the sayings of Socrates that his friends have left us we approve only out of respect for the universal approval these sayings enjoy, not by our own knowledge. They are beyond our usage. If anything of the kind were brought forth at this time, there are few men who would prize it. (792)

The multiple levels of irony in this opening become clear as the essay unfolds. If Socrates were, in fact, to come back to sixteenth-century France—as Christ to Chicago—he would find few followers. Montaigne's bitter indictment of his times contains, however, one of his characteristic paradoxes. We moderns, he says, worship or at least give lip service to the classics because everyone else has and does, and perhaps that is as a good a reason to defend the classics as any other. Such figures as the Socrates of

Plato and Xenophon hold up an enduring moral measure by which we can judge our own behavior for better or worse: and Montaigne appears to argue that these classical exemplars check any impulse that the present may have to condescend with moral superiority toward the past. Yet, since we will not emulate them—since their teachings do not fit the way that we live, our "usage"—do they really have any practical use for a modern world?[19]

This restatement of the central dilemma of Renaissance Humanism itself becomes complicated as the essay holds up the conduct of Montaigne against that of Socrates, and in this substitution of personal experience for ancient authority "De la phisionomie" anticipates the logic of "De l'experience," the essay that follows it and that concludes Montaigne's book. Thus Montaigne might seem to be one of those moderns who may dutifully admire the Socrates he reads about, but is not about to follow his example when different times call for different behavior. But to compound matters, Montaigne, far from reducing Socrates to an anachronism, depicts himself in the course of the essay as a genuine disciple of the Athenian philosopher, a Socrates, it must be said, made suspiciously in Montaigne's likeness. It may be *Montaigne* who presents "quelque chose de pareil" to the present time, and who thus risks being out of step with his age and who already wonders if his message will find any takers. Montaigne needs to find a way of being sufficiently *unlike* Socrates in order to update Socratic teachings for his sixteenth-century readership. One way of doing so is to suggest that he is truer to the essence of those teachings than was Socrates himself.

"De la phisionomie," in fact, recapitulates the earlier line of reasoning of "De la cruauté"—once again we are dealing with a series of interrelated essays in Montaigne's larger book—by preferring the easygoing Socrates to the tense Stoic Cato who, Montaigne now remarks, is always mounted on his high horse—"monté sur ses grands chevaux" (1038; 793)—and then doubles this argument against rigid Stoic self-control a few pages later by preferring the writings of Plutarch to those of Seneca up on his "perche" (1040; 795). Socrates replaces Cato as the moral figure whose example teaches the most simple, ordinary, and, above all, natural forms of virtue, and at the beginning of the essay Montaigne transfers the Roman poet Lucan's description of Cato, who knew how to follow nature—*Naturámque sequi* (1037; 793)—from the Stoic hero to Socrates. This naturalness has now been conflated with the skeptical Socratic ignorance that we have seen Montaigne explore in "De l'art de conferer" and it is similarly opposed to philosophical learning and presumption. But when the essay arrives at its final section where it takes up the subject of its title, the ugly face of Socrates is the outward sign of an original vice that he had to overcome through the moral discipline of philosophy; it is the sign, therefore, of philosophy's distance from nature. Montaigne, by contrast, has a *favorable* face—it is to this face that he attributes his escape from his captors in the anecdotes that follow—which suggests that Montaigne's virtue is more natural than that of Socrates.

Montaigne repeats his claim in "De la cruauté" that his behavior is unstudied, and that whatever goodness he has comes to him from his good nature.

> J'ay pris, comme j'ay dict ailleurs, bien simplement et cruement pour mon regard ce precepte ancien: que nous ne sçaurions faillir à suivre nature, que le souverain precepte c'est de se conformer a elle. Je n'ay pas corrigé, comme Socrates, par force de la raison mes complexions naturelles, et n'ay aucunement troublé par art mon inclination. Je me laisse aller, comme je suis venu, je ne combats rien, mes deux maistresses pieces vivent de leur grace en pais et bon accord; mais le lait de ma nourrice a esté Dieu mercy mediocrement sain et temperé. (1059)

> As I have said elsewhere I have very simply and crudely adopted for my own sake this ancient precept: that we cannot go wrong by following Nature, that the sovereign precept is to conform to her. I have not, like Socrates, corrected my natural disposition by force of reason, and have not troubled my inclination at all by art. I let myself go as I have come. I combat nothing. My two ruling parts, of their own volition, live in peace and good accord. But my nurse's milk, thank God, was moderately healthy and temperate. (811)

As Montaigne notes, we have see this argument before, in "De la cruauté." He—and by implication most other people—can get along very well without the efforts of philosophy, particularly of a philosophy that pits the two ruling parts of the human being, mind and body, against one another. He depends on a good disposition that he comes by naturally—and here, as in "De la cruauté," the figure of the nurse's milk blurs the distinction between the gifts of birth and those of nurture, both of which he passively received. So Montaigne's mode of following nature is even more simple and raw, more effortless, than the perfected virtue of Socrates. He has understood the message of Socrates and carried it a step further.

This bald summary of the logic of the essay does not do justice to how, in a way typical of Montaigne's writing, it qualifies, to the point of collapsing, the distinctions it makes. Although they are not my primary focus here, the essay's problematic notion of naturalness and the likeness and unlikeness of Montaigne to Socrates frame the final opposition of the two figures in its concluding pages. These issues have been well and amply discussed by critics of "De la phisionomie," particularly by Joshua Scodel in a fundamental reading of the essay.[20] Two major strains of the essay suffice to demonstrate the kinds of contradictions that Montaigne introduces into it. Beyond Socrates and himself, Montaigne establishes still another, third term in natural virtue: the behavior of the peasantry, who, in the face of the twin evils of the civil wars and the plague, behave with a patience and fortitude that would put a philosopher to shame. The peasants are not Socratically ignorant—aware that they know nothing—rather they are simply ignorant. They represent a degree of naturalness that is unattainable for Montaigne as much as for Socrates, and that reveals the art, learning, and self-consciousness involved in the essayist's pose as a "naturaliste" (1056; 809). Montaigne's own patient endurance of the ills of his time, furthermore, requires his cajoling himself into believing that they are useful troubles—"utiles inconveniens" (1045; 799)—and he goes on to cite a series of arguments that help to cheer him up: that he is finally forced to adapt the Stoic self-reliance that he has for many years preached to himself, that he enjoys watching the tragic spectacle of France's political upheavals (it is not boring), that France was not in such good political health before the civil wars and has not fallen far. These are all *diversions* of the sort that Montaigne describes in "De la diversion" (3:4), where he explores how we can use the powers of the mind to distract ourselves from ills we cannot avoid, and of which he will give his most spectacular example in "De l'experience," where his mind, in a long second-person address, consoles him for his kidney stones and the pain they are inflicting upon his body.[21] Thus if the two ruling parts of Montaigne's being are in accord, they are so by virtue of a willed and artful method of reasoning that is again at some remove from the natural effortlessness and simplicity he claims for himself. (To be sure, Montaigne puts the mind in the service of the body rather than subordinate the latter, and this may be what is finally most innovative in his version of following nature.)

It is as an interpreter of "simplicité naturelle" that Montaigne presents Socrates speaking to his judges. In the first B-text version of the essay, the speech is indeed simple. At least it is quite short, reduced to seven sentences: this Socrates professes ignorance about the nature of death, and asserts that he cannot fear what he does not know. At the same time, he does know better than to harm his neighbor or to disobey a superior. This drastically distilled version of Plato's *Apology* 29a-b is of a piece with the Socratic ignorance that Montaigne praises toward the beginning of the essay. He tells us that Socrates brought a human wisdom down from heaven, from the metaphysical reaches where it was wasting its time—"ou elle perdoit son temps" (1038; 793)—and teaches us how to discover and rely on our natural "suffisance" beyond which other doctrines and learning are empty and superfluous—"Toute cette nostre suffisance qui est au delà de la naturelle, est à peu pres vaine et superflue" (1039; 794). The passage chimes with the argument that we have seen in "De l'art de conferer" where self-knowledge involves the recognition of the proper limits of one's "suffisance," now defined as the natural residue of reason and common sense that is left over once Socratic skepticism has demolished all other forms of knowing. Socrates showed human nature how much it could do by itself—"combien elle peut d'elle mesme" (1038; 794)—which in the final analysis may not be very much. But, as in "De l'art de conferer" and throughout the larger *Essais*, skepticism, by checking human presumption, leads to Montaigne's favorite political moral: one should bow before higher authority. Such obedience is made to seem an imperative of nature itself.

But the figure of Socrates has assumed a more complicated and aggressive posture toward the authorities who are deciding his fate in the C-text version of "De la phisionomie." Montaigne fills out his speech before his judges with more passages translated and paraphrased from the *Apology*, but he now includes passages that come in Plato's dialogue *after* the court has found Socrates guilty and is about to deliberate on his punishment. Socrates proposes an alternative to the death sentence asked for by his accusers.

> Et, jugeant selon mes actions passées et publiques et privées, selon mes intentions, et selon le profit que tirent tous les jours de ma conversation tant de nos citoyens et jeunes et vieux, et le fruit que je vous fay à tous, vous ne pouvez duement vous descharger envers mon merite qu'en ordonnant que je sois nourry, attendu ma pauvreté, au Prytanée aux despens publiques, ce que souvent je vous ay veu à moindre raison ottroyer à d'autres. Ne prenez pas à obstination ou à desdain que, suivant la coustume, je n'aille vous suppliant et esmouvant a commiseration. J'ay des amis et des parents (n'estant, comme dict Homere, engendré ny de bois ny de pierre non plus que les autres) capables de se presenter avec des larmes et le deuil, et ay trois enfans esplorez de quoy vous tirer à pitié. Mais je feroy honte à nostre ville, en l'aage que je suis et en telle reputation de sagesse que m'en voicy en prevention, de m'aller desmettre à si laches contenances . . . car ce n'est pas à mes prieres de vous persuader, c'est aux raisons pures et solides de la justice. Vous avez juré aux Dieux d'ainsi vous maintenir: il sembleroit que je vous vousisse soupçonner et recriminer de ne croire pas qu'il y en aye. Et moy mesme tesmoigneroy contre moy de ne croire point en eux comme je doy, me desfiant de leur conduicte et ne remettant purement en leurs mains mon affaire. Je m'y fie du tout et tiens pour certain qu'ils feront en cecy selon qu'il sera plus propre à vous et à moy. (1053)

> And if you judge according to my past actions, both public and private, according to my intentions, and according to the profit that so many of our citizens, young and old, derive every day from my conversations, and the good I do you all, you cannot duly discharge your obligation to my merit except by ordering that in view of my poverty I be maintained in the Pryta-

neum at the public expense; which I have often known you to grant to others with less reason. Do not take it as obstinacy or disdain that I do not follow the custom and supplicate you and try to move you to commiseration. I have friends and relatives—not being, as Homer says, born of wood or stone any more than others—capable of presenting themselves in tears and mourning, and I have three weeping children to move you to pity. But I would bring shame on my city, at my age and with such a reputation for wisdom as I here stand accused of, to stoop to such cowardly countenances . . . for you should not be persuaded by prayers, but by the pure and solid reasons of justice. You have sworn to the gods thus to comport yourselves; it would seem that I wanted to suspect you and countercharge you with not believing that there are any gods. And I would actually be testifying against myself that I did not believe in them as I should, distrusting their guidance and not committting my affair purely into their hands. I trust in them for everything and hold it for certain that in this they will do what is most fitting for you and for me. (806)

It was this speech that did Socrates in. For while he remarks in the *Apology* (36a) that the vote for his conviction was close enough that a swing of thirty votes would have acquitted him, it is reported by Diogenes Laertius (2.41–42) that after his proposal that he be "punished" by being rewarded with free meals at the Prytaneum, an honor received by Olympic victors, some eighty more votes from his outraged fellow citizens joined the majority that condemned him to death. No longer the simple skeptic whose ignorance leads him to yield to his superiors, this Socrates of the C text is unrepentant, not to say self-righteous in his assertion of his usefulness to the city as a seeker after wisdom. He all but asks for the death sentence, and his judges are only too willing to pronounce it over him. In the *Apology* (37a), Socrates goes on to acknowledge that the punishment he suggests for himself will be taken as a sign of obstinacy like his earlier refusal before the verdict, which Montaigne now inserts, to pursue the customary course of supplication (34e–35d). The judges recognize in both instances a defiance of their court; even Socrates' explanation that he puts his case purely into the hands of the gods—answering the main charge of impiety that has been brought against him—carries the not-so-hidden implication that the judges are as much on trial as he is. I do not hold you in contempt ("desdain"); I am not counterCharging you with unbelief, this Socrates says, thereby intimating that he is doing just that. He takes his irony a step further and makes a mockery of their proceedings by his request for a meal ticket at state expense. Mockery was, Montaigne later notes in another C-text addition, Socrates' customary usage—"il se mocquoit suivant son usage" (1058; 810).

Whether openly or ironically defiant—and the judges have no difficulty reading through his irony—this Socrates joins the *Essais*' gallery of figures of heroic resistance to superior power, of inflexible valor in the face of death, that began in its opening essay. Montaigne keeps coming back to that essay and its first sentence. The heroic Socrates will not go supplicating and moving his judges to commiseration—"esmouvant a commiseration"—thus eschewing the common course of softening the hearts of one's adversaries described at the outset of the *Essais*: moving them to commiseration through submission—"les esmouvoir par submission à commiseration." Should one have heard from the mouth of Socrates a suppliant word—"Eust-on ouy de la bouche de Socrates une voix suppliante?" (1054; 807)—asks the essayist in another C-text addition that follows Montaigne's version of the philosopher's defense. He echoes the ending of the same first essay, where Alexander asks whether his captive Betis has let escape any word of supplication—"lui est-il eschappé quelque voix suppliante" (9; 5), but receives only an obstinate silence and a lofty and even insolent look in return. The refusal of Socrates to court pity by lowering himself to "laches contenances," his own tears or the tears of his family— recalls not just Betis in that essay but the stoically imperturbable and defiant Phyto as well, who maintains a "visage ferme" under the tortures and insults of Dionysius; Phyto also threatens the vindictive tyrant with imminent divine punishment (9; 4). It further makes Socrates similar, surprisingly so, to the bravest, and perhaps most morally troubling of all of Montaigne's defiant heroes, the Brazilian cannibals, who never admit defeat and prefer death to relaxing, either in countenance or speech, their invincible courage—"de relascher, ny par contenance, ny de parole, un seul point d'une grandeur de courage invincible"(210; 156).[22] The brave fronts these figures put up normally do not soften, but rather harden the hearts of those who have them in their power. They invite and collaborate in their own destruction, and Montaigne appears to follow the testimony of Xenophon that Socrates willfully chose a glorious death rather than decline into old age or prolong his decrepitude by even one year—"pour allonger un an sa decrepitude" (1054; 807). He went out when he was still in top form, the sacred image of the human form—"saincte image de l'humaine forme"—which, Montaigne says, he owed to the world as an "exemple" (1054; 807).

Between the B and C texts, then, Montaigne decided to supplement and change his portrayal of Socrates at his trial. His additions in the final version of the essay emphasized Socrates the philosophical martyr for justice and truth—a Socrates now courting death—in order to contrast his resistance to his judges with the different behavior that Montaigne himself exhibited in his two deliverances from deadly adversaries in the anecdotes that conclude "De la phisionomie." Montaigne also made a C-text addition earlier in the essay, well *before* his version of the speech of Socrates, that instead suggests his own erstwhile similarity to the Socrates he will subsequently depict. He describes his conduct during the civil wars when he was suspected, as a moderate, by all sides.

> J'ayde ordinairement aux presumptions injurieuses que la Fortune seme contre moy par une façon que j'ay dés tousjours de fuir à me justifier, excuser et interpreter, estimant que c'est mettre ma conscience en compromis de playder pour elle. "*Perspicuitas enim argumentatione elevatur.*" Et comme si chacun voyoit en moy aussi clair que je fay, au lieu de me tirer arriere de l'accusation, je m'y avance et la renchery plustost par une confession ironique et mocqueuse; si je ne m'en tais tout à plat, comme de chose indigne de responce. Mais ceux qui le prennent pour une trop hautaine confiance ne m'en veulent guere moins que ceux qui le prennent pour foiblesse d'une cause indefensible, nomméement les grands, envers lesquels faute de summission est l'extreme faute, rudes à toute justice qui se cognoist, qui se sent non demise, humble et suppliante. J'ay souvent heurté à ce pilier. (1044-45)

> I ordinarily assist the unfair presumptions against me that fortune sows about by a way I have always had of avoiding justifying, excusing, and interpreting myself, thinking that it is compromising my conscience to plead for it. *For clarity is lessened by argument* [Cicero]. And as if everyone saw into me as clearly as I do myself, instead of retreating from the accusation, I advance to meet it and rather enhance it by an ironic and mocking confession, if I do not flatly keep silent about it as about something unworthy of an answer. But those who attribute this to an over-haughty confidence show me hardly less ill will than those who attribute it to the weakness of an indefensible cause—especially the great, toward whom lack of submission is the ultimate offense, and who are rough on any righteousness that is aware of itself and does not feel itself to be abject, humble, and suppliant. I have often bumped myself on that pillar. (799)

When he answered those who accused him, Montaigne adapted either the ironic, mocking stance of a Socrates or the taciturnity of a Betis—that is, he gave no answer to their charges. His refusal to justify himself and his sense of his own "justice" were taken by others as offensive gestures just as Socrates anticipates that his judges will regard him as disdainful and obstinate, and Montaigne's text carefully spells out the resemblance through the synonymous "hautaine / desdain" and "confiance / obstination."

But the nub of the issue, which returns us to the discussion of our first chapter, is that those in power, the greater power that they have ("les grands")—like the tyrannical Alexander the Great at the end of "Par divers moyens"—demand nothing less than submission and words of supplication. The powerful want their power acknowledged. They cannot stand the prospect of an individual who stands up to them, for the cause of justice or for himself—and they see the former exclusively as the latter. They see such resistance as an affront to their power and to themselves—which they also identify as one and the same. The result is to turn all human relations, including and especially the process of justice, into struggles for dominance between selves who would be all-powerful. Montaigne has learned from practice that to face such judges is to encounter immovable objects, and that to put up opposition to them, even of an ironic kind, is a dead end. It was a literal dead end for Socrates.

Montaigne adds this passage to "De la phisionomie" pages before he turns to the example of Socrates at his trial in order to reverse, at least in the narrative logic of the essay, the relationship of Renaissance imitation to ancient model: it is as if Socrates essayed at his trial a course of behavior whose drawbacks Montaigne already knows about from his own experience. He does not, it appears, need the classical authority of Socrates that he invokes at the essay's beginning. In the personal anecdotes that conclude the essay, experience reemerges to displace authority, as Montaigne presents his conduct when menaced with death as a substitute for that of Socrates, although this conduct, we shall see, may still remain "Socratic." It is an ethical model for Montaigne's own modern times: "selon nostre usage," as he puts it in his preliminary remarks, and he will later speak of writing for the fancy of the age—"la fantasie du siecle" (1055; 808). In the stories he recounts, he insists upon the pressure of the times upon action. "I was not unaware in what sort of an age I was living"—"Je n'ignorois pas en quel siecle je vivois" (1060; 812)—he recalls of his first encounter with hostile forces who came disguised as friends in need, and that the second armed ambush into which he fell had become just through custom—"devenue juste par l'usage" (1062; 814). These are the times of civil war, when, Montaigne complains earlier, custom—"coustume"—has corrupted men of good nature and capable of justice—"natures debonnaires et capables de justice" (1042; 797)—and where Plato's worst form of injustice is about to be realized: that what is unjust is held to be just—"que ce qui est injuste soit tenu pour juste" (1043; 798). If his irony and refusal to submit could not save Socrates in a better age, how is the just man—"justice qui se cognoist"—to act with self-respect, that is, without humbling himself abjectly before power, in such abnormal times?

The answer, Montaigne's example will suggest, is: act as normally, that is, as naturally as possible and present a favorable bearing to the world. We shall see that such action and bearing are much the same thing in the stories that Montaigne tells about how his favorable face saved his life during a time of civil wars. "J'ay un port favorable" (1059; 811), the essayist declares, and exploits the punning possibilities of the term for all they are worth. At moments, it seems that he is talking about a physical attractiveness that is opposed to the ugliness that nature unjustly gave Socrates—"Nature luy fit injustice" (1057; 809)—and this seems especially the case when he laments, through a Latin quotation from Terence, its loss through old age (1059–60; 811). Such beauty is a simple gift of nature. But the idea of a bearing or a face equally suggests a manner of conducting oneself that is a willed or habitual second nature. That the two meanings continually slip into one another helps, of course, to carry Montaigne's argument that his behavior is a way of following nature. Yet we should be aware that it is the second kind of bearing—a bearing that promises or is evidenced by action—that Montaigne is usually talking about.

In fact, Montaigne has shortly before defined the nature of a favorable physiognomy: it is important to emphasize that such a face has *nothing* to do with physical beauty.

> Il y a des phisionomies favorables; et en une presse d'ennemys victorieux, vous choisirés incontinent, parmy des hommes incogneus, l'un plustot que l'autre, à qui vous rendre et fier vostre vie; et non proprement par la consideration de la beauté. (1058–59)

> There are favorable physiognomies; and in a crowd of victorious enemies you will instantly choose, among men unknown to you, one rather than another to whom to surrender and entrust your life; and beauty has no real part in the choice. (811)

This is not the face of beauty, but of clemency. In what is yet another return to the situation of the first essay of Montaigne's book—the vanquished of "Par diver moyens" seeking mercy from triumphant enemies— the favorable face belongs to the man to whom you can surrender and entrust yourself, the one who will do you the ultimate favor of saving your life. This face is the one that the *Essais* have presented to us in their self-portrait: a Montaigne who from that first essay has told us that he is wonderfully lax in the direction of mercy and who hates cruelty and bloodshed so much that he cannot bear to watch the slaughtering of a chicken. It is a face that would then claim to correspond to the inner nature of the man— and here it may differ from the ironic, mocking front of Socrates.

But Montaigne's claim is larger. In the stories he goes on to tell he asserts that such a face of clemency, the clemency for which his book continuously pleads, corresponds to ordinary human nature itself.

In the first vignette, a neighboring gentleman and marital relation of Montaigne attempts treacherously to capture Montaigne and his chateau; he feigns that he and his men are seeking refuge after having been themselves attacked by an enemy with whom he is feuding; his troops straggle in behind him until some twenty-five or thirty stand outside the chateau. Montaigne first naively and naturally—for "nayfvement" (1060; 812) has both of these connotations—admits the gentlemen to his house, as he notes he normally does to everyone. When the well-armed retainers arrive, Montaigne's suspicions are aroused, but he admits them as well, adapting the most natural and most simple course: "je me laissay aller au party le plus naturel et le plus simple." He becomes, like Socrates before his judges, an interpreter of "la simplicité naturelle." This movement, however, from unthinking naiveté to conscious simplicity and naturalness is not in itself simple, despite its tautological appearance: Montaigne calculatingly *chooses* to continue his former behavior. Not to do so, he reasons, would have been to break everything—"tout rompre" (1060; 812)—to break, above all, the pretense that nothing out of the ordinary is taking place. His conduct is not, then, quite the effortless following of nature that he represents it to be; nonetheless, he takes a path of least resistance, which is tantamount to submitting himself into his enemy's hands. The story is related to and should be read alongside the C-text addition that Montaigne placed at the end of "Que nostre desir s'accroit par la malaisance" (2:15), where he describes how he has refused to fortify his chateau in times of civil war, since the very preparations to resist assault *wear the visage* of war and aggression—"Toute garde porte visage de guerre" (617; 467)—and invite attack. The very ease of entrance, has, he claims, protected his house from violence, not least because it takes away from soldiers the elements of risk and military glory. In fact, having gained a too easy victory, the gentleman simply leaves, taking his astonished troops with him.

Montaigne's natural behavior is thus very much a strategy for self-preservation, a front that he presents to the world like his favorable face: these are virtually identical. It is this face and his free and open behavior—"mon visage et ma franchise" (1061; 831)—that disarmed his would-be assailant in the latter's own recollection of the event. Yet if this front is a conscious social mask, its appearance of yielding accommodation and of a naive trust in the fronts put up by others—including those who may be bent on treachery—is supposedly connected to a true inner nature that is registered in Montaigne's initial response of naiveté when his two-faced enemy presents himself at his door. So Montaigne explains in a long aside.

> —Aussi à la verité, je suis peu deffiant et soubçonneus de ma nature; je penche volontiers vers l'excuse et interpretation plus douce; je prens les hommes selon le commun ordre, et ne croy pas ces inclinations perverses et desnaturées si je n'y suis forcé par grand tesmoignage, non plus que les monstres et miracles. Et suis homme en outre qui me commets volontiers a la fortune et me laisse aller à corps perdu entre ses bras. . . . [C] Nous faillons, ce me semble, en ce que nous ne nous fions pas assez du ciel de nous, et pretendons plus de nostre conduite qu'il nous appartient. (1060–61)

Besides the truth is that I am by nature little given to distrust and suspicion. I am apt to lean toward the milder excuse and interpretation. I take men according to the common order, and do not believe in these perverted and unnatural inclinations unless I am forced to by strong testimony, any more than in monsters and miracles. And besides, I am the sort of man who readily commits himself to Fortune and abandons himself bodily into her arms. . . . [C] We err, it seems to me, in that we do not trust ourselves enough to heaven, and we expect more from our own conduct than belongs to us. (812)

Montaigne *naturally* expects other human beings not to be *denatured*: such an expectation, in fact, defines his idea of what it is not to be denatured oneself. The passage is glossed by a C-text addition one page earlier that attributes to all men who are not denatured a universal reason that governs ethical conduct—"la raison universelle empreinte en tout homme non desnaturé" (1059; 811). It also alludes to the preceding essay, "Des boyteux" (3:11), where Montaigne famously discounts belief in witchcraft or any *supernatural* behavior (1031; 789).[23] He thus expects others to belong to a common order of nature—to be ordinary and to act with common human decency—and he acts normally in accordance. His lack of distrust in his fellow men matches, and is perhaps the same thing as, his trust in fortune and in Heaven.[24]

In "Que nostre desir s'accroit par malaisance," he similarly entrusts his undefended chateau purely to heaven—"fié purement au ciel" (617; 468). In a deliberate parallel to the Socrates who had claimed at his trial to entrust his case purely into the hands of the gods ("remettant purement en leurs mains mon affaire. Je m'y fie du tout"), Montaigne entrusts his body to the arms of fortune as he places himself and his house in the hands of other men, even of potential enemies.

Yet in the episode that Montaigne recounts it is—*ostensibly*—the other gentleman who is placing himself and his men in the hands of Montaigne, who shields them from their enemy. The shape of the story dramatizes, however ironically at first, the reciprocity that is the logical consequence of the common human nature in which Montaigne chooses to believe. Clemency, Montaigne has repeatedly argued, is a matter of trust—at least a suspension of the fear—that those whom you pardon will not try to harm you in the future: it puts you in the same position of vulnerability as those you spare. Thus the man who bears a clement "port favorable" is the one who trusts in the good nature of others. Such a face, like the "visage" of Montaigne's chateau, is not so much defenseless as nonthreatening, and it inspires the trust of others. Montaigne has told us how his presence and bearing have caused strangers both greatly to trust in him—"grandement fiées"—and to shower him with rare favors—"faveurs singulieres et rares" (1060; 812). Montaigne's "natural" willingness to take in and protect his neighbor—a reaction that is instinctive and then, in a second self-conscious moment, when he may be said to *put on* his favorable bearing, imitates this same normal instinct of human decency—produces in the end the same response from the would-be traitor.

This reciprocity is the more striking in the second story, where Montaigne, setting out on a journey in a supposed time of truce, is captured, robbed, and held for ransom by marauding, masked gentlemen of another party, Huguenot or Ligueur. Once again, his face saves him. So he is told by the leader of the marauders who takes his mask off and names himself, and then asks Montaigne to assure him of similar treatment should the occasion arise—"me demanda asseurance d'une pareille" (1062; 814). The act of clemency and the removal of the mask are one and the same gesture: they both reveal underneath a shared human nature—the ordinary humanity that links men in bonds of mutual trust. Montaigne chooses to act in accord with this human nature—it is *his* public mask—and he converts others to act in the same natural way.

Do unto others as you would have them do unto you—and trust them to do it. If Montaigne's example seemingly boils down to the reciprocity of the Golden Rule, it is nonetheless phrased in terms of an exchange of aristocratic favor, the same exchange to which we have seen Montaigne refer when he spoke of doing a *courtesy* to an adversary in "Couardise mere de la cruauté." When Montaigne asserts that his favorable bearing has won him singular favors in return, he summons up an aristocratic world held together by favors that place noblemen under mutual obligation to one another. When in the story that follows he admits the gentleman and his soldiers into his house, he says he has done so "à faire plaisir"—to do him a pleasure or favor (1060; 812).[25] One favor produces another, and the gentleman in return leaves Montaigne his life and home intact. The gentleman-bandit of the second episode similarly looks for a future favor from Montaigne when he sets him free. It is important that in both cases Montaigne is dealing with members of his own class: their mutual recognition—beautifully told in the removal of the gentleman's mask—is Montaigne's substitution for that class recognition of the sacred image of valor ("saincte image de la vertu") that takes place at swordpoint in the opening essay of the book. We may feel that this substitution has already been anticipated in Montaigne's praise of the exemplary Socrates and his "saincte image de l'humaine forme." One nobleman knows another not because of a valor that has now become "populaire" in France's civil strife—of which the transformation of the gentleman into a masked bandit might be an emblem—but on the basis of a clement disposition that is both trusting and trustworthy. Such a disposition may be itself merely the natural human form, shared by the common run of humanity, but then nobility based on birth and blood also claims to be natural. The paradoxical argument that Montaigne makes, in the appeal for ethical reform that he addresses to the members of his class, is that this nobility will tell by the naturalness of its conduct: a conduct that is ordinary, clement, and humane.

We are made to feel, nonetheless, that there is something valorous and quietly heroic—something old-fashionedly aristocratic too—in Montaigne's behavior. In these moments of danger his countenance is as firm and unafraid as it is favorable and open: like Socrates at his trial, Montaigne does not resort to "laches contenances." The vignettes recall, as I have mentioned, the story of how Montaigne faced down the mutinous troops in Bordeaux, which he recounted in "Divers evenemens de mesme conseil." There, too, the front that he put up saved his life and created a relationship of mutual trust—"une mutuelle et utile confience" (131; 96). The moral of that episode applies to these stories near the end of Montaigne's book as well. I repeat it here.

> C'est un excellent moyen de gaigner le coeur et volonté d'autruy, de s'y aller soubsmettre et fier, pourveu que ce soit librement et sans contrainte d'aucune necessité, et que ce soit en condition qu'on y porte une fiance pure et nette, le front au moins des chargé de tout scrupule. (130)

> To submit and entrust oneself to others is an excellent way to win their heart and will, provided it be done freely and without the constraint of any necessity, and that the situation be such that we bring to it a pure and clean trust, and at least a countenance free of any misgiving. (95)

The pure trust with which Montaigne acts when he is in the hands of his enemies transforms and ennobles what seems to be a submission to the inevitable—the constraint of necessity—into a free act of will. In the first story recounted in "De la phisionomie" his former adversary tells him that it was his "franchise" along with his face that led to his escape. The double meaning of this frankness seems to be translated into the liberty and firmness of his words—"mon visage, liberté et fermeté de mes parolles" (1062; 814)—that are attributed to him by his captor in the second. Such freedom is possible, we observed in our discussion of "Divers evenemens," only if one is not afraid to die—this is, finally what it means to trust oneself to fortune. Montaigne thus carries out in his own conduct the same lack of fear of death that Socrates declares at the beginning of his speech to his judges.

This conduct, of course, has the approval of Stoicism. In a passage from Seneca's Epistle 66 (16) that Montaigne probably has in mind, the Roman sage asserts that "nothing is honorable/virtuous [*honestum*] that is enacted against one's will, that is coerced . . . everything honorable is voluntary . . . that which is not free cannot be honorable: for one serves what one fears." The "liberté" of his behavior on which Montaigne insists—he repeats the word three times in the space of six sentences toward the end of "De la phisionomie"—recaptures and morally rehabilitates the Stoic "fermeté" and independence that Montaigne so often condemns in its other guises. It does so, as my translation of Seneca's class-inflected "honestum" as "honorable" indicates, by suggesting that there is a way of submitting and trusting to others that allows one to retain one's aristocratic honor intact. His indiscreet liberty—"liberté indiscrete" (1062; 814)—gives the impression that Montaigne is not afraid of anyone and is his own man. Montaigne has thus dialectically combined what seemed to be the opposed paths of submission and heroic resistance to power in order to suggest that submission may contain its own form of heroism, that it may represent true freedom.

The larger political moral of this idea is clear enough: you may submit with honor to a greater power, the power of a king for instance, especially if you are a nobleman with a sense of honor to lose. Much as in "De l'art de conferer," where this submission was depicted as an act of self-mastery and a free and knowing choice, Montaigne's "liberté" here appears to be aligned with a new ethos of the royal servant: a servant who behaves *as if* he bows before power not out of necessity—this would imply fear and in Seneca's terms servitude—but as a free act of will. The voluntary servitude to the king-tyrant that appalled Montaigne's friend La Boétie and made him long for republican Venice is, Montaigne argues, not servitude at all.

Montaigne concludes his discussion of the two episodes by noting that his behavior may appear uncivil and ill adapted to the usage of his times— "incivile et mal accommodée à nostre usage" (1062; 814)—and so echoes the beginning of the essay where it was feared that Socrates' manner of conduct would not fit modern usage. In fact, his example has shown how Socratic doctrine can be improved upon and updated for Montaigne's times and for his aristocratic class who are probably also included in that "nostre"; how furthermore by acting against the prevailing enmities and cruelties of his age, he can effect moral changes on those around him and begin to repair the social and human fissures of civil war. Just as importantly Montaigne finds a way to survive where Socrates failed.[26] He has managed to incorporate the linked precepts of Socrates—he trusts in heaven, he overcomes his fear of death—while simplifying further what he presents as the central Socratic lesson of simplicity and following nature: an ordinary human nature that Montaigne redefines as a clement, trusting demeanor toward others. The ambiguity of the figure of Montaigne's favorable face—we cannot tell to what extent he is talking about a gift of nature or a willed mask of doing what comes naturally that he presents to the world—suggests how close, in fact, the clemency and trust that others read into it are to the essence of human nature itself. (And they are the essence as well of noble conduct, to the extent that nobility itself is a gift of nature, nature in its noblest form.) Montaigne's simpler, more effortlessly natural behavior takes the place of a Socratic mask of mockery and resistance to authority—the ugly Silenus-like face of Socrates—that the essayist had himself tried and found wanting when he confronted the powerful who demand submission. Like Socrates, he refuses to supplicate in order to summon pity from those who hold him in their power, but neither does he antagonize them. Rather he finds a way to submit to them with a liberty that preserves his self-respect and honor, and that finally moves them to *both* pity for his plight—the normal human response—and to esteem for an image of courage. Montaigne holds up an image of mercy and fearless trust in which his captors *want* to recognize themselves and they adapt their own behavior accordingly. Even better than Socrates, Montaigne shows them the image of the human form, and his example has the power to convert others, overriding differences of religion and political allegiance.[27] Montaigne has become the Socrates for his modern age.

Montaigne does not, I think, expect his reader to feel entirely comfortable with the conclusion the essay has reached: that one does better to imitate the example of Montaigne rather than that of Socrates. There can hardly be a more prestigious model in the Western tradition for resistance to authority and martyrdom than the trial and death of Socrates, who died for the right to pursue and teach philosophical wisdom. It was a death frequently compared to the sacrifice of Christ, as Montaigne well knows from the interplay of his essay with Erasmus's adage on the ugliness of Socrates and the Silenus of Alcibiades.[28] Most importantly for the ethical and political arguments of the *Essais*, Socrates stood up for *justice*, the justice that has become a major casualty of the French civil wars. He called his judges to account and refused to accept their verdict as just. Montaigne may find a way for the just man to submit to power without abasing himself and losing honor, but at the cost of leaving the claims of justice itself behind. In the same earlier passage where he condemns the injustice brought about by the civil wars, Montaigne cites with approval the opinions of Favonius and Plato that no political evil, even tyrannical usurpation, can sanction taking arms against the state: all that the "homme de bien" can do is to leave things be and pray to God—"de laisser tout là; seulement de prier Dieu" (1043; 796). This is explicitly an argument against civil war, but it is not clear that Montaigne can approve of any form of resistance to unjust power. He asserts in "De l'utile et de l'honneste" that he may refuse to carry out dishonorable actions for the good of the state, but he concedes that someone else will be found to perform the dirty work: it is perhaps possible to avoid becoming an accomplice to a regime that one will not oppose.[29] Socrates was an active opponent of injustice, as Montaigne further documents toward the end of "De l'experience," where he recalls how Socrates attempted to rescue Theramenes, whom the thirty tyrants were putting to death, even though he had only two followers against the tyrants' many satellites (1109–10; 852). At his trial, Socrates is once again ready to put his life on the line for justice, to the point, Montaigne suggests, of inviting the death sentence passed on him. Compared to such heroism, Montaigne's nonconfrontational style could look rather cowardly, its primary objective physical survival. While Socrates does not prolong his decrepitude, Montaigne lives on to write about his: his essays, themselves, he pointedly says a few pages later, are his failing old age put into print—"decrepitude soubs la presse" (1057; 809). Montaigne may live on, but is life without justice worth living? Even the liberty and self-respect that Montaigne claims that he and others can retain in the act of submitting to power may appear to be a diversion, a way of cheering himself up in the face of unpleasant political realities to which he sees no remedy, much as he distracted himself from the pain of his incurable kidney stones.

Montaigne, that is, does not set up the contrast between himself and Socrates in a wholly one-sided way. The example of Socrates suggests the limits of the ethical model that Montaigne advances and claims to embody in his own person. He explicitly lays these limits bare in the extraordinary coda that ends "De la phisionomie" and that concerns precisely Montaigne's behavior as judge and dispenser of justice: he had extensive experience as a magistrate. He hates no one, he says, and he is so weak about hurting others—"si láche à offenser"—that he cannot bring himself to pass harsh sentences even when they are justly deserved. He is merciful—"misericordieux"—to the man if not to the crime he has committed (1063; 814), reiterating his "merveilleuse lacheté vers la misericorde" declared at the outset of the *Essais* in "Par divers moyens"; he goes on to reiterate his hatred of cruelty asserted in "De la cruauté" that makes him shrink from the death penalty (or at least from death by torture) even for murder: the first cruelty, he notes here, does not justify cruel and unusual punishment—"la haine de la premiere cruauté m'en faict hayr toute imitation" (1063; 814). So far, this is the Montaigne we have come to admire—clement, easygoing, the opponent of cruelty. Montaigne already suggests that there may be a problem with being excessively merciful and lax toward evildoers, and he adduces the authority of Aristotle and Plutarch to that effect. But up to this point we may be inclined to agree with what he notes Plutarch observing in another place: that such mild behavior is indeed the indication of a good nature. But the last sentence of "De la phisionomie" marks a sticking point: *in cauda venenum*.

> Comme aux actions legitimes, je me fasche de m'y employer quand c'est envers ceux qui s'en deplaisent, aussi, à dire verité, aux illegitimes je ne fay pas assez de conscience de m'y employer quand c'est envers ceux qui y consentent. (1063)

> As I do not like to take a hand in lawful actions against people who resent them, so, to tell the truth, I am not scrupulous enough to refrain from taking a hand in unlawful actions against people who consent to them. (814)

This convoluted if perfectly balanced sentence contains a startling revelation at its end.[30] Montaigne's passive goodness that stops him from justly persecuting evildoers has, he somewhat shamefacedly admits ("à dire verité"), as its corollary a lack of conscience or will that allows him to go along with an unjust legal action if its victims do not object and let him get away with it. Montaigne is easygoing to a fault; he does not want to hurt you, but he will not trouble himself to stop unless you let him know that he is hurting you. This passivity may be aligned with what Montaigne says in another moment of what feels like genuine self-criticism, another moment where we see Montaigne's face, warts and all, in "De l'institution des enfans": the danger his tutors felt was not that he would do evil, but that he would do nothing—"Le danger n'estoit pas que je fisse mal, mais que je ne fisse rien" (175; 130). Such moral inertia is the other face of Montaigne's professed reliance on the ordinary goodness and decency of his human nature instead of on a philosophical discipline that, however denaturing, upholds standards of justice. When in "De l'experience," Montaigne cites the opinion of the Stoics that nature itself proceeds against justice in most of its works—"nature mesme procede contre justice, en la plus part de ces ouvrages" (1071; 820)—we may feel the full implications of Montaigne's anti-philosophical naturalism.

Perhaps most remarkably, this last sentence of "De la phisionomie" reopens the question of whether one should submit or put up resistance in order to soften the hearts of those who have power over you, a question that seemed to have been decided in favor of submission—though an honorable submission to be sure. It behooves those on the other end of Montaigne's judicial actions against them—whether they are guilty or innocent—to resist and show their displeasure: the good-natured Montaigne will desist. To submit and consent to suffering an injustice, on the other hand, is to help to perpetuate it; even a good-natured man like Montaigne can be corrupted—as other "natures debonnaires et capables de justice" have been corrupted by the civil wars—unless they are forced to confront their actions. It is also possible that resistance and consent can become entangled: in the martyr, like Socrates, who stands up to his unjust judges and also accedes to his own destruction. Would the clement Montaigne have condemned Socrates to death?

We seem at the end of "De la phisionomie" to have returned to where we started at the beginning of the *Essais* with the same issues still open. This inability to close off argument, we should recognize by now, is as much the moral of Montaigne's book as the doctrine it espouses: he could argue all day, he says in "De l'art de conferer."[31] The last word of the *Essais* does make an attempt at closure; it reasserts a central tenet of that doctrine and it, too, returns to the book's beginning. At the end of "De l'experience" Montaigne makes a final declaration.

> Les plus belles vies sont, à mon gré, celles qui se rangent au modelle commun [C] et humain, avec ordre, mais [B] sans miracle et sans extravagance. (1116)

> The most beautiful lives, to my mind, are those that conform to the common [C] human [B] pattern, [C] with order, but [B] without miracle and eccentricity. (857)

The first words of the *Essais* are "La plus commune façon . . ." and here Montaigne, in another gesture toward providing a frame to his book, restates his preference for such a common fashion of behavior, the behavior of men who do nothing out of the ordinary. This ethical stance seems to make a final choice between the political alternatives posed in that first sentence: it is better to follow the common course of submission, rather than heroic resistance. "Don't try to be a hero," Montaigne concludes here, and suggests that it is heroic enough to be a human being. But, in effect, the *Essais* end twice in "De la phisionomie" and "De l'experience," and the ending of the former, penultimate essay suggests his awareness of just what his moral position can and cannot do. Montaigne's morality for everyman, which enjoins one to rediscover one's own best natural instincts—at the basis of which is a human trust that makes possible both submission and clemency to others, trust above all that others at heart share the same instincts—is the best ethical model that he knows. But he also acknowledges the shortcomings of this model, because he has the classics and Socrates as witnesses to a rival morality based on justice. Montaigne's ethics can hope to make men behave more humanely to one another, perhaps to lead his countrymen out of their civil wars and so restore the conditions of justice that the wars have abrogated, but they cannot guarantee justice itself. We may return and reconsider just where the emphasis falls in the advice that Montaigne gives to the prince in "De la praesumption," a passage that was cited in our first chapter (see p. 27 above): if he recommends first of all that the prince be humane and clement—"Qu'il reluise d'humanité . . ."—he enjoins him, above all, to be just—"et sur tout de justice" (647; 490). Yet Montaigne knows that in many cases one cannot have both. He knows that between humanity and justice his choice lies with the former, but he knows that to have to choose is itself unsatisfactory. His is indeed a modern morality.

It is one of the weaknesses, we have just seen, of Montaigne's ethics and of the political submission they underwrite that he appears to suggest that there is little if anything one can do to oppose the actions of a ruler. But this was not strictly true in his own life. On January 18, 1590, that is, two years after the publication of the second B text of the *Essais* in 1588 and while he was presumably working on the additions that would fill out the posthumous C text, Montaigne wrote to Henri of Navarre, now King Henri IV but still constrained to fight for his crown, especially against the citizens of Paris who had risen against him with the Catholic League and whom Henri's army had attacked the previous November. In the letter, Montaigne took on the role of royal counselor that he had recommended for himself in "De l'Experience."

> J'eusse bien desire que le guein particulier des soldats de vostre armee et le besouin de les contanter ne vous eut desrobe nomeemant en cette ville princi-

pale la belle recomandation d'avoir treté vos subjetz mutins en pleine victoire avec plus de solagemant que ne font leurs protecteurs & qu'a la differance d'un credit passagier et usurpé vous eussies montré qu'ils estoint vostres par une protection paternelle et vraïemant royalle A conduire tels affaires que ceus que vous aves en main il se faut servir de voies non communes Si s'est il tousjours veu qu'ou les conquestes par leur grandeur et difficulté ne se pouvoint bonemant parfaire par armes et par force elles ont esté parfaictes par clemance et magnificence excellans leurres a attirer les homes specialemant vers le juste et legitime parti S'il y eschoit rigur et chastiemant il doit estre remis apres la possession de la maistrise. Un grand conquerur du temp passé se vante d'avoir doné autant d'occasion a ses enemis subjuguez de l'eimer qu'as ses amis Et icy nous sentons desja quelqu'effaict de bon prognostique de l'impression que reçoivent vos villes desvoiees par la comparaison de leur rude tretemant a celluy des villes qui sont sous vostre obeissance. Desirant à Vostre Majesté une felicité plus presante et moins hasardeuse & qu'elle soit plus tost cherie que creinte de ses peuples. . . . Je reçois a grace singuliere qu'ell'aie deigné me faire sentir qu'elle pranderoit a gre de me voir, persone si inutile mais siene plus par affection encore que par devoir. Elle a treslouablemant rangé ses formes externes a la hautur de sa nouvelle fortune mais la debonaireté & facilité des ses humeurs internes elle faict autant louable de ne les changer. . . .[32]

I would have wished, to be sure, that the individual profit of the soldiers in your army and the need to content them had not robbed you, especially in that principal city, of the fine recommendation of having treated your mutinous subjects, in the height of victory, with more solace than do their protectors; and that you had shown that they were yours, not by a passing and usurped claim, but by a paternal and truly royal affection. To conduct such affairs as those you have in hand it is necessary to use uncommon ways. Moreover, it has always been observed that where conquests, because of their greatness and difficulty, could not be thoroughly completed by arms and by force, they have been completed by clemency and magnificence, excellent lures to attract men, especially toward the just and legitimate side. If rigor and punishment occur, they must be put off until after the possession of mastery. A great conqueror of the past boasts that he has given his subjugated enemies as much occasion to love him as his friends. And here we already feel a somewhat promising effect from the impression received by the towns that have strayed from you when they compare their harsh treatement [by the League] with that of the towns that are obedient to you. Wishing Your Majesty, as I do, a more present and less hazardous felicity, and that you may be rather loved than feared by your people . . . I take it as a singular favor that you have deigned to make me feel that you take pleasure in seeing me, a person so useless, but yours even more by affection than by duty. Your Majesty has very laudably adapted your outward appearance to the height of your new fortune, but you act just as laudably in not changing the good nature and ease of your inward disposition . . . (1092–95)

Beneath his deference and courtly praise, Montaigne is offering his king both criticism and advice that reads like a quick précis of those ethical and political issues we have traced through the *Essais*. It is too bad, he says, that you did not restrain your troops from pillaging and committing atrocities against the Parisians, since it would have distinguished you as their rightful ruler rather than the various claimants to the crown thrown up by the League. In other words, Henri had better adapt a policy of clemency if he ever wants the Parisians to be lured to recognize his legitimacy. The argument for clemency is made in perfectly Machiavellian terms of realpolitik, only to overturn Machiavelli's conclusion that it is better to be feared than to be loved. If Montaigne begins by suggesting that leniency is uncommon, he immediately asserts that, to the contrary, it has *always* been the case that force alone cannot suffice to achieve a total conquest of a people and that clemency must play a part. Rigor and punishment may be necessary, but it is equally necessary to defer them until Henri has control of the situation (and then, perhaps Montaigne hopes, they will not be necessary after all).[33] He couples clemency with *magnificence*, a display of nobility and personal grandeur, much as he does in "De la diversion," where we saw him write of having swayed a young prince—presumably the same Henri—from revenge to clemency by appealing to the prince's ambition and pointing out to him the honor and favor—"l'honneur, la faveur" (835; 634)—his mildness would accrue to him. In the guise of a humanist advisor, Montaigne cites to Henri the same saying of Scipio the elder that he was contemporaneously adding into the C text of "De la vanité," a Scipio who, Montaigne writes there, was prouder of his "debonnaireté et humanité" than of his "hardiesse" and his victories (970; 741). Finally, in a gesture of gratitude for Henri's condescension to his own lowly self, Montaigne praises the king for retaining, even as he adapts his outward form—what we might call his physiognomy—to the greatness of his station, a similar kind of "debonnaireté & facilité," the good-naturedness and easygoingness of a Scipio, of Montaigne's ideal Epaminondas, above all, of Montaigne himself. Such courtly praise in the Renaissance is also an exhortation: Henri should live up to the accolade paid to him and remember his humanity. Montaigne puts the idea more colorfully in a C-text addition just before the end of the *Essais* in "De l'Experience": on the highest throne in the world, he notes, we are still only sitting on our ass—"Et au plus eslevé throne du monde si ne sommes assis que sus nostre cul" (1115; 857).

The letter is precious evidence that Montaigne practiced what he preached in the *Essais*: that is, he made the same ethical arguments to Henri IV that he made in his book. It shows us a Montaigne who did not hesitate to oppose and try to moderate his king's policies even as he declares himself the affectionate, as well as dutiful servant of Henri: an obedient Montaigne who nonetheless exercises his indiscreet "liberté" to say what he thinks. His resistance takes the form of persuasion rather than force, and we can see how the free-speaking *Essais* may be engaged in a similar task. The letter, in fact, indicates the direct political application and context of the moral thought of the *Essais*: this is an ethics designed to end France's civil strife. For Montaigne the knottier, perhaps ultimately intractable questions of justice—of rigor and punishment—will always have to wait for revenge and cruelty to stop, for the simple mutual recognition of adversaries as fellow human creatures, for the rebuilding of trust. He offers Henri two admonitions or "advertissements": an appeal for clemency and an appeal to Henri's good nature. These two teachings are inextricable and virtually identical: for, as we have seen the *Essais* argue, it is by holding to one's own good nature, a shared human nature, that a moral basis can be found both for the subject's submission and for the ruler's policy of clemency that together are Montaigne's most urgent goal. It is a morality fit alike for a king and for the reader of Montaigne's book.

NOTES

CHAPTER ONE
CLEMENCY AND REVENGE

1. Citations of Montaigne's text will be drawn from the edition of Pierre Villey, *Les Essais de Michel de Montaigne* (Paris: Presses Universitaires de la France, 1965); the English translations that follow are cited from Donald Frame, *The Complete Works of Montaigne* (Stanford, Cal.: Stanford University Press, 1957). The respective page references are given in parentheses. In some cases I have slightly altered Frame's translation in order to emphasize key words that are repeated from essay to essay.

2. A valuable discussion of the A-text version of "Par divers moyens" is found in Edwin Duval, "Le début des 'Essais' et la fin d'un livre," *Revue d'Histoire Littéraire de la France* 88, no. 5 (1988): 896–907; Duval argues for the integrity of the original 1580 essay and notes how the subsequent additions of 1588 and 1595 change the focus of the essay from the defeated to the conqueror. The tendency of critical discussions of the essay is to move away from the concrete issues of clemency and revenge, submission and defiance in the anecdotes to the larger, more abstract question of diversity announced in the title, to problems of writing, and to Montaigne's generally skeptical reflections on human judgment. Some useful readings are Marcel Gutwirth, "'By diverse means . . .'(I.1)," in *Montaigne: Essays in Reading*, ed. Gerard Defaux, *Yale French Studies* 64 (1984): 180–87; Steven Rendall, *Distinguo: Reading Montaigne Differently* (Oxford: Clarendon Press, 1992), pp. 15–21; Lawrence D. Kritzman, *Destruction/Découverte: Le fonctionnement de la rhétorique dans les "Essais" de Montaigne*, French Forum Monographs 21 (Lexington, Ky.: French Forum Publishers, 1980), pp. 21–33; Karlheinz Stierle, "L'Histoire comme exemple, l'exemple comme histoire: contribution à la pragmatique et à la poétique des textes narratifs," *Poétique* 10 (1972): 176–98; Robert D. Cottrell, "Croisement chiasmique dans le premier *Essai* de Montaigne," *Bulletin de la Société des Amis de Montaigne*, 6e série, 11–12 (1982): 65–71; Michael O'Loughlin, *The Garlands of Repose* (Chicago and London: University of Chicago Press, 1978), pp. 244–52; Frieda S. Brown, "'By Diverse Means We Arrive at the Same End': Gateway to the Essays," in *Approaches to Teaching Montaigne's "Essays*,"ed. Patrick Henry (New York: MLA, 1994), pp. 138–45. A more thematic reading that sees the "temptation of stoicism" first embraced and then rejected in the evolution of the essay from 1580 to the later editions of the *Essais* is offered by Gabriel-A. Pérouse, "Le seuil des *Essais*," in *Études Montaignistes en hommage à Pierre Michel*, ed. Claude Blum and François Moureau (Paris: Champion, 1984), pp. 215–21.

3. The question of Montaigne's class identification is taken up in Chapter 2. Some critical discussions of the subject are James J. Supple, *Arms versus Letters: The Military and Literary Ideals in the "Essais" of Montaigne* (Oxford: Clarendon Press,

1984); J. P. Boon, *Montaigne gentilhomme et essayiste* (Paris: Éditions Universitaires, 1971); Hugo Friedrich, *Montaigne* (1949, 1967; Eng. trans. Berkeley, Los Angeles, and Oxford: University of California Press, 1991), pp. 9–11; Arlette Jouanna, "Montaigne et la noblesse," in *Les écrivains et la politique dans le sud-ouest de la France autour des annés 1580* (Bordeaux: Presses Universitarires de Bordeaux III, 1982), pp. 113–23; Jacques de Feytaud, "Valet de trèfles ou l'Honneur des Armes," *Bulletin de la Société des Amis de Montaigne*, 6e série, 5–6 (1981): 43–72; 7–8 (1981): 11–37; 9–10 (1982): 7–26; David Posner, "Stoic Posturing and Noble Theatricality in the *Essais*," *Montaigne Studies* 4 (1992): 127–55.

4. One need only think of the opening of d'Aubigné's *Les Tragiques*, where the Huguenot poet, imitating the *Pharsalia* of Lucan, identifies himself with Caesar crossing the Rubicon in order to initiate civil war. Montaigne sides with Pompey as the defender not of republicanism but of the established political order of Rome—which, in terms of the analogy to France, would correspond to the traditional monarchy and Catholic religion. See the condemnation of Caesar's political innovation in "L'histoire de Spurina" (2:33); in "De la vanité" (3:9), Montaigne comments: "Or, j'ay attaqué cent querelles pour la deffence de Pompeius et pour la cause de Brutus" (996), and two pages earlier, "Entre Cesar et Pompeius je me fusse franchement declaré. Mais entre ces trois voleurs [i.e., the second triumvirate of Augustus, Antony, and Lepidus] qui vindrent depuis, ou il eust fallu se cacher, ou suvyre le vent" (994). See Eric MacPhail, *The Voyage to Rome in French Renaissance Literature*, Stanford French and Italian Studies 68 (Stanford, Cal.: Anma Libri, 1990), pp. 200–202.

5. Every example "limps"—"tout exemple cloche" (1070; 819)—Montaigne famously declares in "De l'experience." The skepticism that the *Essais* turn against the historical example has been most acutely analyzed by Timothy Hampton, *Writing from History: The Rhetoric of Exemplarity in Renaissance Literature* (Ithaca and London: Cornell University Press, 1990); see also John D. Lyons, *Exemplum: The Rhetoric of Example in Early Modern France and Italy* (Princeton: Princeton University Press, 1989); Stierle, "L'Histoire comme exemple." See also the remarks of George W. Pigman III, who relates Montaigne's skepticism toward the lessons of history to the "Ricordi" of Guicciardini, and who also reminds us that we cannot dispense with the example as a means both of cognition and deliberation, in "Limping Examples: Exemplarity, the New Historicism, and Psychoanalysis," in *Creative Imitation: New Essays on Renaissance Literature in Honor of Thomas M. Greene*, ed. David Quint et al. (Binghamton, N.Y.: Medieval and Renaissance Texts and Studies, 1992), pp. 281–95. The phrase "Historia ... magistra vitae" derives from Cicero, *De oratore* 2.9.36. For the tradition of humanist reflection on history and its teachings with which Montaigne appears to be engaged here, see Myron P. Gilmore, "The Renaissance Conception of the Lessons of History," in *Facets of the Renaissance*, ed. William H. Werkmeister (New York, Evanston, and London: Harper and Row, 1963), pp. 73–101; Beatrice Reynolds, "Shifting Currents in Historical Criticism," in *Renaissance Essays*, ed. Paul O. Kristeller and Philip P. Weiner (New York and Evanston: Harper and Row, 1968), pp. 115–36. Montaigne read, and both cites (2.19) and responds to (2.36) the *Methodus* of his contemporary Jean Bodin, a work that assesses and attempts to systematize the kinds

of lessons taught by the past; see Reynolds's translation, *Method for the Easy Comprehension of History* (1945; rpt. New York: W. W. Norton, 1969).

6. See Villey, *Les sources et l'évolution des "Essais" de Montaigne* (1907; Paris: Hachette, 1933), 2 vols., and his elegant and concise *Les Essais de Michel de Montaigne* (Paris: Nizet, 1932). Pérouse, "Le seuil des *Essais*," 216–17, suggests that the 1580 text of "Par divers moyens" still belongs to Montaigne's "Stoic" stage. For a restatement of Villey's thesis, see Kyriaki Christodoulou, "Montaigne et la vertu stoïque," in *Le parcours des "Essais": Montaigne 1588–1988*, ed. Marcel Tetel and G. Mallary Masters (Paris: Aux Amateurs des Livres, 1989), pp. 175–85.

7. Villey's view has been challenged by David Lewis Schaefer, who sees the *Essais* engaged in a polemic against Stoicism from their inception; see *The Political Philosophy of Montaigne* (Ithaca and London: Cornell University Press, 1990), esp. pp. 29–30, 201–26. Schaefer's book is among the most ambitious and problematic of recent studies of Montaigne and it requires separate comment. Schaefer is an often acute close reader of Montaigne's text and has many sensible and insightful things to say about it. In places his conclusions dovetail with mine and he has also come to similar readings of textual details and connections; I have tried to indicate where this is the case. Chapters 6–9, pp. 177–288, of Schaefer's study seem to me particularly rewarding.

Both Schaefer's approach and larger conclusions, however, need to be approached with considerable caution and critical distance.

In keeping with its methodological debt to Leo Strauss, Schaefer's study largely ignores the historical and topical context of Montaigne's thought. A more serious problem is Schaefer's argument, developed in the book's second half and also familiar from the writings of other Straussian adepts, that Montaigne is a kind of ironist/allegorist who disguises his true doctrine from the vulgar though not from the fit but few readers he counts on. The problems with this approach, among them the difficulty of criticizing it from the outside, are taken up in a good critique of Schaefer by John Christian Laursen in *The Politics of Skepticism in the Ancients, Montaigne, Hume, and Kant* (Leiden, New York, and Cologne: E. J. Brill, 1992), pp. 131–38. Beyond this overall scheme of Schaefer's study, some of its specific arguments are tendentious. Few reader will be persuaded by his further contention against Villey's magisterial study of the phases of Montaigne's thought and of his book's composition that "the changes of style and in the *Essays* were *a thoroughly planned rhetorical technique* adopted by Montaigne so as to have a maximal influence on his readers at minimal danger to himself" (p. 27). Schaefer flattens the differences between Montaigne's thought and that of Machiavelli, and his concluding argument bizarrely locates the modern telos of Montaigne's political thought in the trickle-down economics of Milton and Rose Friedman (393). Judith N. Shklar offers a more limited, but for that much more powerful description of how Montaigne stands at the beginning of the modern liberal tradition (and she carefully distinguishes his thought from the illiberal dimensions of Machiavelli's political theory) in *Ordinary Vices* (Cambridge, Mass., and London: Harvard University Press, 1984).

8. Fausta Garavini notes how the essay shifts back and forth from the perspectives of the victors and the vanquished in her *Monstres et chimères: Montaigne le texte et le fantasme* (Paris: Champion, 1993), pp. 241–45.

9. Montaigne discusses the relationship between the virtue of valor and virtue proper in essay 2:7, "Des récompenses d'honneur."

He notes the Latin etymology of "virtus" in Roman usage: "Car la generale appellation de vertu prend chez eux etymologie de la force." (384; 277). See I. D. McFarlane, "The Concept of Virtue in Montaigne," in *Montaigne: Essays in Memory of Richard Sayce*, ed. I. D. McFarlane and Ian Maclean (Oxford: Clarendon, 1982), pp. 77–100. Marianne Meijer has looked at Montaigne's ethical reclamation of a semantics of relaxation and softness by examining the scandalized reaction of Pascal; see "Mourir lâchement et mollement," in *Études Montaignistes en hommage à Pierre Michel*, pp. 173–82. See also Carol Clark, *The Web of Metaphor: Studies in the Imagery of Montaigne's "Essais,"* French Forum Monographs 7 (Lexington, Ky.: French Forum, 1978), pp. 90–97.

10. Gordon Braden suggests the opposite: that the Stoic sage becomes an inverted mirror image of the emperor; see his penetrating discussion in *Renaissance Tragedy and the Senecan Tradition: Anger's Privilege* (New Haven and London: Yale University Press, 1985), 5–27.

11. Citation from both Seneca's *De Clementia* and *De Constantia* are taken from Seneca, *Moral Essays*, trans. John W. Basore, Loeb Classical Library (Cambridge Mass.: Harvard University Press, 1985), Volume 1.

12. One can compare this aesthetic ploy of persuasion to the appealing image of virtue that Montaigne proposes that one paint for the young student in a C-text addition to "De l'institution des enfans" (1:26; 161–62; 119–20). On diversion, see Marianne S. Meijer, "The Significance of 'De la Diversion' in Montaigne's Third Book," *Romance Notes* 32 (1991): 11–17. On the range of tropes of persuasion in the *Essais* see Margaret M. McGowan, *Montaigne's Deceits: The Art of Persuasion in the "Essais"* (Philadelphia: Temple University Press, 1974).

13. I disagree here with the contention of Robert D. Cottrell in *Sexuality/Textuality: A Study of the Fabric of Montaigne's "Essais"* (Columbus, Ohio: Ohio State University Press, 1981), p. 18, that the citation of *De Clementia* in the B text is a kind of philosophical dressing placed on the earlier, less bookish version of "Par divers moyens." Cottrell may be correct about other instances of Montaigne's additions to his text, but this essay from its opening evocation of "constance" seems to have been conceived in Stoic terms.

14. On the opposition of "molle" and "forte" in "Par divers moyens" and their relationship to a rhetorical tradition that defined a masculine versus a feminine style, see Cottrell, "Croisement chiasmique," and more generally his *Sexuality/Textuality*. A more recent study that relates this stylistic opposition to Montaigne's reflections on sexuality and impotence in "Sur quelque vers de Virgile" (3:5) is Patricia Parker, "Gender Ideology, Gender Change: The Case of Marie Germain," *Critical Inquiry* 19 (1993): 337–64. "Mollesse" is also related to impotence by Yves Citton in a reading that places Montaigne confessions of weakness in the context of politics and class; see Citton, *Impuissances: Défaillances masculines et pouvoir politique de Montaigne à Stendhal* (Paris: Aubier, 1994), pp. 199–226.

15. Alexander is typically cast as a villain in Stoic writings. See Johannes Stroux, "Die stoische Beurteilung Alexanders des Grossen," *Philologus* 88 (1933): 222–40. Montaigne, who praises Alexander in the 1580 A text of the *Essais*, has turned against him by the 1588 B text; it is possible that he is using the Stoics' butt of

criticism against Stoicism itself by suggesting the similarity of Alexander to the Stoic. Perhaps, Braden suggests in *Renaissance Tragedy*, p. 18, there was once a similar identification within Stoicism itself. Braden follows the argument of M. H. Fisch, "Alexander and the Stoics," *American Journal of Philology* 58 (1937): 59–82, 129–51; Fisch, in a rejoinder to Stroux, p. 151, argues that Seneca expressed hostility to Alexander "with an eye to Nero's Alexander-complex." The example of Seneca's occasional praise of Alexander that Fisch cites, the anecdote of Alexander and Philippus in *De Ira* 2.23, turns up in a similarly approving moment in "Divers evenemens de mesme conseil," discussed below.

16. On the other hand, the following essay, "De la punition de la couardise" (1:16), coupled with "On est puny pour s'opiniastrer," tell of the execution and degradation of defenders who surrender too easily to besiegers. In the political and military world of the opening of the *Essais*, you are damned if you do, damned if you don't.

17. For a somewhat different construction of the opposition of enemies that haunts the early essays of Montaigne's book, see Thomas M. Greene's analysis of the scenes of negotiation between warring forces in "Si le chef d'une place assiégée doit sortir pour parlementer" and "L'heure des parlemens dangereuse" in "Dangerous Parleys—*Essais* 1:5 and 6," in *Montaigne: Essays in Reading*, pp. 3–23. These scenes ultimately turn for Greene into allegories of the writing of the *Essais*, Montaigne pitting his own voice against other writers and readers. On the same pair of essays, see Frieda S. Brown, "'Si le chef d'une place assiegée doit sortir pour parlementer' and 'L'heure des parlemens dangereuse': Montaigne's Political Morality and Its Expression in the Early Essays," in *Oh un amy!: Essays on Montaigne in Honor of Donald M. Frame*, ed. Raymond La Charité, French Forum Monographs 5 (Lexington, Ky.: French Forum, 1977), pp. 72–87.

18. Kahn, *Rhetoric, Prudence, and Skepticism in the Renaissance* (Ithaca and London: Cornell University Press, 1985), pp. 115–151.

19. My demonstration of the symmetrical relationship between the two essays is anticipated in the brief remarks of Gérald Nakam in *Montaigne: La manière et la matière* (Paris: Klinksieck, 1992), pp. 168–71.

20. Montaigne will return to a consideration of François de Guise's assassination in the B-text addition that formed the ending of the 1588 version of "De la vertu" (2:29; 711; 537–38). In that essay, he treats the assassin ironically as the highest embodiment of virtue, when virtue is defined in terms of sheer courage and constancy in the face of death. The C-text ending of the essay recalls the original Assassins of the Levant, who disdained all dangers and held that "the most certain way to deserve Paradise was to kill someone of a contrary religion"—"le plus certain moyen de meriter Paradis, c'est tuer quelqu'un de religion contraire" (710; 538). It is the murderousness of this "virtue," a mixture of fanaticism and steadfast valor, that the *Essais* repeatedly expose. The passage is an evident enough allusion to the assassinations that had been carried out in Montaigne's own France in the name of religion. Between the 1588 B text and Montaigne's death in 1592 as he was preparing the C text France had experienced two other great political assassinations: first the double assassination of the sons of François, Henri, duke of Guise, and Louis, cardinal of Lorraine, killed at the orders of Henri III at Blois in 1588, then of Henri himself in the following year. There is some retrospective irony,

moreover, in reading the counsel of clemency advocated in "Divers evenemens" in relationship to the similar counsel that Montaigne offered to the new King Henri IV in a letter of 1590, presumably the same young prince whom Montaigne diverts from revenge in "De la diversion." Henri was assassinated in 1610. The questions that Montaigne addresses in "Divers evenemens" had only acquired greater contemporary urgency as the course of his life and his book progressed.

21. Both the two-book installment of the *Essais* of 1580 and the three-book versions of 1588 and 1595 ended with essays that addressed the ailment of kidney stones that Montaigne had inherited from his father: "De la ressemblance des enfans aux peres" (2:37) and "De l'experience" (3:13). Both contain polemics against the failures of medicine. The relationship to Montaigne's essays about the uncertainty of political remedies is made clear in a passage from the 1580 text of "De la ressemblance" that disappeared after the lightly revised 1582 edition of the *Essais*. Speaking of doctors, Montaigne had originally written: "Or, ainsi, quand ils nous conseillent une chose plus tost qu'une autre, quand ils nous ordonnent les choses aperitives, commes sont les eaus chaudes, ou qu'ils nous les deffendent: ils le font d'une pareille incertitude, et *remettent sans doubte à la mercy de la fortune l'evenement de leur conseil*" (776; 589; my emphasis). For how Montaigne's discussion of his own health takes up metaphors of disease applied to the body-politic, see Gérald Nakam, *Les "Essais" de Montaigne miroir et procès de leur temps* (Paris: Nizet, 1984), pp. 272–310, 424–36; Carol E. Clark, "Montaigne and the Imagery of Political Discourse in Sixteenth-Century France," *French Studies* 24 (1970): 337–55 and *The Web of Metaphor*, 64–77. See also Jean Starobinski, *Montaigne in Motion*, trans. Arthur Goldhammer (1982; English trans. Chicago and London: University of Chicago Press, 1985), pp. 147–56.

22. See the various essays in *La catégorie de l'"honneste" dans la culture du XVIème siècle* (St. Etienne: Institute d'études de la Renaissance et de l'age classique, Université de Saint-Etienne, 1985); Marianne Meijer, "De l'honnête, de l'utile e du repentir," *Journal of Medieval and Renaissance Studies* 12 (1982): 259–74. Montaigne's key description of "honnêteté" is found in "De trois commerces" (3:3; 824; 625–26), where he describes the circle of friends with whom he enjoys conversation. It is an attribute that, he says, depends above all on nature, on having a soul that is "bien née": the ambiguity here, which suggests either noble birth or just having a good disposition (or both at once), is similar to what we will see Montaigne say about his own noble nature in "De la cruauté" (see Chapter 2 below): it still *looks* as if noble lineage is involved in making a man honorable and honest.

23. For a discussion of this passage, see Supple, *Arms versus Letters*, pp. 185–89. See also I. D. McFarlane, "The Concept of Virtue in Montaigne."

24. Gérald Nakam describes paintings made after 1561 that show the members of the ancient Roman Triumvirate enjoying the spectacle of the proscriptions they had ordered, paintings that had obvious polemical applications to the contemporary French situation. See Nakam, *Montaigne et son temps: Les événements et les "Essais"* (1982; Paris: Gallimard, 1993), pp. 128, 149.

25. The connection of this scene to the stories of Montaigne's escapes in "De la phisionomie" has been noted by other readers; see Nakam, *Montaigne: la manière et la matière*, 178–79; Jouanna, "Montaigne et la noblesse," p. 113. For

the biographical background of the anecdote at Bordeaux, see Donald Frame, *Montaigne: A Biography* (1965; San Francisco: North Point Press, 1984), pp. 237–40.

26. One should compare the B-text addition that Montaigne makes to the end of "Si le chef d'une place assiegée doit sortir pour parlementer" (1:5): "Je me fie ayseement à la foy d'autruy. Mais mal-aiseement le fairoy je lors que je donnerois à juger l'avoir plustost faict par desespoir et faute de coeur que par franchise et fiance de sa loyauté" (27).

27. This connection between the first and last essays of Montaigne's book has been noted by Schaefer, *Political Philosophy*, p. 232, in the context of a discussion of "De la cruauté," the subject of our next chapter. In this exceptionally rich passage, Schaefer also cites "On est puny pour s'opiniastrer a une place sans raison," and writes: "Pity being a passion that results from the painful perception of an undeserved evil befalling someone else which we might expect to befall ourselves, it follows that the greater people think themselves to be in comparison with others, the less prone they will be to experience pity or compassion for others's sufferings. Hence the Stoical understanding of virtue as a kind of self-conquest, by means of which the virtuous human being rivals or surpasses God, amounts—as the title of II, xi, suggests—to an education in cruelty. The archetype of people so convinced of their transcendent greatness that they display a cruelty unmitigated by compassion, for Montaigne, is Alexander the Great."

28. All citations from the letters of Seneca are taken from *Ad Lucilium Epistulae Morales*, trans. Richard M. Gummere, Loeb Classical Library (London: William Heinemann and New York: G. Putnam's Sons, 1925), 3 vols.

29. Hampton, *Writing from History*, pp. 138–39. See also Kyriaki Christodoulou, "Le portrait d'Epaminondas chez Montaigne et chez Pascal: Texte et intertexte," in *Le lecteur, l'auteur et l'écrivain: Montaigne 1492-1592-1992*, ed. Ilana Zinguer (Paris: Champion, 1993), pp. 121–36.

30. See Villey's headnote to "Des plus excellens hommes," p. 751. In *Les sources et evolution*, 1:111, Villey dates Montaigne's reading of Quintus Curtius to 1587.

31. Amyot, *Oeuvres morales et meslees de Plutarque* (Lyon: Estienne Michel, 1579), p. 807. In fact, Amyot has either mistranslated Plutarch or was in possession of a faulty Greek text: the passage reads: "It is true, in a battle one should avoid that enemy *who is skillful in handling his weapon*" (my emphasis); *Plutarch's Morals*, ed. William W. Goodwin (New York: The Athenaeum Society, 1905), 2: 396. *Vive la différence!*

32. The ancient testimony on Epaminondas is collected and assessed in Marcello Fortina, *Epaminonda* (Torino: Società Editrice Internazionale, 1958); on the mildness of the hero, see p. 7, n. 26.

33. One could complicate this scheme further by noting that Epaminondas also appears in the first and last essays of Montaigne's book, though not in their concluding passages in the way that Alexander does. In 1:1, he is seen before his judges in Thebes (8; 4), defying them by recounting his great deeds—and here he anticipates the Socrates of "De la physionomie" who similarly defies his Athenian judges. Several pages from the end of 3:13, he reappears, here explicitly linked to Socrates whose own example almost directly follows, as a man for all seasons who dances alongside the boys of Thebes with his tell-tale "facilité": "Le relachement et facilité

honore, ce semble, à merveilles et sied mieux à une ame forte et genereuse. Epaminondas n'estimoit pas que de se mesler à la dance des garçons de sa ville, [C] de chanter, de sonner [B] et s'y embesongner avec attention fut chose qui desrogeat à l'honneur des ses glorieuses victoires et à la parfaicte reformation de meurs qui estoit en luy." (1109; 851).

CHAPTER TWO
CRUELTY AND NOBLESSE

1. Montaigne's abhorrence of *physical* cruelty makes him the hero of Judith N. Shklar's august *Ordinary Vices*. Shklar argues that hatred of cruelty places Montaigne at the origins of the liberal tradition, and she opposes his position both to Machiavelli's notion of a limited "well-used cruelty" and to Nietzsche's elitist hatred of moral cruelty that ends in a Machiavellian admiration for brute physical power. See especially pp. 7–44; 212–25. I consider Shklar's reading indispensable, but I place Montaigne's discussions of cruelty more closely in their political and historical context, where "cruautez" was, in fact, a charge leveled by the belligerents of the Wars of Religion against one another; see for example the two treatises of 1589 listed by Robert O. Lindsay and John Neu in *French Political Pamphlets 1547–1648: A Catalog of Major Collections in American Libraries* (Madison, Milwaukee, and London: University of Wisconsin Press, 1969), p. 100: *Les cruautez commises contre les Catholiques de la ville de Vandosme, par le roy de Navarre* ... (Paris: R. Thieery, 1589); *Les cruautez sanguinaires, exercees envers feu monseigneur le cardinal de Guise, pair de France & archevesque de Reims ... Avec le remonstrance faicte au roy par madame la duchesse de Nemours, sur le massacre de ses enfans* (1589). I also suggest how they fit into an overarching argument of Montaigne's book and its corollary topics: the drawbacks of Stoic virtue, the nature of true nobility, above all the twin political imperatives of submission and clemency.

2. Nakam, *Les "Essais" de Montaigne*, p. 438, notes that the two essays on cruelty in Book 2 are arranged symmetrically with relationship to the central essay of the book, "De la liberté de conscience" (2.19), and its figure of Julian the Apostate who, for all his irreligion, nonetheless detested cruelty.

3. For the role of the nobility in the civil wars, see Arlette Jouanna, *Le devoir de revolte: La noblesse française et la gestation de l'État moderne (1559–1661)* (Paris: Fayard, 1989); J.H.M. Salmon, *Society in Crisis: France in the Sixteenth Century* (New York: St. Martin's Press, 1975); Mack Holt, *The French Wars of Religion, 1562–1629* (Cambridge: Cambridge University Press, 1995).

4. Nakam admits that she is simplifyng when she presents this scenario in *Montaigne et son temps*, p. 168: "A travers le conflit de deux christianismes, dans lequel la passion religieuse ne fait souvent qu'habiller ou attiser l'ambition du pouvoir, les guerres civiles sont la manifestation d'un regain de l'esprit féodal exacerbé devant une monarchie divisée et faible. Ce sont des guerres féodale triangulaires: le heurt des clans rivaux entre eux, leur lutte pour dominer ou amoindrir le pouvoir monarchique, et les ripostes de ce dernier pour mater, circonvenir ou éliminer à tour de rôle ses trop puissants ennemis et partenaires féodaux." This social interpretation of the Wars of Religion goes back to early in this century; see the 1917 essay of Lucien Romier, translated and reprinted as "A Dissident Nobility Under the Cloak of Religion," in J.H.M. Salmon, ed., *The French Wars of Religion: How Important*

Were Religious Factors? (Boston: D. C. Heath, 1967), pp. 24–29. A recent turn in the historical literature has newly emphasized the importance of religion in the struggles. Mack P. Holt discusses this development in a review essay, "Putting Religion Back into the Wars of Religion," *French Historical Studies* 18, no. 2 (1993): 514–51; Holt argues for a Durkheimian understanding of religion as culture, a collection not of doctrines but of believers. Denis Crouzet has insisted upon the pious motivation of the combatants, particularly on their apocalyptic expectations, on Huguenot and especially Catholic sides, in his monumental examination of the mentality of religious psychosis (this might not, however, be his own description of his study), *Les guerriers de Dieu: La violence au temps des troubles de religion* (Paris: Champ Vallon, 1990), 2 vols. At least one intelligent contemporary observer, Montaigne, saw, or claimed to see, matters otherwise. The vocabulary of feudal duties used to justify aristocratic ambition and revolt was already in place in the fifteenth century; see P. S. Lewis, *Later Medieval France: The Polity* (London: Macmillan; and New York: St. Martin's Press, 1968), pp. 94–101, 226–37.

5. Neuschel, *Word of Honor: Interpreting Noble Culture in Sixteenth-Century France* (Ithaca and London: Cornell University Press, 1989), p. 18.

6. Significant critical discussions of "De la cruauté" are found in Philip P. Hallie, "The Ethics of Montaigne's 'De la cruauté,'" in Charité, ed., *Oh un amy!*, pp. 156–71; Hampton, *Writing from History*, pp. 159–71; Starobinski, *Montaigne in Motion*, pp. 132–36; Schaefer, *The Political Philosophy*, pp. 227–50. Donald Stone, Jr., discusses some of Montaigne's revisions of the essay in "Montaigne Reads Montaigne (II, 11)," *Modern Language Review* 80 (1985): 802–9. See also the remarks of Arthur Kirsch on forgiveness in *The Tempest* in "Montaigne and *The Tempest*," in *Cultural Exchange between European Nations during the Renaissance*, ed. Gunnar Sorelius and Michael Srigley, *Acta Universitatis Upsaliensis: Studia Anglistica Upsaliensis* 86 (Uppsala: Uppsala University, 1994), pp. 111–21.

7. The relative sublimity of the poets and of their treatments of Cato is discussed by J. L. Logan, "Montaigne et Longin: Une nouvelle hypothèse," *Revue d'Histoire Littéraire de la France* 83 (1983): 355–70.

8. On the staginess of Stoicism, the need for the sage to act as if an external audience were watching him, see the remarks of Braden, *Renaissance Tragedy*, pp. 25–27; Hampton, *Writing from History*, pp. 161–66, discusses the way that Montaigne's Cato is a kind of "stage-manager" of his suicide, at once actor and audience.

9. On Montaigne's refusal of a classical model of virtue that involves self-division, see Hallie, "The Ethics," and an essay that acknowledges its debt to Hallie, Donald M. Frame, "Montaigne's Rejection of Inner Conflict and His Chapter 'De la Cruauté' (II:11)," *Melanges sur la littérature de la Renaissance* (Geneva: Droz, 1984): 481–89. See also I. D. McFarlane, "The Concept of Virtue in Montaigne." On Montaigne's "innocence," see Starobinski, *Montaigne in Motion*, 133–36.

10. Montaigne's attitude here, I think, must qualify Shklar's view in *Ordinary Vices*, pp. 13–14, that the essayist idealized and "came to overrate" the animal world.

11. Starobinski argues along somewhat similar lines in *Montaigne in Motion*, pp. 135–36.

12. Versions of this debate contemporary with Montaigne are discussed by Arlette Jouanna, *L'idée de race en France au XVIe siècle et au début du XVIIe*, Édition

revue (Montpellier: Presses de l'imprimerie de Recherche Université Paul Valéry, 1981), 2 vols.; and by Ellery Schalk, *From Valor to Pedigree: Ideas of Nobility in France in the Sixteenth and Seventeenth Centuries* (Princeton: Princeton University Press, 1986). See also Davis Bitton, *The French Nobility in Crisis, 1560–1640* (Stanford, Cal.: Stanford University Press, 1969), pp. 77–91. The humanist contribution to the debate that Jouanna discusses in pp. 601–28 already had a long tradition; see the texts gathered and translated by Albert Rabil, Jr., in *Knowledge, Goodness, and Power: The Debate over Nobility among Quattrocento Italian Humanists* (Binghamton, N.Y.: Medieval and Renaissance Texts and Studies, 1991).

13. On noble nature and nurture, see Jouanna, *L'idée de race*, pp. 51–70.

14. Braden, *Renaissance Tragedy*, pp. 80–83. Forcione, in a powerful discussion of the concept of nature in humanist thought in relationship to *La gitanilla* of Cervantes, places less emphasis on the aristocratic dimension of "good birth"; the outcome of the tale—and our retrospective understanding of how Preciosa has proved virtuous in her gypsy environment—hinge, however, on the discovery of her noble lineage. See *Cervantes and the Humanist Vision: A Study of Four "Exemplary Novels"* (Princeton: Princeton University Press, 1982), pp. 157–92.

15. Rabelais, *Gargantua*, ed. Ruth Calder and Michael Screech (Geneva: Droz and Paris: Minard, 1970), pp. 302–3.

16. Whigham, *Ambition and Privilege: The Social Tropes of Elizabethan Courtesy Theory* (Berkeley, Los Angeles, and London: University of California Press, 1984), p. 33.

17. On *sprezzatura* and Montaigne's style, see the rich essay of Antoine Compagnon, "A Long Short Story: Montaigne's Brevity," in *Montaigne: Essays in Reading*, 24–50, p. 39.

18. Supple, *Arms versus Letters*, pp. 27–44, carefully considers the scathing remarks of Brantôme and Joseph Scaliger; see also Friedrich, *Montaigne*, pp. 9–11. This passage in "De la cruauté" is closely paralleled by a B-text addition to "De mesnager sa volonté" (3:10): "Ma fortune le veut ainsi. Je suis nay d'une famille qui a coulé sans esclat et sans tumulte, e de longue memoire particulierement ambitieuse de preud'hommie" (1021; 782). See also Margaret McGowan, "Montaigne: A Social Role for the Nobleman?" in *Montaigne and His Age*, ed. Keith Cameron (Exeter: University of Exeter Press, 1981), pp. 87–96.

19. For the conflict between sword and robe ideas of nobility and attempts to bridge it, see Jouanna, *L'idée de race*, pp. 323–574. Jonathan Dewald has stressed the integration among nobles of sword and robe in the sixteenth and seventeenth centuries in *Aristocratic Experience and the Origins of Modern Culture: France, 1570–1715* (Berkeley, Los Angeles, and Oxford: University of California Press, 1993), and *The Formation of a Provincial Nobility: The Magistrates of Rouen, 1499–1610* (Princeton: Princeton University Press, 1980). See also Donna Bohanan, "The Sword as the Robe in Seventeenth Century Provence and Brittany," in *Society and Institutions in Early Modern France*, ed. Mack P. Holt (Athens, Ga., and London: University of Georgia Press, 1991), pp. 51–62. That there was, nonetheless, a distinctive robe culture and outlook is the thesis of George Huppert in *Les Bourgeois Gentilshommes* (Chicago and London: University of Chicago Press, 1977); see also the study of the Séguier family of Parisian high magistrats by Denis Richet in *De la Réforme à la Révolution: Études sur la France moderne* (Paris: Aubier, 1991).

The question of Montaigne's class sympathies is the subject of Supple, *Arms versus Letters.* Supple's valuable study judiciously weighs the evidence of the *Essais* and notes how Montaigne qualifies his admiration for military valor; his conclusions, however, present a Montaigne more wedded to the ethos of the sword nobility than the one for which I argue here. His study plays down Montaigne's robe experience as magistrate and mayor and, perhaps along the same lines, treats "Letters" as mere learning or literary attainment; to be fair, Montaigne, in keeping with his snobbish pose, consistently depreciates learning to professional ends as beneath a nobleman's dignity. The debate betwen arms and letters of Supple's title often, in fact, encoded a class divide between the military nobility and the new legal and bureaucratic class that aspired to noble status: see the debate between arms and letters in the seventh day of Annibale Romei's influential *Discorsi* (1585), where the speaker for letters is not a poet but the lawyer Cati.

20. Cervantes, *Don Quixote*, trans. Walter Starkie (New York and Scarborough, Ontario: The New American Library, 1964), pp. 776–77.

21. Erasmus, *The Praise of Folly*, trans. Hoyt Hopewell Hudson (Princeton: Princeton University Press, 1941), p. 54.

22. See Margaret Mann Phillips, *Erasmus on His Times* (Cambridge: Cambridge University Press, 1967), pp. 113–16. This passage is linked to the condemnation of hunting in *The Praise of Folly* by Robert M. Adams, *The Better Part of Valor: More, Erasmus, Colet, and Vives on Humanism* (Seattle: University of Washington Press, 1962), pp. 43–54.

23. More, *Utopia*, ed. Edward Surtz, S.J., and J. H. Hexter, *The Complete Works of St. Thomas More* 4 (New Haven and London, Yale University Press, 1965), p. 171. Another satirical view that equates hunters with butchers can be found in a text more contemporary (1584) with the *Essais*; see Giordano Bruno, *Spaccio de la bestia trionfante*, ed. Michele Ciliberto (Milan: Biblioteca Universale Rizzoli, 1988), pp. 293–94.

24. *Don Quixote, loc. cit.* I have altered Starkie's translation.

25. Hampton, *Writing from History*, p. 170, writes: "In a discussion of the hunt—an epic locus for the demonstration of heroic action—Montaigne simply switches sides, allying himself with the victim instead of the hunter." Montaigne may also be recalling Ovid's story of Actaeon, the hunter who is changed into the hunted and vainly supplicates his pursuers. See *Metamorphoses*, 3.240–41.

26. R. A. Sayce, in *The Essays of Montaigne: A Critical Exploration* (London: Weidenfeld and Nicolson, 1972), pp. 239–40, takes a similar line of argument when he makes Montaigne out to be a proto-bourgeois: "he criticizes the members of the nobility who surround him and their semi-barbarous immersion in war and hunting. The self-portrait may be the first major expression in European literature of the individualism which has been associated with the middle class." It seems less anachronistic to see Montaigne as retaining the values of the robe even as he presents himself, certainly as a rhetorical ploy, probably also out of personal snobbery, as a member of the sword nobility.

27. Hallie, "The Ethics," p. 171.

28. For remarks on "Couardise mere de la cruauté," see Géralde Nakam, "Les temps en miroir ou les dialogues du passé et du présent," in *Montaigne et l'histoire*, ed. Claude-Gilbert Dubois (Paris: Klincksieck, 1991), pp. 39–52, pp. 43–47; Shklar, *Ordinary Vices*, pp. 212–14.

29. Our knowledge of the opinion of the papal censor comes from Montaigne's

travel journal; see the splendid recent edition of François Rigolot of the *Journal de Voyage de Michel de Montaigne* (Paris: Presses Universitaires de France, 1992), p. 119; Frame, *The Complete Works*, p. 955. For a further discussion that appears to see the papal censor as the equivalent of a friendly modern editor, see Malcolm Smith, *Montaigne and the Roman Censors* (Geneva: Droz, 1981), pp. 75–86.

30. For a later Renaissance expression of the same ideas, see the chorus that ends Act 4 of Elizabeth's Cary's *The Tragedy of Mariam*. Cary is, I suspect, indebted both to Montaigne and to Seneca's *De Clementia*:

> The fairest action of our human life
> Is scorning to revenge an injury:
> For who forgives without a further strife,
> His adversary's heart to him doth tie.
>   And 'tis a firmer conquest truly said,
>   To win the heart than overthrow the head.
>
> If we a worthy enemy do find,
> To yield to worth, it must be nobly done:
> But if of baser metal be his mind,
> In base revenge there is no honour won.
>   Who would a worthy courage overthrow,
>   And who would wrestle with a worthless foe?
>
> We say our hearts are great and cannot yield;
> Because they cannot yield it proves them poor:
> Great hearts are task'd beyond their power but seld,
> The weakest lion will the loudest roar.
>   Truth's school for certain doth this same allow,
>   High-heartedness doth sometimes teach to bow.
>
> A noble heart doth teach a virtuous scorn:
> To scorn to owe a duty overlong,
> To scorn to be for benefits forborne,
> To scorn to lie, to scorn to do a wrong,
>   To scorn to bear an injury in mind,
>   To scorn a freeborn heart slavelike to bind.
>
> But if for wrongs we needs revenge must have,
> Then be our vengeance of the noblest kind:
> Do we his body from our fury save,
> And let our hate prevail against our mind?
>   What can 'gainst him a greater vengeance be,
>   Than make his foe more worthy far than he?

The virtuous scorn of Cary's noble protagonist is a kind of aristocratic/Stoic *sprezzatura*; one cannot be bothered or let one's tranquil mind be bothered with blood vendetta. The vengeance of the true noble—"vengeance of the noblest kind" with a quibble on kind—desists from killing and even from continuing to hold a grudge. To be truly noble—and this is Montaigne's central argument as well—is to learn to yield. Unfortunately, the chorus goes on to comment, Mariam, the play's titular heroine, could not control her desire for revenge. See *The Tragedy of Mariam, the Fair Queen of Jewry*, ed. Barry Weller and Margaret W. Ferguson (Berkeley and Los Angeles: University of California Press, 1994), pp. 137–39, and p. 37 of the editors' Introduction.

31. Supple, *Arms versus Letters*, p. 37.

32. On the duel, see François Billacois, *The Duel: Its Rise and Fall in Early Modern France*, trans. Trista Selous (1986; English trans. New Haven and London: Yale University press, 1990); Billacois discusses the use of seconds that Montaigne's essay decries on pp. 65–66. For the Italian treatises on dueling that circulated through sixteenth-century Europe, see Francesco Erspamer, *La biblioteca di Don Ferrante: Duello e onore nella cultura del Cinquecento* (Rome: Bulzoni, 1982); Frederic R. Bryson, *The Sixteenth-Century Italian Duel* (Chicago: The University of Chicago Press, 1938), and *The Point of Honor in Sixteenth-Century Italy* (New York: Columbia University Press, 1935). For the larger history of the duel, see V. G. Kiernan, *The Duel in European History* (Oxford: Oxford University Press, 1988). On the relationship of the duel and the vendetta, see Edward Muir, *Mad Blood Stirring: Vendetta & Factions in Friuli during the Renaissance* (Baltimore and London: The Johns Hopkins University Press, 1993), pp. 247–72.

33. Stone, *The Crisis of the Aristocracy 1558–1641* (1965; abridged second edition London, Oxford, and New York: Oxford University Press, 1967), p. 97; on dueling, see pp. 118–21.

34. Bertrand de Loque answers a would-be duelist who asks why else should he carry a sword by his side in *Deux traitez, l'un de la guerre, l'autre du duel* (Lyons, 1588), p. 93: "Dequoy donc (dis-tu) me sert l'espee à mon costé? Tu la portes en quelque temps que ce soit ou de paix ou de guerre, non point pour te venger toy-mesmes: Car tu n'es point Magistrat: ains pour aider au Magistrat à bien regir le païs, à repousser l'ennemy, à brider ses courses, à empescher le fourragement & degast de la campagne, à chasser tous vices & meschancetez bien loing de la patrie, en somme à maintenir & defendre la Pieté, la Iustice, la Loy, la Republique."

35. Girolamo Muzio, *Il Duello* (Venice: Gabriel Giolito, 1550), p. 93 verso, writes that the injured party on such occasions is not dishonored, even if he seeks redress in the duel; rather the traitor or bully who uses "soperchiaria" has dishonored himself. "Che qual riputeremo noi, che piu honorato, e piu svergognato debba rimanere, o quel cavaliero, il quale a tradimento sara stato offeso? o quell'altro il quale haveva il mancamento commesso? Et quello, che detto ho del tradimento, dico ancora della soperchiaria, del ferire altrui di dietro, et de gli altri tristi modi di oltraggiare altrui."

36. Pierre de Brantôme, the contemporary who scorned Montaigne's pretensions to soldiery, devotes a section of his *Discours sur les duels* to the "courtoisies" shown by combatants to one another. See Brantôme, *Oeuvres complètes* (Paris: Foucault, 1823), 6:99–119. He notes, p. 119, that the proper formula to spare one's adversary is not "Rends-toy, ou je te tueray; demandes-moy la vie, ou je t'acheveray," but rather "Je te donne la vie par courtoisie et gentillesse." He also agrees with Montaigne, p. 112, that clement courtesy is the duelist's duty and that it adds to his glory: "En ces combat hastifs et precipitez, et qui donnent du premier coup la mort, il ne faut parler de la vie: mais, quand on respire encore, il faut estre courtois sur le vaincu; la gloire en est très-belle et pie."

37. Neuschel, *Word of Honor*, p. 76 and, more broadly, pp. 69–102.

38. Schaefer, *The Political Philosophy*, p. 269, argues that the passage "suggests a naturalistic explanation of Christ's resurrection."

CHAPTER THREE
THE CULTURE THAT CANNOT PARDON

1. The issue of pardoning may be prompted by a passage in one of Montaigne's principal "cosmographic" sources, the *Histoire d'un voyage faict en la terre du Brésil* (1578) by the Protestant Jean de Léry, who describes the unrelenting nature of the cannibals' hatred and draws—as Montaigne will—an analogy to the civil wars in France, with a particular accusation against the French disciples of Machiavelli—that is, the Florentine Catherine de' Medici and her Catholic party: "De plus, sitôt que la guerre est une fois déclarée entre quelques-unes de ces nations, tous allèguent que, puisque l'ennemi qui a reçu l'injure s'en ressentira à jamais, c'est agir trop lâchement que de le laisser échapper quand on le tient à sa merci: leurs haines sont donc tellement invétérées qu'ils demeurent perpétuellement irréconciliables. A ce propos on peut dire que Machiavel et ses disciples (dont la France pour son malheur est maintenant remplie) sont les vrais imitateurs des cruautés barbaresques: car ces athées, contrairement à la doctrine chrétienne, enseignent et pratiquent aussi que les nouveaux services ne doivent jamais faire oublier les vieilles injures: *c'est-à-dire que les hommes, tenant du naturel du diable, ne se doivent point pardonner les uns aux autres.*" (My emphasis.) I quote from the modern edition of M.-R. Mayeux, *Journal de bord de Jean de Léry en la terre du Brésil 1557* (Paris: Editions de Paris, 1957), p. 296.

2. Schaefer, *The Political Philosophy*, p. 187, notes that the cannibals' lack of a word for pardon is a sign of their cruelty. See also his remarks, p. 217, on the cannibals and martial valor.

3. Important critical discussions of "Des cannibales" are found in Edwin M. Duval, "Lessons of the New World: Design and Meaning in Montaigne's 'Des Cannibales' (I:31) and 'Des coches' (III:6)," in *Montaigne: Essays in Reading*, pp. 95–112, where Duval demonstrates the reversals the essay effects on such key terms as art, nature, simplicity, barbarism; in Frank Lestringant's many studies of the essay, notably in his books *L'Huguenot et le sauvage: L'Amérique et la controverse coloniale en France, au temps des Guerres de Religion (1555–1589)* (Paris: Aux Amateurs de Livres, 1990), pp. 133–48, and *Le cannibale: Grandeur et décadence* (Paris: Perrin, 1994): Lestringant places "Des cannibales" within larger sixteenth-century thought and ethnographic writing about the New World; and in Claude Rawson, "'Indians' and Irish: Montaigne, Swift, and the Cannibal Question," *Modern Language Quarterly* 53 (1992): 299–363. See also Guy Mermier, "L'Essai *Des Cannibales* de Montaigne," *Bulletin de la Société des Amis de Montaigne* 7 (1973): 27–38; Caroline Locher, "Primary and Secondary Themes in Montaigne's 'Des Cannibales' (I:31)," *French Forum* 1 (1976): 119–26; Steven Rendall, "Dialectical Structure and Tactics in Montaigne's 'Of Cannibals,'" *Pacific Coast Philology* 12 (1977): 56–63; O'Loughlin, *The Garlands of Repose*, pp. 257–68; Kritzman, *Destruction/Découverte*, 79–87; and the essays on "Des cannibales" and "Des coches" collected in *Montaigne et le nouveau monde*, ed. Claude Blum,

Marie-Luce Demonet, and André Tournon (Mont de Marsan: Éditions InterUniversitaires, 1994) (= *Bulletin de la Société des Amis de Montaigne* 7e série, nos. 29-32 [1992-93].)

4. "Icy on vit de chair humaine; là c'est office de pieté de tuer son pere en certain aage . . ." (114; 82); "Darius demandoit à quelques Grecs pour combien ils voudroient prendre la coustume des Indes, de manger leurs peres trespassez (car c'estoit leur forme, estimans ne leur pouvoir donner plus favorable sepulture, que dans eux-mesmes), ils luy repondirent que pour chose du monde ils ne le feroient; mais, s'estant aussi essayé de persuader aux Indiens de laisser leur façon et prendre celle de Grece, qui estoit de brusler les corps de leurs peres, il leur fit encore plus d'horreur. Chacun en fait ainsi, d'autant que l'usage nous desrobbe le vray visage des choses . . ." (116; 84). On "De la coustume," se Ullrich Langer, "Montaigne's Customs," *Montaigne Studies* 4 (1992): 81-96. For the larger question of Montaigne's relativism, see Zachary Schiffman, *On the Threshold of Modernity: Relativism in the French Renaissance* (Baltimore and London: The Johns Hopkins University Press, 1991), pp. 53-77.

5. For suggestive remarks on the class-inflected role of the servant in the essay, see Stephen Greenblatt, *Marvelous Posessions* (Chicago: University of Chicago Press, 1991), pp. 146-50.

6. Defaux, "Un cannibale en haut de chausses: Montaigne, la différence et la logique de l'identité," *MLN* 97 (1982): 919-57. For Defaux's discussion of the rhetoric of the Golden Age, see pp. 951-56.

7. Post-structuralist anthropology seems to agree with Defaux and has emphasized a "linguistic turn" toward self-consciousness. It has targeted for examination the ethnographer's own discursive practice and cultural makeup as much as— sometimes to the point of replacing as focus of interest—the culture that is his or her declared object of study. See for example the essays collected by James Clifford and George E. Marcus in *Writing Culture* (Berkeley, Los Angeles, and London: University of California Press, 1986); James Boon, *Other Tribes, Other Scribes* (Cambridge: Cambridge University Press, 1982); Karl-Heinz Kohl, *Exotik als Beruf* (1979; 2nd ed. Frankfurt and New York: Campus Verlag, 1986).

8. Montaigne does attack European—that is, Spanish—colonialism in the New World in "Des Coches," where the Amerindians are depicted suffering the cruelties inflicted upon them by the conquistadors, and here he may indulge, as Shklar argues in *Ordinary Vices*, pp. 15-19, in idealizing them as victims as a way of escaping misanthropy. But these victims of foreign conquest should not, I think, be confused with the cannibals and their internecine wars.

9. For episodes of real cannibalism and of the role of cannibalism in the polemical rhetoric of the struggle between French Catholics and Protestants, see Lestringant, *Le cannibale*, pp. 124-42, and his "Le Cannibale et ses paradoxes: Images du cannibalisme au temps des Guerres de Religion," *Mentalities/Mentalités* 1 (1983): 4-19.

10. In his *Cosmographie Universelle* (Paris, 1575), Book 21, Chapter 15, p. 945, André Thevet writes of his conversation with the cannibals' captives: "Que si je leur parlois de les delivrer, et racheter, des mains de leurs ennemis, ils prenoient tout en mocquerie, me faisans la mouë, disoient que nous *Aiouroiou* (ainsi nous nomment ils, combien que ce soit un nom d'une espece de gros Perroquets), n'es-

tions point hommes de coeur: . . ." See the modern edition of Thevet's text in *Les Français en Amérique pendant la deuxième moitié du XVIe siècle: Le Brésil et les Brésiliens par André Thevet*, ed. Suzanne Lussagnet (Paris: Presses Universitaires de France, 1958), p. 198.

11. On Montaigne's care to identify the cannibalism of the Brazilians as a ritual of revenge rather than as a necessary dietary supplement, see the two-part article of Frank Lestringant, "Le canibalisme des 'cannibales,'" *Bulletin de la Societé des Amis de Montaigne* 6 ser. 9–10 (1982): 27–40; and 11–12 (1982): 19–38. See also Lestringant, *Le cannibale*, pp. 193-248.

12. Compare *Republic* 461d. See also Léry, *Journal*, ed. Mayeux, p. 348.

13. The influence of Girard's thought on my reading of Montaigne's essay will be obvious. See *La Violence et le sacré* (Paris: Grasset, 1972).

14. André Thevet, *Les Singularitez de la France antarctique . . .* (Antwerp, 1558), 74v. Compare another version of this song in the *Cosmographie Universelle*, p. 945 (*Les Français en Amérique*, p. 198): "Nos amis les Margageaz sont gens de biens, fortz et puissants en guerre: ils ont prins et mangé plusieurs de voz parents noz ennemis, et de ceux qui me tiennent pour me faire mourir: mais ils vengeront bient tost ma mort, et vous mangeront quand il leur plaira, et voz enfans aussi: quant à moy j'ay tué et mangé plusieurs amis de ce malin Aignan, qui me tient prisonnier. Je suis fort, je suis puissant: c'est moy qui ay mis en route plusieurs fois vous autres coüards, qui n'entendez rien à faire guerre, et plusieurs autres parolles disent-ils, qui monstre le peu de compte qu'ils ont de la mort, et que la crainte d'icelle ne peut en rien esbranler leur plus que brutale asseurance." Compare as well analogous words of defiance by a cannibal captive in Léry, *Journal*, ed. Mayeux, p. 311: "avec une audace et une assurance incroyables, il se vantera de ses prouesses passées, et dira à ceux qui le tiennent lié: 'Le premier j'ai moi-même, vaillant que je suis, lié ainsi et garotté vos parents.' Puis, s'exaltant toujours de plus en plus, avec la contenance de même, il se tournera de côté et d'autre, et dira à l'un: 'J'ai mangé ton père', à l'autre: 'J'ai assommé et boucané tes frères'; 'Bref,' ajoutera-t-il, 'j'ai en général tant mangé d'hommes et de femmes, voire des enfants, de vous autres *Toüoupinambaoults*, pris en guerre, que je ne saurais en dire le nombre. Et au reste ne doutez pas que pour venger ma mort, les *Margaias* de la nation d'où je suis n'en mangent encore plus tard autant qu'ils en pourront attraper.'" Léry's passage may be slightly closer to Montaigne's text, but it is in Thevet that the cannibal's defiance takes the form of a song. There is, however, no notion in these texts that the cannibal invites his enemies to eat the flesh of their own relatives.

15. The peasant insurrections that had accompanied the Wars of Religion since 1561 culminated in widespread rural uprisings in the final phase of the conflict in the early 1590s. See Salmon, *Society in Crisis*, pp. 276–91.

16. de Certeau, *Heterologies: Discourse on the Other*, trans. Brian Massumi (Minneapolis: University of Minnesota Press, 1986), p. 77.

17. Castiglione's *Book of the Courtier* itself links fencing to the courtier's art: see the crucial passage in Book 2, section 40. For an Elizabethan attack on Italian fencing and the rapier and a defense of the old English short sword, see George Silver, *Paradoxes of Defense* (London, 1599), collected and reprinted in *Three Elizabethan Fencing Manuals*, ed. James L. Jackson (Delmar, N.Y.: Scholars' Facsimiles and Reprints, 1972).

18. Supple, *Arms versus Letters*, pp. 195–97, attempts to account for Montaigne's admiration of the cannibals' warfare, which he does not find ironic even though he acknowledges, p. 195, that it is "none the less surprising coming as it does in the midst of a description of men who tie their prisoners up and then hack them to pieces." He links, p. 196, the cannibals to the Roman gladiators of "Des mauvais moyens."

19. On aristocratic competition see Dewald, *Aristocratic Experience*, pp. 15–44, especially pp. 43–44; Neuschel, *Word of Honor*, pp. 101–2; Norbert Elias, *The Court Society*, trans. Edmund Jephcott (1969; English trans. New York: Pantheon Books, 1983), pp. 100–104, 207–8; Mark Motley, *Becoming a French Aristocrat: The Education of the Court Nobility: 1580–1715* (Princeton: Princeton University Press, 1990), pp. 192–208.

20. I cite *Les Tragiques* from Agrippa d'Aubigné, *Oeuvres*, ed. Henri Weber (Paris: Gallimard, 1969). The "constance" of the Huguenot martyrs is attested to over and over again by Jean Crespin in his *Histoire des Martyrs* (1619). Good examples are two victims executed at Tours in 1562, the sieur Moreau and a townswoman la Glee; see the *Histoire des Martyrs*, ed. Daniel Benoit (Toulouse: Société des Livres Religieux, 1880), 3:318–19.

21. In his *Discours des misères de ce temps* (1562), Ronsard describes, vv. 121f., the mythological birth of Opinion, who is responsible for France's present troubles. Ronsard, *Oeuvres complètes*, vol. 11, ed. Paul Laumonier, Société des Textes Français Modernes (Paris: Marcel Didier, 1973), pp. 25f. "Nouvelle opinion" is a derogatory term, like "pretendue Religion reformée," that runs through Catholic pamphlet literature of the Wars of Religion to describe Protestantism, and it appears in official documents. The terms are paired together in a 1569 edict of the Parlement of Paris, item 651 in the great collection of French political pamphlets gathered and microfilmed by Robert O. Lindsay and John Neu, which declares that all royal offices are to be filled by Catholics "en lieu de ceux qui se trouveront chargez de la nouvelle opinion ou pretendue Religion." See the titles of items 658, 686, 730, 745–46, 920, 1141, and 1144 listed in Lindsay and Neu, *French Poltical Pamphlets*.

22. I am grateful to John Christian Laursen for this formulation.

23. Rawson, "'Indians' and Irish," pp. 318–30; for other comments on the connection between the ending of "De la moderation" and "Des cannibales," see McGowan, *Montaigne's Deceits*, p. 116; Schaefer, *The Political Philosophy*, p. 187.

24. It may be significant that the essay that follows "Des cannibales" is "Qu'il faut *sobrement* se mesler de juger des ordonnances divines" (1:32; my emphasis), where Montaigne refuses to see success in war as the sign of divine favor. The essay on cannibalism is flanked by two appeals for sober moderation in matters of religion.

25. I am indebted for this suggestion to Nicole Minnick, who has been preparing a study of Montaigne's policy of moderation in the Wars of Religion. For cases, one can consult the index of Crespin, *Histoire des Martyrs* (3:954); typical are the accounts of the Flemish martyrs Chrestien de Quekere, Jaques Dienssart, and Jeanne de Salomez, executed in 1560 (3:75–76) and of Pierre Blance and Pierre Savret, hanged in Aurillac in 1561, who died "constamment & chantans à haute voix le Pseau. 27" (3:211).

26. That understanding is *interested*, reflecting the desires, situation, and needs of the understander—who is still capable of self-criticism and not condemned to a merely relativistic vantage point—is a guiding tenet of Frankfurt School thought; see Jürgen Habermas, *Knowledge and Human Interests*, trans. Jeremy J. Shapiro (Boston: Beacon Press, 1971). See also, from a different perspective, David Bromwich, "The Genealogy of Disinterestedness," in Bromwich, *A Choice of Inheritance: Self and Community from Edmund Burke to Robert Frost* (Cambridge, Mass. and London: Harvard University Press, 1989), pp. 106–32.

27. Clendinnen, "The Cost of Courage in Aztec Society," *Past and Present* 107 (1985): 44–89, pp. 72–74. See also Clendinnen's elaboration of her argument in *Aztecs* (Cambridge: Cambridge University Press, 1991), pp. 87–98, 141–52.

CHAPTER FOUR
AN ETHICS OF YIELDING

1. The political alignments in France and the distinct *politique* position are succinctly outlined by Nakam in *Montaigne et son temps*, pp. 329–33; see also Salmon, *Society in Crisis*, pp. 291–306.

2. Most accounts of Montaigne's conservatism end up calling him a liberal as well; Laursen provides a balanced overview of the various constructions that have been put on the essayist's political thought in Laursen, *The Politics of Skepticism*, pp. 125–44. See also the thoughtful analyses of Frieda S. Brown, *Religious and Political Conservatism in the "Essais" of Montaigne*, Travaux d'Humanisme et Renaissance 59 (Geneva: Droz, 1963), and Sayce, *The Essays of Montaigne*, pp. 233–59, whose view that Montaigne's conservatism counters an awareness of a world continually in motion anticipates Starobinski. Starobinski is, I think, mistaken in *Montaigne in Motion*, p. 288f., when he locates Montaigne in a prescientific and premodern moment in which it was not possible to think of progress and place hope in the future. For Starobinski, Montaigne missed out by one generation, for Bacon was around the corner. Such a contention ignores the long Renaissance humanist tradition in which truth was understood to be the daughter of time—an idea embraced both by Protestant chiliasts and the protolibertine Giordano Bruno, who in the *Cabala del cavallo pegaseo* rehearses the same skeptical views of Montaigne's "Apologie" only to reject skepticism. A future of progress was certainly thinkable for Montaigne, and his not thinking it should be understood as a deliberate choice, most likely directed to a political situation in which change and innovation inevitably evoked the Protestant challenge to national stability. In a different reading of Montaigne's political thought in a premodern (i.e., pre-Cartesian) world, Timothy J. Reiss emphasizes the importance of late Renaissance juridical theory that deduced a kind of universal reason vested in the state; see Reiss, "Montaigne and the Subject of Polity," in *Literary Theory/ Renaissance Texts*, ed. Patricia Parker and David Quint (Baltimore and London: The Johns Hopkins University Press, 1986), pp. 115–49.

3. This is the contention of Max Horkheimer, who crudely assimilates Montaigne to an emergent bourgeosie in "Montaigne et la fonction du sceptisme" in *Théorie critique* (1938; French trans. Paris: Payot, 1978), pp. 261–312. Horkheimer argues that Montaigne's position is no longer tenable *after* the mod-

ern triumph of bourgeois capitalism and what Horkheimer took in 1938 to be its evolution into National Socialism. Our view of the monarchomachs has been greatly influenced by Michael Walzer, *The Revolution of the Saints: A Study in the Origins of Radical Politics* (1965; New York: Atheneum, 1970), especially pp. 68–92. Walzer, p. 87, concedes that "Perhaps the Protestant *vicomtes* of the second civil war still resembled gallant knights, or more likely, marauding feudal barons," but he prefers the Huguenot view of their troops as disciplined godly soldiers, early versions of what would later be a fateful combination of revolutionary radicalism and moral puritanism.

4. In the large critical literature on Montaigne's relationship to La Boétie, the studies of François Rigolot stand out. In addition to "Montaigne's Purloined Letters," in *Montaigne: Essays in Reading*, pp. 145–66, his more recent study, "Montaigne et la 'servitude volontaire': pour une interprétation platonicienne," in *Le lecteur, l'auteur et l'écrivain*, pp. 85–103, suggests how "De l'amitié" substitutes itself for La Boétie's tract, playing on the description of friendship in Plato's *Symposium* as (in Ficino's and Le Roy's translations) "servitude volontaire." Along similar lines, see Eric MacPhail, "Friendship as a Political Ideal in Montaigne's *Essais*," *Montaigne Studies* 1 (1989): 177–87. For the antitolerationist views of La Boétie expressed in his unpublished *Mémoire touchant L'Edit de janvier 1562*, see Brown, *Religious and Political Conservatism*, pp. 24–27.

5. On Montaigne and Venice, see Frame, *Montaigne: A Biography*, pp. 205–6. See also Isida Cremona, "Montaigne et la République de Venise," in *Montaigne et les Essais 1580–1980*, ed. François Moureau, Robert Granderoute, and Claude Blum (Paris: Champion; and Geneva: Slatkine, 1983), pp. 279–88.

6. Tasso, *Dialoghi*, ed. Ezio Raimondi (Florence: G. C. Sansoni, 1958), pp. 83–84.

7. An analogous story in sixteenth-century England, where the crown established itself as the arbiter of noble honor and identity, has been traced by Mervyn James in his study "English Politics and the Concept of Honour, 1485–1642," collected in James, *Society, Politics, and Culture: Studies in Early Modern England*, Past and Present Publications (Cambridge: Cambridge University Press, 1986), pp. 308–415.

8. Elias, *The Civilizing Process*, Volume 1: *The History of Manners*, Volume 2: *Power and Civility*, trans. Edmund Jephcott (1939; English trans. New York: Pantheon Books, 1982).

9. Richard Regosin offers a helpful discussion of "De l'art de conferer" in *The Matter of My Book: Montaigne's "Essais" as the Book of the Self* (Berkeley, Los Angeles, and London: University of California Press, 1977), pp. 111–22; see also Bénédicte Boudou, "L'accomplissement des *Essais* dan 'De l'art de conferer,'" in *Montaigne et les Essais 1588–1988*, ed. Claude Blum (Paris: Champion, 1990), pp. 41–53 (= *Bulletin de la Société des Amis de Montaigne*, 7e série, 13–16 [1988–89]). Less helpful are two collections of studies on "De l'art de conferer" that appeared in 1980, when the essay was chosen as a subject for examination in the competition for entrance to the Grandes Écoles Scientifiques: *Lectures de "L'art de conférer" de Montaigne, Theme: Ironie*, ed. Pascal Mathiot (Paris: Belin, 1980); *De l'art de conferer· Essais, Livre III, chapitre 8, l'ironie de Michel de Montaigne*, ed. Jacques Martin (Paris: Ellipses, 1980).

10. Jules Brody remarks on the imagery and language of "pointiness" in the essay that suggest the stinging or prickly character of conversation in "'Of the Art of Discussion': A Philological Reading," in *Approaches to Teaching Montaigne's Essays*, pp. 159–65.

11. One can compare such statements with analogous passages in the Italian treatises on civility which lie behind "De l'art de conferer." In the *Galateo* (1558), Giovanni della Casa writes, "Ed alcuni, che si oppongono ad ogni parola e quistionano e contrastano, mostrano che male conoscano la natura degli uomini, che ciascuno ama la vittoria, e lo esser vinto odia non meno nel favellare che nello adoperare: senzaché il porsi volentieri al contrario ad altri è opera di nimistà e non d'amicizia ... anzi si dee sforzare di essere arrendevole alle openioni degli altri d'intorno a quelle cose che poco rilevano" (18); della Casa, *Galateo*, ed. Giorgio Manganelli and Claudio Milanini (Milan: Biblioteca Universale Rizzoli, 1977), p. 95. Stefano Guazzo similarly inveighs against speakers who are "contenziosi" in the first book of *La civil conversazione* (1574), and then recommends a pugnacious conversation that remains friendly and is directed toward the truth: "A quel che dite poi de' filosofi, vi rispondo che non solamente a loro ma a tutti gli altri uomini, quando s'acozzano insieme per disputare, è lecito e convenevole il contrasto, ed è più degno d'onore quel che difende la più difficil parte; e se ben sono discordanze nelle parole, non discordano però nell'amore e nella scambievole benivolenza, anzi vanno d'accordo cercando la verità ..." Guazzo, *La civil conversazione*, ed. Amedeo Quondam (Modena: Panini, 1993), 1:63–64.

12. Constance Jordan examines the figure of the endless hunt for truth in Montaigne's book in "Montaigne's 'Chasse de Cognoissance': Language and Play in the *Essais*," *Romanic Review* 71 (1980): 265–80.

13. One should compare the closely related description of conversation in "Des trois commerces": "La fin de ce commerce, c'est simplement la privauté, frequentation, et conference: l'exercise des ames sans autre fruit. En nos propos, tous subjects me sont égaux; il ne me chaut qu'il n'y ait ny poix ny profondeur: la grace et la pertinence y sont tousjours; tout y est teinct d'un jugement meur et constant, et meslé de bonté, de franchise, de gayeté et d'amitié" (824; 625).

14. This passage seems concordant with Starobinski's reading of the *Essais*, in which Montaigne's skepticism strips away the masks of culture, custom, and human illusion only to accept their necessity. With the ending of "De l'utile et de l'honneste" in mind, Starobinski sees a residue of negation—what in this passage in "De l'art de conferer" would be Montaigne's understanding that does not bow to the king—as a saving feature that does not allow Montaigne quite to turn into a proponent of the status quo: "This power of negation through free thought (which is also a power of liberation through refusal) is what Montaigne retains from his initial revolt against mask and appearance even after his reconciliation with them" (*Montaigne in Motion*, p. 305). In a critique of Starobinski, Gregory Sims demonstrates how much this interpretative scheme of unmasking and ultimately conforming is indebted to Pascal's *Entretien avec M. de Saci*; see Sims, "Stoic Virtues/Stoic Vices: Montaigne's Pyrrhic Rhetoric," *Journal of Medieval and Renaissance Studies* 23 (1993): 235–66. Sims's contention, however, that the excessiveness of Montaigne's writing, the motion that Starobinski describes, undermines its ethical

themes of moderation, seems to me to require more robust textual evidence than he provides: such excess may be in the mind of the beholder. I acknowledge my own prejudice as a reader who attempts what Sims regards as misguided, one who "insists, come what may, on reading Montaigne as a moralist" (252n.46).

15. Patrick Henry has commented on some of the links between the two essays in "Reading Montaigne Contextually: 'De l'incommodité de la grandeur' (III, 7)," *The French Review* 61 (1988): 859–64. John Michael Archer discusses the isolation and friendless state of the monarch of "De l'art de confere," in his chapter on Montaigne in *Sovereignty and Intelligence: Spying and Court Culture in the English Renaissance* (Stanford: Stanford University Press, 1993), pp. 31–38.

16. Oestreich, *Neostoicism and the Early Modern State*, trans. David McLintock (Cambridge and London: Cambridge University Press, 1982).

17. For the antinoble sentiment produced by League radicalism, see Jouanna, *L'idée de race*, pp. 681–97, and *Le devoir de révolte*, pp. 200–206. A key text of the period is François Cromé, *Dialogue d'entre le maheustre et le manant*, ed. Peter Ascoli (Geneva: Droz, 1977); for a brief discussion, see David Quint, *Epic and Empire* (Princeton: Princeton University Press, 1993), pp. 205–7.

18. At the end of the essay, Montaigne declares that he is "Roy de la matiere" of his book, which becomes another realm of personal freedom that he obtains in exchange for political obedience. See Henry, "Reading Montaigne," p. 863; Archer, *Sovereignty and Intelligence*, p. 38. For the locus classicus, see Horace, *Odes* 2.2.9–12.

19. On the problem of the exemplar, see once again Hampton, *Writing from History*, and Pigman, "Limping Examples," cited in Chapter 1, note 5. See also by Pigman, "Imitation and the Renaissance Sense of the Past: The Reception of Erasmus' *Ciceronianus*," *Journal of Medieval and Renaissance Studies* 9 (1979): 155–77. Thomas M. Greene discusses the problem of anachronism for a humanism that seeks models in the past in *The Light in Troy: Imitation and Discovery in Renaissance Poetry* (New Haven and London: Yale University Press, 1982), pp. 28–53.

20. Scodel, "The Affirmation of Paradox: A Reading of Montaigne's 'De la Phisionomie' (III:12)," in *Montaigne: Essays in Reading*, pp. 209–37. Other fine critical discussions of the essay are found in Hampton, *Writing from History*, pp. 171–88; Raymond B. Waddington, "Socrates in Montaigne's 'Traicté de la phisionomie,'" *Modern Language Quarterly* 41 (1980): 328–45; Terence Cave, *The Cornucopian Text: Problems of Writing in the French Renaissance* (Oxford: Clarendon Press, 1979), pp. 302–12; Hope H. Glidden, "The Face in the Text: Montaigne's Emblematic Self-Portrait (*Essais* III, 12)," *Renaissance Quarterly* 46 (1993): 71–97. On broader issues that surround the essay, see Frederick Kellerman, "The *Essais* and Socrates," *Symposium* 10 (1956): 204–16; Jean-Marie Compain, "L'imitation Socratique dans les *Essais*," in *Montaigne et les Essais 1588–1988*, pp. 161–71, and James G. Beaudry, "Virtue and Nature in the *Essais*," *Kentucky Romance Quarterly* 1 (1976): 93–103.

21. Starobinski, *Montaigne in Motion*, pp. 175–84, writes very well about this passage in "De L'experience"; see also Meijer, "The Significance of 'De la Diversion'."

22. The resemblance between Socrates and the cannibals is noted, though with

a different valorization, by Ian Winter in "'Cest bien le bout, non pourtant le but de la vie': La question de la mort dans 'Des cannibales' et dans 'De la phisionomie'," in *Montaigne et le Nouveau Monde*, pp. 133–41.

23. See Maryanne Cline Horowitz, "Montaigne's Doubts on the Miraculous and the Demonic in Cases of His Own Day," in *Regnum, Religio et Ratio: Essays Presented to Robert M. Kingdon*, ed. Jerome Friedman, Sixteenth Century Essays and Studies Volume 8 (Kirksville, Mo.: Sixteenth Century Journal Publishers, 1987), pp. 81–92.

24. For similar remarks on natural and denatured behavior in "De la phisionomie," see Nakam, *Les "Essais" de Montaigne*, pp. 306–8.

25. Jouanna, *Le devoir de révolte*, p. 74, writes of the exchange of gifts and favor among nobles and their clients: "Ces relations étaient caractérisées par l'emploi d'un vocabulaire affectif particulier où le mot 'amitié' voisine avec ceux d' 'affection', 'contentement', 'bonne volonté', 'bon plaisir', 'bonnes graces'." See the chapter, "The Exchange of Favor," in Neuschel, *Word of Honor*, pp. 69–102.

This exchange of favor also evokes Seneca's discussion of gifts in the *De beneficiis* and the philosopher, too, includes among such gifts the sparing of another's life (see, for example, II.11; II.20). Here, too, Montaigne, the devoted reader of Seneca even when he disagrees with him, may recuperate an element of Stoic doctrine—its sense of *noblesse oblige*. For Seneca, as for Montaigne, one does good deeds both for their own sake and as an act of faith in one's fellow men and women. So Seneca declares near the end of his unfinished treatise: "Persistent goodness wins over bad men, and no one of them is so hard-hearted and hostile to kindly treatment as not to love a good man even when they wrong him, when even the fact that they can fail to pay back with impunity is made an additional source of indebtedness to him" (VII.31.1). Seneca, *Moral Essays*, 3:523.

26. Waddington gives a somewhat different construction to the likeness/difference between Socrates and Montaigne in their respective confrontations with deadly adversaries in "Socrates," pp. 340–43.

27. What I speak of as reciprocity and conversion is memorably described by Nakam in *Montaigne: La manière*, p. 178, as a "contagion" of goodness: "Le pari sur l'efficacité d'un beau geste et la contagion de la générosité est au coeur des *Essais*. Montaigne s'est mêlé aux troupes de la milice bordelaise "la tête droite et le visage ouvert". Visage et coeur ouverts. Parler ouvert. Porte ouverte. Ouvrir par la confiance la confiance d'autrui. . . . Par cette attitude active, par son pouvoir de contagion, Montaigne désire aimanter, forcer la confiance d'autrui, la libérer à son tour, aider à se faire jour sa vertu native." The openness of which Nakam speaks is closely related to the frankness that Montaigne ascribes to his speech and, by extension, to the *Essais* themselves, which are "un livre de bonne foy," as Montaigne announces in his address to his reader, where he also wants to be seen in his fashion that is "simple, naturelle et ordinaire" (3; 2). Antoine Compagnon offers a perceptive analysis in "Montaigne ou la parole donnée,"in *Rhétorique de Montaigne*, ed. Frank Lestringant (Paris: Champion, 1985), pp. 9–19.

28. See Scodel, "The Affirmation of Paradox."

29. In a C-text addition to the "Apologie de Raimond Sebond," Montaigne comments on how the monarchomach doctrine sanctioning rebellion against one's prince has been transferred from the Huguenots, who originally theorized it but

who now defended the divine right of kings when the king in question was Henri IV, to the Catholic Ligueurs: "Cette proposition si solenne: S'il est permis au subjet de se rebeller et armer contre son prince pour la defence de la religion, souvienne-vous en quelles bouches, cette année passée, l'affirmative d'icelle estoit l'arc-boutant d'un parti, la negative de quel autre parti c'estoit l'arc-boutant; et oyez à present de quel quartier vient la voix et instruction de l'une et de l'autre; et si les armes bruyent moins pour cette cause que pour cette là!" (443; 323). He will have none of this solemn proposition himself.

30. Raymond C. La Charité is one of the few commentators who notes that this sentence really *is* a problem in "'Of Physiognomy': The Staging and Reading of Facial Narrative," in *Approaches to Teaching Montaigne's "Essays,"* pp. 166–72, p. 172. M. A. Screech is perhaps unsettled by its implications, for he mistranslates the sentence in *The Essays of Michel de Montaigne* (London: Allen Lane and The Penguin Press, 1991), p. 1206.

31. Mary B. McKinley has discussed the conclusion of the "Apologie de Raimond Sebond" as paradigmatic of the open-endedness of the *Essais*; see *Les terrains vagues des "Essais": Itinéraires et intertextes* (Paris: Champion, 1996), pp. 91–103.

32. I cite the text of the letter in Montaigne, *Oeuvres complètes*, ed. Albert Thibaudet and Maurice Rat (Paris: Gallimard, 1962), p. 1398.

33. This glimpse of the historical Montaigne may show him sweeping aside problems of justice in this counsel of clemency, and it fits my argument. But clemency is the necessary first step for the establishment of a political order that can guarantee the justice in which the same historical Montaigne took a passionate and professional interest. On other occasions, we find him advising his royal masters about judicial reform. His official letter to Henri III of August 31, 1583, complains about the increasing venality of the judiciary (*Oeuvres complètes*, ed. Thibaudet and Rat, p. 1376; *Complete Works*, ed. Frame, p. 1070). In 1584, he was consulted by Henri of Navarre about projects to reform the courts; see Nakam, *Montaigne et ses temps*, 313–14.

INDEX

Adams, Robert M., 155n.22
Albon, Jacques d', 28
Alexander the Great, xi, 4, 14–20, 29–30, 33–38, 40–41, 54–55, 67, 79–80, 82, 87, 94–95, 129–30
Alexander, Tyrant of Pherae, 66
Amyot, Jacques, 22, 40, 151n.31
Appian, 28
Archer, John Michael, 165nn.15 and 18
Aristotle, 48, 139
Aubigné, Agrippa d', 93, 146n.4

Beaudry, James G., 165n.20
Betis, 14–20, 34–35, 41, 55, 67, 79–80, 82, 87, 94–95, 129–30
Billacois, François, 157n.32
Bitton, Davis, 154n.12
Bodin, Jean, 37, 146n.5
Bohanan, Donna, 154n.19
Boon, J. P., 146n.3
Boon, James, 159n.7
Boudou, Bénédicte, 163n.9
Braden, Gordon, 59, 148n.10, 149n.15, 153n.8, 154n.14
Brantôme, Pierre de, 157n.36
Brody, Jules, 164n.10
Bromwich, David, 162n.26
Brown, Frieda S., 145n.2, 149n.17, 162n.2, 163n.4
Bruno, Giordano, 155n.23, 162n.2
Bryson, Frederick R., 157n.32
Burckhardt, Jacob, x

Caesar, Augustus, 23–24, 26, 28–29, 33, 55
Caesar, Julius, 26, 28, 37, 146n.4
Cary, Elizabeth, 156n.30
Casa, Giovanni della, 108, 164n.11
Castiglione, Baldassarre, 59, 72, 160n.17
Cato, Marcus Porcius, the younger, 45–51, 56–57, 91, 124
Cave, Terence, 165n.20
Certeau, Michel de, 89, 91, 160n.16
Cervantes, Miguel de, 59, 61, 63
Charles IX, king of France, 61, 102
Christodoulou, Kyriaki, 147n.6, 151n.29

Cinna, 23–24, 33, 55
Citton, Yves, 148n.14
Clark, Carol, 148n.9, 150n.21
Clendinnen, Inga, 100–101, 162n.27
Compagnon, Antoine, 154n.17, 166n.27
Compain, Jean-Marie, 165n.20
Corneille, Pierre, 23
Cottrell, Robert, 145n.2, 148nn.13 and 14
Cremona, Isida, 163n.5
Crespin, Jean, 161nn. 20 and 25
Cromé, François, 165n.17
Crouzet, Denis, 153n.4

Defaux, Gérard, 77–78, 159n.6
Dewald, Jonathan, 154n.19, 161n.19
Diogenes Laertius, 128
Dionysius of Syracuse, 12–15, 19, 29–30, 33, 129
Duval, Edwin, 145n.2, 158n.3

Edward, prince of Wales, 4–5, 14, 17
Elias, Norbert, ix, 109, 161n.19, 163n.8
Epaminondas, xi, 4, 6, 9, 14, 17, 37–41, 64, 73, 143, 151n.33
Erasmus, Desiderius, 59, 62, 138
Erspamer, Francesco, 157n.32
Eyquem, Pierre, father of Montaigne, 61

Feytaud, Jacques de, 146n.3
Fisch, M. H., 149n.15
Forcione, Alban, 59, 154n.14
Fortini, Marcello, 151n.32
Frame, Donald, 25, 145n.1, 151n.25, 153n.9, 156n.29, 163n.5
Friedrich, Hugo, 146n.3, 154n.18

Garavini, Fausta, 147n.8
Gilmore, Myron, 146n.5
Girard, René, 83, 160n.13
Glidden, Hope H., 165n.20
Greenblatt, Stephen, 159n.5
Greene, Thomas M., 149n.17, 165n.19
Guazzo, Stefano, 108, 164n.11
Guise, François, duke of, 23–26, 28–30, 45, 149n.20

Gutwirth, Marcel, 145n.2

Habermas, Jürgen, 162n.26
Hallie, Phillip, 65, 153nn.6 and 9, 155n.27
Hampton, Timothy, 37, 146n.5, 151n.29, 153nn.6 and 8, 155n.25, 165nn.19 and 20
Homer, 15, 37
Horkheimer, Max, xiv, 162–63n.3
Horowitz, Maryanne Cline, 166n.23
Henri II, king of France, 111
Henri III, king of France, 104, 107, 150n.20, 167n.33
Henri de Navarre, later Henri IV, king of France, 10, 104, 107, 141–44, 150n.20, 167n.33
Henry, Patrick, 165nn.15 and 18
Holt, Mack, 152n.3, 153n.4
Huppert, George, 154n.19

James, Mervyn, 163n.7
Jordan, Constance, 164n.12
Josephus, 74, 95
Jouanna, Arlette, 146n.3, 150n.25, 152n.3, 153n.12, 154nn. 13 and 19, 165n.17, 166n.25
Julian, Roman emperor, ix, 152n.2

Kahn, Victoria, 20, 149n.18
Kellerman, Frederick, 165n20
Kiernan, V.G., 157n.32
Kirsch, Arthur, 153n.6
Kohl, Karl-heinz, 159n.7
Kritzman, Lawrence D., 145n.2, 158n.3

La Boétie, Etienne de, 37, 104–8, 137
La Charité, Raymond C., 167n.30
Langer, Ullrich, 159n.4
Laursen, John Christian, 147n.7, 161n.22, 162n.2
Léry, Jean de, 158n.1, 160nn.12 and 14
Lestringant, Frank, 158n.3, 159n.9, 160n.11
Lewis, P. S., 153n.4
Lindsay, Robert O., 152n.1, 161n.21
Lipsius, Justus, 120
Livia, 23–24, 26, 29
Locher, Caroline, 158n.3
Logan, J. L., 153n.7
Loque, Bertrand de, 157n.34
Lucan, 124, 146n.4

Lyons, John D., 146n.5

Machiavelli, Niccolò, 143
MacPhail, Eric, 146n.4, 163n.4
Martial, 76
Mattecolom, sieur de, brother of Montaigne, 71
McFarlane, I. D., 148n.9, 150n.22, 153n.9
McGowan, Margaret M., 148n.12, 154n.18, 161n.23
McKinley, Mary B., 167n.31
Medici, Catherine de', 22
Meijer, Marianne, 148nn.9 and 12, 150n.22, 165n.21
Mermier, Guy, 158n.3
Minnick, Nicole, 161n.25
Montaigne, Michel de, *Essais*
 1:1, "Par diver moyens on arrive à pareille fin," xi, 3–21, 24, 26, 31–31, 40–41, 43, 52, 55, 65–67, 79–80, 85, 87, 92, 94–95, 99, 129–30, 132, 139
 1:5, "Si le chef d'une place assiegée doit sortir pour parlementer," 151n.26
 1:14, "Que le goust des biens et des maux depend en bonne partie de l'opinion que nous en avons," 5–6, 9
 1:15, "On est puny pour s'opiniastrer à une place sans raison," 17–19, 94
 1:16, "De la punition de la couardise," 149n.16
 1:23, "De la coustume et de ne changer aisément une loy receüe," x, 70, 77, 103, 105, 159n.4
 1:24, "Divers evenemens de mesme conseil," xi, 3–4, 21–34, 43, 55, 107–8, 136, 149n.15
 1:26, "De l'institution des enfans," 99, 140
 1:27, "C'est folie de rapporter le vray et le faux à nostre suffisance," 110–11
 1:28, "De l'amitié," 104–5
 1:30, "De la moderation," 96
 1:31, "Des cannibales," xi, 75–102,
 1:32, "Qu'il faut sobrement se mesler de juger des ordonnances divines," 161n.24
 1:37, "Du jeune Caton," 46–48
 1:39, "De la solitude," 13, 71, 119
 1:42, "De l'inequalité qui est entre nous," 106–7, 120
 2:1, "De l'inconstance de nos actions,"

10, 35, 38, 41
  2:2, "De l'yvrongnerie," xii, 94–96
  2:5, "De la conscience," 35
  2:7, "Des récompenses d'honneur," 26, 91–92, 148n.9
  2:10, "Des livres," 60, 76
  2:11, "De la cruauté," xi, 42–65, 68–69, 73, 80, 85, 92, 114, 125, 139
  2:12, "Apologie de Raimond Sebond," x, 20, 31, 36–37, 102–3, 106, 108, 110, 165–66n.22
  2:13, "De juger de la mort d'autruy," 46–48
  2:15, "Que nostre desir s'accroit par la malaisance," 133–34
  2:17: "De la praesumption," 27–28, 54, 99, 135, 141
  2:19, "De la liberté de conscience," ix
  2:21, "Contre la faineantise," 48–49
  2:23, "Des mauvais moyens employez à bonne fin," xii, 76, 85–88, 92, 98
  2:27, "Couardise mere de la cruauté," xi, 26, 43, 45, 65–74, 80–82, 90–91, 135
  2:28, "Toutes choses ont leur saison," 49
  2:29, "De la vertu," 149n.20
  2:32, "Defence de Seneque et de Plutarque," 37, 93
  2:33, "L'histoire de Spurina," 146n.4
  2:36, "Des plus excellens hommes," 37–41
  2:37, "De la ressemblance des enfans aux peres," 150n.21
  3:1, "De l'utile et de l'honneste," 39–41, 44, 53, 64, 73, 138
  3:2, "De repentir," xiv
  3:3, "Des trois commerces," 107, 109, 150n.22, 164n.13
  3:4, "De la diversion," 10–11, 26, 74, 126
  3:6, "Des coches," 159n.8
  3:7, "De l'incommodité de la grandeur," 118–19
  3:8, "De l'art de conferer," xii, 42, 61, 105, 108–22, 126–27, 137, 140
  3:9, "De la vanité," 105, 143, 146n.4
  3:10, "De mesnager sa volonté," 7, 154n.18
  3:11, "Des boyteux," 112, 134
  3:12, "De la phisionomie," xii, 30–31, 44, 60, 108, 122 41

  3:13, "De l'experience," 34–36, 41, 119, 124, 126, 138, 140–41, 143, 146n.5, 150n.21, 151–52n.33
  Letter to Henri of Navarre, 141–44
Montmorency, Anne de, 28
More, Thomas, 62–63
Motley, Mark, 161n.19
Muir, Edward, 157n.32
Muzio, Girolamo, 157n.35

Nakam, Géralde, xiii, 149n.19, 150nn.21, 24, and 25, 152nn.2 and 4, 155n.28, 162n.1, 166nn.24 and 27, 167n.33 Nero, 10, 12, 24, 33, 54
Neu, John, 152n.1, 161n.21
Neuschel, Kristen B., 44, 73, 153n.5, 158n.37, 161n.19, 166n.25

Oestreich, Gerhard, 120, 165n.16
O'Loughlin, Michael, 145n.2, 158n.3

Parker, Patricia, 148n.14
Paul, Saint, 96
Pelopidas, 6, 9
Pérouse, Gabriel-A., 145n.2, 147n.6
Philippus, 29, 35
Philotas, 35–36, 41
Phyto, 12–15, 18–19, 29, 31, 129
Pico della Mirandola, Giovanni, x Pigman, George W., III, 146n.5, 165n.19 Plato, 75, 83, 110, 124, 126–28, 131, 138
Plutarch, 37, 40, 60, 110, 139, 151n.31
Pompey, 7, 36, 41
Posner, David, 146n.3
Prudentius, 95

Quintus Curtius, 15, 35, 38

Rabelais, François, 59
Rabil, Albert, Jr., 154n.12
Rawson, Claude, 96, 158n.3, 161n.23
Reiss, Timothy J., 162n.2
Rendall, Michael, 145n.2, 158n.3
Reynolds, Beatrice, 146n.5
Richet, Denis, 154n.19
Rigolot, François, 156n.29, 162n.4
Romei, Annibale, 155n.19
Romier, Lucien, 152n.4
Rousseau, Jean-Jacques, 75

Salmon, J.H.M., 152n.3, 160n.15

Sayce, R. A., 155n.26, 162n.2
Scaliger, Joseph, x, 69
Scanderbeg, 4, 6
Schaefer, David Lewis, 147n.7, 151n.27, 153n.6, 158nn.38 and 3, 161n.23
Schalk, Ellery, 154n.12
Schiffman, Zachary, 159n.4
Scipio the Elder, 143
Scipio Aemilianus, 37
Scodel, Joshua, 125, 165n.20, 166n.28
Screech, M. A., 167n.30
Sechel, George, 74
Seneca, Lucius Annaeus, 8–14, 17, 21, 23–24, 26, 32–33, 36, 52–56. 60, 62, 90, 93, 119–20, 124; *De Beneficiis* 166n.25; *De Clementia*, 10–12, 14, 17, 21, 23–24, 26, 32–33, 54–55, 62; *De Constantia*, 8, 13, 90; *De Providentia*, 90; *Epistle 66*, 136; *Epistle 73*, 119–20; *Epistle 90*, 53, 55–56; *Epistle 92*, 36
Shakespeare, William, 14, 75
Shklar, Judith, xiii, 147n.7, 152n.1, 153n.10, 159n.8
Sims, Gregory, 164–65n.14
Smith, Malcolm, 156n.29
Socrates, xii, xiv, 3, 45, 47–51, 56–57, 64, 91, 110, 117–18, 123–32, 134–35, 137–41

Starobinski, Jean, xiii, 150n.21, 153nn.6, 9, and 11, 162n.2, 164n.14, 165n.21
Stierle, Karlheinz, 145n.2, 146n.5
Stilbo, 13
Stone, Donald, 153n.6
Stone, Lawrence, 69, 157n.33
Stroux, Johannes, 148n. 14
Sulla, 7–8, 20
Supple, James J., 145n.3, 150n.23, 154nn.18 and 19, 157n.31, 161n.18

Tacitus, 111
Tasso, Torquato, 106
Terence, 131
Thevet, André, 84, 159n.10, 160n.14
Thou, Jacques de, 105

Venice, 105–7, 137
Villey, Pierre, xiv, 8, 21, 38, 81, 145n.1, 147n.6 and 7, 151n.30
Virgil, 37, 64

Waddington, Raymond, 165n20, 166n26
Walzer, Michael, 163n.3
Whigham, Frank, 59–60, 154n.16
Winter, Ian, 166n.22

Xenophon, 61–62, 124, 129

ABOUT THE AUTHOR

DAVID QUINT is the George M. Bodman Professor of English and Comparative Literature at Yale University. He is the author of *Epic and Empire: Politics and Generic Form from Virgil to Milton* (Princeton, 1993).

GPSR Authorized Representative: Easy Access System Europe - Mustamäe tee 50, 10621 Tallinn, Estonia, gpsr.requests@easproject.com

www.ingramcontent.com/pod-product-compliance
Lightning Source LLC
Chambersburg PA
CBHW051525230426
43668CB00012B/1740